# Log Rafts to Freedom

One teenager's extraordinary journey of survival from Poland to England via exile in Siberia

Linda Gallagher
Jerzy Dąbrowski

Log Rafts to Freedom: One teenager's extraordinary journey of survival from Poland to England via exile in Siberia

Copyright © 2023 Linda Gallagher

ISBN: 9798391908586

All rights reserved. Except for brief excerpts for review purposes, no part of this book may be reproduced or used in any form or media without permission from the publisher.

Any websites, books or other references recommended throughout this work are offered as a resource to you. These are not intended in any way to imply an endorsement on the part of the author or publisher. The information in this book was correct at the time it was published.

The map on page 266 was produced by Ben Childs of Tracemaps LTD, using a base map © Mapbox © OpenStreetMap, see:

https://www.mapbox.com/about/maps

https://www.openstreetmap.org/copyright

Cover design: Sarah Clarke, Jerzy Dąbrowski

Survival is the ability to swim in strange water.
— Frank Herbert, *Dune*

# DEDICATION

To my children and my grandchildren, so that they will know a little more of their Polish background.

# CONTENTS

| | | |
|---|---|---|
| | Introduction | i |
| | Original Preface | v |

**Part One: From Poland to Siberia**
**"Here You Shall Live"**

| | | |
|---|---|---|
| | *In the Background: The Invasions* | 3 |
| 1 | A Happy Childhood in Pre-War Poland | 13 |
| 2 | War Begins in Poland | 22 |
| 3 | Journey to Siberia | 29 |
| | *In the Spotlight: Deportation — Arrests and Cattle Trucks* | 38 |
| 4 | 'Here you shall live' | 47 |
| | *In the Spotlight: Arrival and Conditions in the Settlement* | 54 |
| 5 | Labour in the Logging Camp | 60 |
| | *In the Spotlight: Surviving and Working in Siberia* | 66 |
| 6 | Beauty and Grief in the Taiga | 72 |
| | *In the Spotlight: The Taiga Forest* | 80 |
| | *Maps, Drawings and Photos* | 83 |

**Part Two: From Siberia to Palestine**
**"Amnesty and Freedom"**

| | | |
|---|---|---|
| | *In the Background: The Allies* | 91 |
| 7 | Leaving Siberia on Log Rafts | 98 |
| | *In the Spotlight: Amnesty* | 106 |
| 8 | On the Train to Kazakhstan | 111 |
| 9 | Waiting around in Uzbekistan | 118 |
| 10 | Freedom in the Middle East | 125 |
| | *In the Spotlight: Across the Caspian Sea to Persia* | 133 |

| 11 | Arriving in the 'Promised Land' | 140 |
|---|---|---|
| | *In the Spotlight: The Katyn Massacres* | 148 |
| | *In the Spotlight: Death of Sikorski, the Polish Prime Minister* | 153 |
| 12 | Palestine – Exploration and Education | 156 |
| 13 | Sailing to Britain | 164 |
| | *Drawings and Photos* | 172 |

**Part Three: From Palestine to Britain "A New Start"**

| | *In the Background: The Poles* | 181 |
|---|---|---|
| 14 | Faldingworth Bomber Command | 187 |
| 15 | Wireless, Radar and Resettlement | 195 |
| | *In the Spotlight: Settling the Poles in Britain* | 203 |
| | *In the Spotlight: Soviets at the Nuremberg Trials* | 208 |
| 16 | Architecture, a Wife and a Death | 213 |
| | *In the Spotlight: The Polish School of Architecture* | 220 |
| 17 | A Career and Family | 222 |
| 18 | Moving and More Moving | 231 |
| | *In the Spotlight: Jerzy Dąbrowski's Major Architectural Projects* | 240 |
| 19 | Back to Poland at Last | 242 |
| | *In the Spotlight: Rebuilding Warsaw* | 252 |
| 20 | Epilogue: Travels and Retirement | 255 |
| | *Photos* | 259 |
| | *Map of Jerzy's Journey* | 266 |
| | *Key events of WW2 and Jerzy's Journey* | 268 |
| | *Jerzy's family tree and descendants* | 275 |
| | Further Reading | 277 |
| | Acknowledgements | 280 |

# INTRODUCTION

Poland, an incredibly beautiful country, is a land of many contrasts. It has sand-dunned beaches on the north Baltic coast, impenetrable forests of fir trees in the west, and the majestic, craggy peaks of the Tatra Mountains in the south. There are charming, traditional timber houses and churches, mediaeval castles and acres of farmland. But Poland, bordered by both Germany and Russia, is mostly very flat – the perfect terrain for hostile, military troops to cross.

Now one of the largest countries in Central Europe, Poland itself didn't exist at all for over a hundred years: in the 18th century, Poland had been divided up three ways between the Germanic Kingdom of Prussia, the Russian Empire and the Austro-Hungarian Empire. It was only formally reinstated as an independent country with well-defined, political borders at the end of the First World War, when the 1919 Treaty of Versailles brought the Polish Second Republic into being.

After WWI, many countries were discontented with their new borders, especially Germany and Russia. There was also the unsolved *'Polish Question'*: should Poland actually be allowed to exist as an independent nation with its own identity? Poland's newly-gained independence only existed for twenty years until 1939, when first Germany then Russia invaded and divided up the land up between them.

My father, Jerzy Henryk Dąbrowski, was born in Skarżysko-Kamienna, in central Poland in 1926, during a time of enormous political change throughout all of Europe. He had a fascinating, and at times, harrowing life story. Very few people, even now, are aware of the fate of at least one and a half million Polish people who were deported by the Soviets to Siberia at the beginning of WW2. Thousands of Poles, whose only 'crime' was being Polish, died either on the cruel journey to Siberia in cattle-trucks, or in the labour camps and settlements there. My father survived both.

During the 'amnesty', when they were released from Siberia, the survivors, starving and ill from their maltreatment by the Soviets, had to find their own way back to some sort of civilisation with little transport, no food and no maps. Less than ten percent of those who managed to leave Siberia were able to make a new life somewhere after the war. There are enormous Polish cemeteries in certain countries in Soviet and Central Asia full of the bodies those who did not survive the journey. My father and his brother Stanisław (Stach) were among the Poles who managed to reach one of the recruitment centres of Anders' Army, and who eventually found safety in Great Britain.

Ever since Jerzy (usually known as 'Terry' in England) died in 2018 at the age of 92, I have had it in my heart to research the background to his story as well as to edit his memoirs. It is quite poignant for me as I am now a similar age to him when he wrote his story. I needed to know the 'whys' of what had happened to him for myself – why was he in Siberia, why in Palestine and why here in Great Britain? I have wished, so often, that we could have worked on this project together before he died because I am not sure he really understood the bigger picture of what had happened to him. His memories were mainly those of the teenager he was and have little detail of the progress of the war, while I had no real idea of the horrors he had endured.

Now, nearly thirty years after my father first wrote his life-story, a number of books of personal memoirs about the Siberian deportations have appeared. There are also many well-researched historical and factual books regarding the Polish perspective of the Soviets and the British during WW2. Finally, truths, which had been suppressed to appease Stalin during the war, are beginning to be acknowledged.

Despite his fear that he would once again be deported to Siberia, Jerzy did manage to return to Poland several times to reconnect with his remaining relatives and to visit his mother's grave; these journeys seem to have been the catalyst for enabling him to write down his recollections. I have visited Poland twice myself and have met a few of his family members. I felt at the time very much that I belonged there.

Jerzy wrote his 'Memoirs' in the early 1990s, under the title *'This and That, Siberrrria Too!'* These are his memories of a happy childhood in Poland, of his survival during the war despite deportation to Siberia, and of his long trek back to civilisation through much of Asia. He became a cadet in the Polish Army, joined the Polish Air Force in Britain and finally settled there as a British citizen, a successful architect and a family man.

Jerzy used an ancient word processor and photocopier to print off several copies of his memoirs himself in 1994, and these he gave to close family and friends, but he never saw his story actually published. The narrative chapters in this book are my father's own writing (although I have edited the spelling, grammar and format somewhat and removed hundreds of exclamation marks!) – his optimistic and mischievous personality is very evident in the anecdotes he relays to the reader. His time-line of events is very accurate and hopefully my more factual features – 'In the Background' and 'In the Spotlight' – will give his story a historical, military and political context, and help the reader to understand what was going on around his story.

I have divided the book into three parts, each beginning with an 'In the Background' article, the relevant and simplified narrative of the progress of the war – especially the Soviet shenanigans – which you, the reader, may choose to read, ignore or return to later. After several chapters of my father's memoir, I have added 'In the Spotlight' articles which will give more information about selected topics. I have tried to be as accurate as possible in my writing but I am not a historian nor a specialist in the events of WW2. I am just Jerzy's daughter and as such, any errors in the articles are purely my own.

My father often walked in the Tatra Mountains in Poland during his childhood, and he gave me a deep love for mountains and walking; we both used to say how much better we felt when 'up high'! I also seem to have inherited my father's love of writing poetry. I sincerely hope you enjoy reading about his memories in the context of war, and that Jerzy's story will touch you as much as it does me. I will let his own, original, preface – which follows this introduction – set the scene for his memoirs.

*Linda Gallagher 2022*

# THIS AND THAT, SIBERRRRIA TOO!
# LIFE MEMORIES

## (ORIGINAL PREFACE, 1994)

### JERZY HENRYK DĄBROWSKI

Having a cheerful, optimistic disposition and a mischievous sense of humour has helped me to survive the many, extraordinary events in my life without my spirit being broken. However, lately it has become increasingly hard to resist the frequent nagging from friends, family and work colleagues to write my rather unusual life story for posterity. I am rather lazy and somewhat stubborn by nature but now that I am retired and have time on my hands, I am finding it difficult to find any more excuses to delay this project.

Some of my childhood experiences were inspiring and entertaining; they provided a strong base for helping me to understand and cope with the conditions I later experienced during the war when Poland was under Soviet occupation. The journey to Siberia, and the return through Kazahkstan and Uzbekistan, followed by a time in the Middle east as a Cadet with the Polish Air Force, all have their own tragedies and bright patches. I have always believed there must be a light at the end of every dark tunnel, and I am lucky that I have been able to find something amusing in every situation.

Many of my readers will not have experienced being cooped up in a Soviet cattle-truck on the Trans-Siberian railway. Nor will there be many who have had the rather doubtful pleasure of floating on a raft down a Siberian river with snow already falling in September.

Have you ever slept in the depths of the Taiga forest when a 'friendly' brown bear comes to visit? Are you able to count up more than fifteen occasions when you narrowly escaped death?

The reader will be able to learn a little about the Young Soldiers' Battalion in Palestine and Egypt, the Cadets' Schools for Officer Training, and preparing for the Full Matriculation exam before sailing to Great Britain. They will hopefully also understand what it was like to join the Polish Air Force, to be a Polish immigrant in Britain after de-mobilisation, and to attempt to live a relatively normal life in an alien country after the war.

This is not a diary nor a full documentary, but a collection of personal experiences and reminiscences, written hopefully in chronological order without too much exaggeration!

It contains many important facts intermingled with amusing anecdotes. I hope that you will find much of interest to discover in my story.

Jerzy Henryk Dąbrowski
(TERRY)

# This and That, Siberrrria Too!

## LIFE MEMORIES

# PART ONE:
# FROM POLAND TO SIBERIA

# "HERE YOU SHALL LIVE"

# IN THE BACKGROUND: THE INVASIONS

## WHY DID GERMANY AND RUSSIA INVADE POLAND?

*LINDA GALLAGHER*

**Germany's reasons for invading Poland**

When Hitler came to power, his intention was to regain any German territory that had been given to other countries in border changes after the First World War; this was to provide 'Lebenstraum', or 'extended living space' for Germany's 'superior' race.

Hitler had already annexed Austria, where many ethnic Germans lived, into Nazi Germany in the Anschluss of March 1938. For the sake of peace and in order to appease Hitler, the nations of Germany, Italy, Great Britain, and France signed the Munich Agreement in September 1938, which allowed Nazi Germany to re-arm and also to occupy the mainly German area of Czechoslovakia called the Sudetenland. However, Hitler then invaded the whole of Czechoslovakia without resistance. Now Hitler hoped that his next plan, to invade Poland, would again just be tolerated without any protest. He wanted to get rid of all the 'sub-human' Polish and Jewish people and take their land for Germany.

**Russia's reasons for invading Poland**

Poland had won the Polish-Soviet War of 1920, securing a border further to the east of the artificial demarcation line (the *Curzon Line*), that had been suggested after WW1 between the Soviet Union and Poland. This area had originally been part of Poland and most of the people living there were ethnic Poles.

The Russian Communists felt humiliated by this victory and therefore hated the Polish Officers; in retaliation, they decided Poland needed to be 'liberated' from its capitalist history. The Communists wanted the whole of Poland to eventually be controlled by the vast Soviet Republic.

## Germany and Russia working together – Plans for Invasion

The leaders of Germany and Russia met together to work out how to regain the land they both felt they had lost to Poland after the First World War. Both countries believed that Poland should never have been re-established as an independent nation by the Treaty of Versailles in 1919.

On August 23rd 1939, just a week before the Germans invaded Poland, Hitler and Stalin signed a non-aggression agreement, the Ribbentrop-Molotov Pact, which stated they would never start hostilities against each other. Only during the Nuremberg War Crime Trials after WW2 did it come to light that this pact had included a secret protocol, agreeing that they would divide Poland up between them along the Curzon Line.

The Germans would invade first, and the Russians would wait until Poland was on its knees; then the Red Army would stealthily invade from the east without any declaration of war. Stalin would use deceitful propaganda to inform the rest of Europe that the Soviet Army had come to liberate the Polish people from the Nazis.

For both Hitler and Stalin, the key to controlling the Poles would be to eliminate the ruling elite which meant all their intellectuals, politicians, and high-ranking army officers, and anyone else with any level of power or authority. The Poles had already proved excellent at resistance so the leaders of both Germany and Russia, with their police forces (the Nazi Gestapo and the Soviet NKVD), planned together how to totally repress the Polish nation until there was no remaining leadership potential and thus no future underground resistance movement. Lists were written of those who had to be executed, and by the end of the war, nearly half of those Poles who had completed any sort of higher education were dead.

The rumours of possible invasion by Germany were so strong that the French and British signed an Agreement of Mutual Assistance with Poland on August 25th 1939, to ensure that the three countries would be mutual allies, promising military support to each other if any of them were attacked. Hitler, on discovering this agreement, postponed the date of his planned invasion in order to be fully prepared. Instead, he spread malicious propaganda alleging that German speakers in Eastern Poland were being persecuted by the Poles.

### The Gleiwitz Incident

In the afternoon of 31st August 1939, Hitler gave the order for Germany to be ready to invade Poland the next day. At 8 o'clock that evening, a group of Nazi SS troops, dressed in Polish army uniforms, deliberately damaged an important German radio station at Gleiwitz, a border town between Poland and Germany. They also dressed a few dead, concentration camp prisoners in Polish uniform, leaving them on the German side of the border. Finally, they shot some innocent civilians at the border and dressed them in German army uniforms. The Nazis had contrived this phoney act, known as the Gleiwitz incident, to 'prove' that the Poles had attacked Germany first, and Hitler used this lie as his excuse to invade Poland.

## German Invasion

Before dawn the following day, the 1st of September 1939, in spurious 'retaliation' for the Gleiwitz Incident, 1.5 million German troops invaded Poland at many points along the whole length of its 1000 mile border, advancing at a frightening pace in a strategy known as Blitzkreig, or 'lightning war'. Simultaneously, the German Air Force destroyed Polish planes and air fields and bombed random Polish cities, while German U-boats attacked the Polish Navy in the Baltic Sea. Anyone who resisted was executed.

The British demanded that Germany immediately withdraw from Poland, but on Sept 3rd, at 11am, the British ultimatum expired, and Prime Minister Chamberlain announced that Britain was now at war with Germany. By 5.00pm the same day, France also declared war.

The Polish Army managed to mobilise a million troops but their strategy was poor because, as agreed, they were waiting for Britain and France to come to their aid. The allies had encouraged them to fight instead of taking a strong defensive position, so the Poles raced to each invasion point to confront the Germans, and were systematically captured or killed. Poland was massively let down by the allies who just dropped leaflets over Berlin commanding Hitler to withdraw instead of sending troops to help in the battle.

An early strategy of the Germans was to attack and capture all the munitions factories which supplied the Polish military. One of the largest such factories where his father, Michał Dąbrowski, was employed, was in Jerzy's home town of Skarżysko Kamienna. On September 6th, a large group of men from the town, which included Michał and his two sons, fled on bicycles to the Ukraine border in the east to escape the Nazis who were kidnapping men and boys. These captives would then be forced into the German army, deported to concentration camps or even murdered if it was thought they would resist in any way. Everyone thought the war would be short-lived, but no-one knew that the Soviets also intended to invade Poland.

The Germans advanced rapidly and the Polish army, getting no help from their allies, was decimated. Over 10,000 Polish intellectuals from the west of Poland were arrested and sent to concentration camps, and eventually killed; more than 4,000 Polish leaders and 20,000 civilians were murdered near Warsaw, in reprisal for Partisan fighting at the beginning of the war. Another 400,000, now 'stateless', Poles were forcibly deported to the new German General Government, administered from Krakow, where they were treated as slaves.

The Polish Prime Minister, General Sikorski, strongly encouraged both military and civilian convoys to escape westwards over the Carpathian Mountains, to Romania and Hungary, where they would receive a warm welcome. Eighty thousand troops managed to leave before the borders were sealed, and they re-grouped to form the Carpathian Rifle Brigade which later fought alongside the allies. The many civilians who fled gradually made their way to freedom.

**The Soviet Invasion**

Stalin waited until the Polish Army and citizens were weakened by the German onslaught, then sixteen days later, on the 17th September 1939, without any announcement of hostilities, he ordered the Soviet Army to invade Poland from the east.

Half a million Soviet troops overwhelmed what remained of the Polish Border Defence Corps. They said they had come to 'liberate' the country from the Nazis, but the Polish people could not believe that these savage, uncouth hordes riding skeletal horses were a 'victorious' army. Their clothes and bedding were torn and shabby, and the soldiers were starving. Most, including a great number of women, had travelled from the very poor and remote regions of Soviet Asia to arrive at the Ukrainian border with Poland.

These 'Russians' were amazed at the material wealth of the Polish people who were supposed to be inhuman and little better than animals. The women prized the silky nightdresses thinking they were evening wear for special occasions. The men prized the watches and army officers pinned them to their chests, thinking they were military decorations, although they couldn't understand the ticking!

The Soviet soldiers plundered any removable goods the Poles owned, and they allowed any Ukrainians who sided with the Russians to evict the Poles from their homes and inhabit them themselves; hence, the Soviets openly exploited the old animosities between the Polish and the Ukrainians. Several large Polish cities had initially allowed the Soviets peaceful entry through their towns and villages, thinking they were on their way to help Poland against the Nazis, but the Russians quickly imposed the Communist ideology on everyone. Soviet indoctrinators were rapidly exchanged for teachers and clergy, and within three months, the Polish currency, the Złoty, was removed from circulation and prices rose steeply.

**The Polish Premier in Britain**

The day following the Soviet invasion, September 18th 1939, when Poland was near to collapsing, General Władisław Sikorski, with his government, fled Poland. They were interred in Romania at first then went to France where he formed a Polish Government-in-Exile. In Paris, on September 30th, Sikorski became the Polish Prime Minister but without a Military command. Leaving his Government in France, he then travelled London where he was formally acknowledged as the Prime Minister of the Polish Government-in-Exile. This was meant to prove that Poland, as a nation, still existed and would have a say in its own fate.

General Sikorski was held in high regard by Winston Churchill, the British Prime Minister. London was the only European capital that remained free from German occupation; this was partly due to the many brilliant Polish Air Force pilots flying alongside the British RAF in the Battle of Britain in 1940.

**The Soviets in Poland**

On September 28th 1939, Warsaw finally capitulated and surrendered to the relentless German siege, and that same day, Germany and the USSR concluded the secret protocol of the Molotov-Ribbentrop Pact which outlined their new territory. Poland was now divided fairly equally into two along the Curzon Line and geographically ceased to exist. The Germans and Russians both wanted to remove all the Poles and Jews from the areas of Poland they now occupied.

Neither the British nor the French wanted a confrontation with Russia who, under the Tsar, had been their ally in WW1, so their reaction to the Soviet invasion was minimal. They did not even command the Russians to withdraw because war had not actually been declared. This 'Phoney War' (it was not phoney for the Poles!) lasted for six months while the allies, although ready on the sidelines, did nothing at all; they waited to see if Poland was able to defend itself against both invading enemies.

About a month after the Soviet invasion, the Soviets held a National Referendum in Poland in order to 'prove' that the Poles were actually in favour of a Soviet government, and in agreement with East Poland being annexed to the USSR. The Polish civilians were forced to vote in an atmosphere of terror; they were told exactly who to vote for under threat of deportation or execution. But, of course, the referendum was rigged, falsely resulting in a landslide victory for the Soviets.

Many people in the eastern border villages between

Poland and the Ukraine were attacked and murdered, or exiled to Siberia, especially those refugees who had fled from the west of Poland to escape the Nazis. No one realised that trains with cattle trucks had already been prepared beforehand to deport hundreds of thousands of people, arrested at gunpoint in the middle of the night, never to return again. The world wanted to believe that under the protection of the Soviets, the Polish people would be safe from the Germans, but Stalin's plans were to destroy the annexed East Poland and absorb it into the Soviet Union. He confiscated land, property and businesses and stopped all independent political and public institutions. Many thousands of Polish civilians were branded as anti-Soviet and socially dangerous and so were removed from their homes and deported to Siberia.

No one in the west of Europe knew Stalin for the tyrant he really was: the 'Red' Army had spread disinformation everywhere, to give the impression that they were actually assisting the Poles against the Germans and also 'liberating' the Poles from their capitalist, feudal 'Lords'.

Trains full of Polish soldiers and officers retreating from the Germans in the west of Poland, were commandeered by the NKVD, the Soviet secret police, and sent instead to the east. Many ended up in the Siberian Gulag slave labour camps, established under Lenin.

By May the following year, Soviet authorities started issuing Soviet passports to all the inhabitants of the newly annexed east of Poland. People had to choose to either accept the passport thereby effectively becoming a Russian citizen, or return to the west of Poland and live under German occupation. Both options were as terrible as each other.

**Soviet Arrests and Deportations**
Within a few months of the Soviet invasion, the

authorities in Moscow ordered the arrest of all Polish nationals who they regarded as counter-revolutionary and potentially harmful to the Soviet government. The Kremlin was aiming, initially, for a successful communisation of all Polish citizens and so they needed to get rid of any who had served in the pre-war Polish state who could potentially prove resistant or lead an uprising.

A large number of those first arrested were upper-ranking Polish Military personnel, the politicians and scientists, judges and civil servants. Approximately 30,000 people, including 22,000 top level Military Officers and Intelligentsia who were POWs, were interrogated, tortured, executed and buried in mass graves in the Katyn Forest near the Belarus border.

Next, the Soviets arrested professional people with any level of authority or social standing, such as teachers and local government officials; they also arrested any one in uniform such as the police, and even people who just looked well-dressed or well-educated. The NKVD interrogated them until they confessed to crimes against the state that they had not committed, then exiled them to Siberian labour camps. The large civilian population remaining were, in the main, small business owners, women, children, Jews and the elderly. It was decided that anyone who represented the capitalist state in any measure would be deported en masse to the labour camps and settlements in Soviet Russia, leaving East Poland in the hands of the Belorussians and Ukrainian inhabitants. Finally, in order to complete their daily quota of prisoners, they arrested refugees who had fled the Germans from the west, the family members of those already caught, children from summer camps and orphanages, and even random people picked up in the street.

Between 1.25 – 1.7 million Polish nationals (the exact number is unknown) were deported, without trial, to the bleak and remote wastelands of Siberia, the Arctic circle and Soviet Kazakhstan. Such deportations had already been a common occurrence since the beginning of the Russian Revolution and it has been estimated that there were about 30,000 labour camps and settlements of various sizes in the gulag.

There were four major deportations starting in February 1940; my father, Jerzy, with his father, Michał and his brother, Stanisław, were taken on the third and largest deportation, on the 28-29th June 1940, which included any people who would not accept a Soviet passport. Nearly a million people were transported to the Novosibirsk area, and it was such a hot summer, that many died on the train from the heat. They travelled in locked cattle-trucks to the eastern parts of USSR, to Siberia, the Arctic or Soviet Kazakhstan.

For the Polish people, the Soviet Union's policies of ethnic cleansing were arguably harsher even than those of Nazi Germany. The Poles had no idea where they were going, how long they would be there, nor how they would be treated.

# CHAPTER 1: A HAPPY CHILDHOOD IN PRE-WAR POLAND

14/03/1926 – 31/08/1939 (AGE 0-13½)

## JERZY DĄBROWSKI

I was rather small for my age.

At times this proved to be quite useful; for instance, in pre-war Poland, children under 4 years old travelled free on the train. Once, when I was nearly 5, the ticket inspector asked my mother how old I was and she replied, 'Nearly 4'. The inspector then put the same question to me and I replied, 'I must be at least six or seven by now but my mummy always says that I am nearly four!' This made everyone laugh and I was allowed to travel free that day.

My father, Michał Dąbrowski, had been a Lieutenant in the Russian (Tsar's) Army during WW1 and in the Polish-Soviet War of 1919-20, and was discharged from his position in 1933. Both my parents, Michał and Albina Dąbrowski, and their daughter Halina (born 1912), survived the First World War and then settled happily in the small town of Skarżysko-Kamienna in south-east Poland. Michał, fourteen years her senior, was Albina's second husband. Together they brought two boys into the world; Stanisław in 1922 and myself, Jerzy, in 1926.

Skarżysko-Kamienna is a historic town in the valley of the River Kamienna, in central Poland, north-east of Kielce. Originally just a small mine workers' settlement called Kamienna, a very important railway junction was built there in the 1890s to enable the transportation of products of steel production and leather-tanning enterprises between Warsaw and Kraków, and Łódź and

Sandomierz. A Jewish settlement, called Skarżysko, grew up around this junction. The town grew rapidly in the 20 years between the two world wars, when the government decided to build the 'National Armament Factory - Ammunition Plant' there. In 1924 it began production, and became the main supplier of munitions to the Polish Army. Four years later, the town's name was changed to Skarżysko-Kamienna. By the start of the Second World War, the factory employed over 4500 workers, thus becoming the principal employer in the town and driving its growth. The population of the town was 20,000 of which 14% were Jews, who were growing increasingly worried about the growing anti-Semitism in both Germany and Poland.

My father was a building surveyor employed by this large ammunition factory in the town, while my mother successfully ensured that the family was well looked after with lots of love and essential discipline. Thanks to her, I have happy memories of childhood which helped me to get through my life's later difficulties. My sister Halina was thirteen and my brother Stanisław was four in March 1926, when I joined them in this world to put an end to their tranquility. My parents were pleased with this event but I am not sure my brother shared their enthusiasm because he was no longer the centre of attention. My earliest recollection is from the time I was about 2 ½ years old. I came home from playing outside as dirty as any child that age could be. My sister did her best trying to wash me but I kept screaming at the top of my voice 'I don't want to be washed! I want to stay dirty!' Somehow she completed the job but because I was making so much fuss, she threatened to take me outside and rub mud all over me again. At times, when my mother was busy, Halina had to look after me. This did not suit her when she had a date, and I later found out that she used to press my eyes to make me go to sleep quicker – maybe this is why I was so short-sighted and had to wear glasses from childhood!

When I was very young my ambition was to be a

priest. I used to stand on a stool and preach to 'My Dear Parishioners', those unfortunate family members and friends who got caught by me. Later, at age eight or nine, I decided I would rather be a bishop without having to be a priest first. I found myself, on one occasion, sitting on a chair next to a real bishop at the dentist. I took the opportunity to express my plans to him. He promised me that if I allowed the dentist to do his job without me fussing, interrupting or making a noise, he would see to it that I became a bishop without having to be a priest first. To this day I have never become a bishop so I do not trust bishops!

I have never liked chocolate much, particularly milk chocolate. This is because when I was very ill once with tummy problems, the doctor gave me a box of castor oil tablets coated in chocolate. The box was lying on top of my bedside cabinet when a friend came round to see how I was. One by one he consumed the whole box of tablets which gave me great pleasure but for the next few days he was the one with a tummy disorder.

At different times we kept a cat or dog as a pet, but one day we found an injured rook which my brother and I nursed back to health. At first we kept it in a cage but eventually we set it free. It had become so attached to us that if we called his name, 'Kubus, Kubus!', he immediately flew to us to get some food. When he was given too much food, he used to bury it in the garden next door. This did not please our neighbour very much; one day he shot and wounded Kubus. After a few days the bird gave up the ghost, so to get our revenge, we tied a dead rat to the neighbour's door-handle which made us feel much better.

Twice a week, a market was held in the town. Peasants' carts arrived very early, carrying produce and crafts. When the weather was wet or freezing, they still came, the peasants wrapped in furs. About a mile away from my home, surrounded by pine forest, was the beautiful artificial Lake Rejów; it was one mile long and 300 metres wide and as a family, we spent many hot summer days there. We used to row across it to one of its several sandy beaches to have a picnic. Twice I nearly drowned when I tried to walk across the bottom of the lake but thankfully someone pulled me out in time, so I then decided I needed to teach myself to swim. In the winter the lake froze solid allowing us to ice-skate part of the way to our primary school half a mile away.

As well as swimming and ice-skating, I enjoyed playing volleyball and handball, and cycling to the nearby villages. I spent a lot of time in the forest collecting mushrooms, wild strawberries and blueberries, and catching various lizards, beetles and grass snakes which I took to school to frighten the girls and make the boys laugh. At the age of ten, I joined the Boy Scouts and really enjoyed the night exercises and wide games.

One teacher at school thought I looked as if I had a good voice so he enrolled me in the school choir. During rehearsals he realised that someone was not quite singing in tune although public performances went perfectly. It didn't take him long to realise that I was the problem and that during a performance I was only miming the words. Someone at the school must have liked my voice, though, because on many occasions I was asked to recite pieces of poetry from the stage. Fairly early in my life I tried my hand at writing my own poetry which I continued well into adulthood. At the age of nine I wrote short poems to my current girlfriend, but one poem I wrote in 1939, was called 'Old Hitler' and it was not as sweet as the others.

Between the world wars, the now independent Poland had the opportunity to reconstruct a new education system from the remains of the three systems in place during the occupation of the country by Germany, Prussia and Russia in the previous century. School attendance was free and accessible, but compulsory from ages 7-14. There were several different levels of school. Everyone attended the local primary school for the first six years. Any one who wanted to continue into higher education now took the entrance exam and then continued either in the four-year Grammar school, the *gimnazjum,* or in the two-year secondary school. Pupils who didn't want to continue their education finished in the seventh year of primary school and went on to technical, trade or commercial education.

I and four other local children went to a private establishment for our first year and so we started the local primary school in the second year. Like my brother, I had such good results from my sixth year at primary school so was able to enter the grammar school with only an oral interview at age eleven, without taking the exam. The grammar school fees for both my brother and myself, were each equal to my father's monthly salary. He therefore had to sacrifice two months wages each year to pay for our education but somehow we survived financially although it was difficult for him. In the grammar school we were expected to behave in a mature fashion. However, we all delighted in playing tricks on our lecturers or fellow pupils. Our Latin teacher had a habit of walking up and down between our benches when he was teaching; he always asked very predictable questions, so someone would write the answers on a piece of paper in large handwriting, and pin it to the back of his coat-tails. This really helped those who were not concentrating!

On one school trip, we went to the Polish Tatra Mountains, taking a cable car up the mountain called Kasprowy Wierch near Zakopane. There are four mountain crests and paths criss-cross from one to the other following the boundaries of Slovakia and Poland. Later we went by horse-drawn carriage to two beautiful lakes, Morskie Oko whose name means 'The Eye of the Sea' and Czarny Staw, 'The Black Pond' which are, supposedly, the deepest small lakes in the world. There is an old legend that suggests that 'The Eye of the Sea' is connected to the Baltic Sea over 400 miles away, by a secret underground passage! The water was so clear that day, we could see trout and salmon swimming along the bottom. The higher 'Black Pond', is smaller and deep blue not black. On our return journey, we stopped in Kraków, the old capital of Poland, and visited the famous Wawel Castle which contains the tombs of many Polish kings. Finally we saw the well-known church of St Mary, and the legendary Cloth Hall which is full of souvenir shops; both of these historic buildings in Kraków are in the largest Market Square in Europe.

During the summer months, we usually visited various family members who lived in different parts of Poland. My father's brother, a parish priest, lived with his elderly mother in Kamien-Koszyrski in Polesia near the famous Pripyat marshes of northern Ukraine, an enormous natural region of wetlands along the forested Pripyat River. It is one of the largest wetland areas of Europe. The marshes, moors, ponds and streams see many changes in size through the year, with extensive flooding when the winter snow melts in the spring, and when the autumn rainfall causes the river to overflow.

One holiday, we travelled by narrow-gauge railway to visit the historical monastery in Lubieszewo, then followed this by a long walk to swim in a lake. Another time, my older brother Stach (Stanisław's nickname) was chasing me when I tripped and fell on top of one of the broken roofing tiles used for edging a flowerbed. I received a deep cut right to the bone just above my knee. My uncle panicked and poured a whole bottle of iodine on the wound and when the doctor finally saw it, needless to say, he was unable to stitch it; I still have a deep hole there covered only by skin.

We often travelled by train. Once, when returning from one of our frequent visits to a certain aunt, my mother's seat was in the draught from open windows all the way home. This caused a painful inflammation in her jaw which resulted in her spending long periods in hospital. The doctor initially thought it was cancer and treated her jaw with X-rays which made the matter worse, to the point where she finally had to have a sliver of bone from her thigh transplanted there. She never fully recovered from all this but remained cheerful and loving despite her suffering.

I loved walking in the Tatra mountains with my brother, and we had several noteworthy mishaps on our walks. We sometimes lost our way, and on one occasion we found ourselves at the edge of a sheer drop of three metres over a river with no other way back to our holiday villa. My brother finally decided to jump and although I hesitated at first, my mind was quickly made up once I realised that some friendly ants were swarming inside my shorts while I was sitting on the edge!

Another time, with a group, we decided to walk up the Kasprowy Wierch mountain and take the cable car back. I led the walk but somehow happened to take a path to the left instead of to the right. We suddenly realised that Mount Świnica (7,500 feet high) was on our right-hand side when it should have been on our left. Instead of returning the way we had come, we decided to take a short-cut over the mountains but were nearly defeated by the stunted pine trees halfway up the steep slope. These were 'kosodrzewina' or dwarf mountain pines, which only grow about three feet tall but have very long branches (up to 20 feet) which spread all over the ground. There are easier ways to climb a mountain, believe me.

We finally managed to reach the top ridge which we followed across Mount Świnica, and enjoyed the lovely views of valleys and lakes. When we finally got back to Kasprovy Wierch, the main group, having despaired of us ever arriving, had returned to the villa where my parents notified the police that we were lost somewhere in the mountains. In the meantime, my brother and I set off to walk back down because we had too little money for the cable car, although we managed to pay for a lift on a horse and cart for the final few kilometres. We had walked over 30 kilometres in mountains that day and after food, collapsed into bed.

I was always shy with girls and couldn't really understand why they were necessary! However I met my first real girlfriend, Zosia, at the age of 7 and we continued our 'relationship' until war broke out when I was 13. When I was 12, my much older, married sister gave birth to a little boy she called Andrezj, and the girls at school teased me, shouting 'Uncle, Uncle' at me until I wanted to strangle the lot of them. Only Zosia was beyond reproach. Her parents fully approved of me and I was the only boy who was invited to her Name Day celebrations, dressed to kill and carrying the largest bouquet of flowers I could manage. After the war, Zosia and I were able to get back in touch for a little while although by then we lived in different countries.

In Poland at that time, it was the custom to celebrate Name Days, the feast day of the patron saint of our name, rather than birthdays. Almost all Poles have a saint's name and there is a male and female saint for every day of the year. Name Days and their dates, so important in our Polish tradition, are often displayed on buses and trams, so that you would know who to buy flowers and gifts for on that day. Less prominent information on public transport is the name of the next stop. My name, Jerzy, is George in Polish, so I celebrated my 'birthday' on St. George's day. It is said that all the animals have birthdays but only humans can have Name Days.

My brother was very independent and liked to take long cycle rides alone to far away places. At age 16, he started piloting a glider and once very nearly lost his life when the aircraft suddenly rose straight up in the air then nose-dived to the ground. At the last minute he managed to level out the flight just above the ground and so was saved. During my life I experienced over fifteen occasions when I nearly died. One event that remains in my mind happened when I was nine. I was cycling with my friend and we had to cross a double railway track at the crossing which was in a cutting on a bend. We waited for one train to pass then crossed the first track and as we did so, I jokingly called out that there was another train coming the other way, to make my friend panic. Then suddenly, round the bend, a train really did appear and I had to grab my friend and pull him hard over and away from the second track. The train missed us by inches.

In the spring of 1939, while my brother and I were at Grammar school, the dam on Lake Rejów burst. The owner of the small higher lake had been wanting to enlarge his property by collecting more water. This pressure had forced his own dam to break first, sending massive amounts of water downstream and causing the next dam to disintegrate. Large areas of land were flooded and most of the bridges were washed away, including the bridge over the river between our school and our home. A whole corner of a four-storey building vanished and the timber pavilion of the Rejów Lake Club with its tower was also washed away, nearly destroying the nearby, small, electric power station. We were allowed to leave school early that day and had to be personally escorted over the steel railway bridge before walking four kilometres home because no bus could get through.

There were many other adventures and escapades during my childhood, but nothing, however, that could really prepare me for the next few years.

# CHAPTER 2: WAR BEGINS IN POLAND

## 01/09/1939 – 29/06/1940 (AGE 13½-14)

### JERZY DĄBROWSKI

During the hot summer of 1939, it soon became obvious to everybody that Germany was looking for an excuse to invade Poland. There was a lot of political noise about the 'Polish Corridor' which gave Poland access to the Baltic Sea but separated Greater Germany from East Prussia. There were also unfounded accusations about the alleged mistreatment of German minorities by the Poles who lived there. Towards the end of August, the Poles started digging trenches against an attack by German bombers, the Polish army was mobilised and all aircraft, tanks and equipment were overhauled. Every person was issued with a gas-mask because it was possible the Germans would be dropping poison-gas bombs. My 17 year old brother, Stanisław, was put in charge of an observation post on the top of a high building in the town centre, while I, being a 13 year old boy scout, became a messenger.

On Friday 1st September 1939, at about 5 am, the first German bombers appeared and everyone hid in their cellars. The ammunition factory, about half a mile from our home in Skarżysko-Kamienna, was one of the first targets. It seems the Germans had not updated their maps and at that time, Lake Rejów next to the factory was covered in green algae and undergrowth. By mistake, the majority of bombs were dropped on another nearby village with a similar lake surrounded by forest. Later that day I found a fragment of a bomb almost the same shape as Poland, which surprised me.

The Germans were already known to have taken Polish men and boys to be incorporated within their armed forces or to do forced labour in their industrial area, the Ruhr, blackmailing them into obedience by the threat of making their families suffer. To avoid this happening to us, my father, my brother and myself joined a group of about forty other men from the town. After collecting essentials from home and saying goodbye to our mother, we started cycling, myself still on a child's cycle, towards eastern Poland at about 9.30 am on Wednesday 6th September. My brother-in-law was already a Polish Officer and had to join the Polish Army, so my sister and her baby were left behind to keep my mother company. We truly believed that, because Britain and France had now joined the war, a swift defeat of the Germans was inevitable and in a few days we would be able to return home.

We could already see and hear gunfire in several directions, but when cycling through the forest, we could never be sure whether the soldiers we noticed were Polish or German. In the middle of the first night, after cycling non-stop through the forest for several hours, my brother fell asleep on his bicycle and instead of taking the bend to the left, he continued in a straight line, ending up in a ditch! This, and the noise of our laughing, soon woke him up! When we arrived at the River Vistula at Solec, the Germans were already dropping bombs on the bridge we were about to cross. Luckily all the bombs fell into the river and so we were able to get safely to the other side. Then the German planes returned and this time managed to destroy the bridge. We decided to get some sleep in some public gardens, hoping we would be safe there, then continued on our journey towards the city of Lublin. The following night was spent sleeping on straw in the barn of a friendly farmer. The early wake-up call was given by a loud cockerel, and after a tasty breakfast of chicken broth, we continued to Piaski where we stopped at a café for some refreshment. Someone took a fancy to my brother's bicycle and decided to take permanent care of it. This resulted in my brother having to walk to the station to catch an appropriate train in the hope of rejoining the party later.

The following day I got a small puncture and every half a mile had to pump up my tyre then race to catch up with the others. At the village of Hrubieszów, my father could only manage to buy a full-sized inner-tube and somehow managed to force it, folded, into my tyre. Here we all split into family groups and went separate ways. Late in the evening of the sixth day of travelling (12th September), we arrived at the house of one of my father's brothers, in Łuck (pronounced 'Woutzk') and spent the evening catching up with family news. The next day, Friday 13th September, we cycled the last leg of our journey, arriving at the village of Wiszenki on the river Styr near the Ukrainian border, where my father's other brother, a parish priest, lived. To our pleasant surprise and great joy, we discovered my brother had arrived there the previous day before us.

As we settled in Wiszenki, I occasionally helped my uncle by serving at mass, and I also enjoyed helping the local boat-owner to ferry people across the river, welcoming the tips I was given. In my plentiful free time I swam in the river. Unfortunately, as I returned across the river one day to retrieve my clothes, I realised my glasses were missing. I had to manage for the next three years without them but found my eyesight improved a little because I was unable to read.

On the 17th September, the Soviet Red Army crossed the Polish border to 'free the inhabitants' although no-one seemed to know what they were freeing us from! They certainly freed people from eating too much or from the necessity of shopping because very quickly the shops were completely empty. For over two weeks, the poorly equipped Polish army had to fight against two powerful adversaries, the Germans in the west and the Russians in the east. After only five weeks fighting, Poland was finally forced to capitulate.

Not many miles from our village of Wiszenki, there was a large horseshoe bend in the river. A detachment of Polish Army cavalry, which happened to be inside this horseshoe, was spotted by two different units of the Red Army, which were both on the same side of the river but opposite the Polish troops. Both units started firing at the Poles who quietly moved out of the horseshoe, leaving the Russians firing at each other across the bends of the river, each thinking that the other group were the Polish cavalry. By the time they realised what had happened, many of those 'brave' Red Army soldiers had lost their lives.

Hoping to gain favour with the Soviets, some local Ukrainian communist youths had organised themselves into militia units to help the Red Army. One day, as a group of Polish cavalry rode through our village, these youths started shooting at them and in retaliation, the Polish Major in charge wanted to burn the whole village down. My uncle pleaded with him and eventually managed to talk him out of that idea. The majority of Ukrainian people were kind and decent and they were grateful that their village was saved from the flames. Another night soon afterwards, the local communist militia gangs from many villages near us, came to execute my uncle, my father and all who were staying in the house, but in gratitude, the villagers then saved our lives by surrounding the house and not allowing anyone to carry out their intention. We only found out about this evil plan the following morning.

Red Army units marched through our village in a deep silence on the 22nd of September. The soldiers, who were used to shortages, removed the altar cloths from the church to use as sheets, and stole the candles and other liturgical items. They took silk night-dresses from the ladies to give to their wives as 'evening dresses' at dances, and confiscated my uncle's typewriter, saying they would reform the letters into their alphabet. It would be an understatement to mention that the Soviet soldiers were not very bright; it was not difficult to sell them our boy scout compasses as watches!

All the shops had to display a large portrait of 'Father Stalin' in their window. The butcher obeyed but also hung an enormous curved Polish sausage in such a way that the lower end of it touched the tip of Stalin's nose.

The Soviet authorities decided to hold 'elections' on October 22nd and installed their polling stations close to churches where people went in large numbers, so that photographs after the Mass could be taken for the newspapers ostensibly showing how happy and eager the people were to vote. There was, of course, only one candidate to vote for and everybody had to prove they had voted, even being taken there at gunpoint and given a sealed vote to put in a box. Also, blank returns were counted as favourable to the Soviets.

Somehow, through unofficial channels, we managed to send a letter to our mother to assure her that we were all alive and well and staying with our uncle. We found out later that she received this letter a couple of days before the German Red Cross advised her of our death near Warsaw three days after we left home! She immediately knew that this was the Germans' way of trying to break the morale of the conquered people.

Winter that year, 1939, was more severe than any I had ever experienced. The temperature reached $-40°C$ and snow covered the ground for four months. At times it was so thick we couldn't open the doors. One time we opened the back door with great difficulty, then with shovels at the ready, we removed three feet of snow from the front door. It was impossible for us to travel anywhere. But then neither could the Soviet soldiers.

Early every morning, my very active 80 year old grandmother, who also lived with us, would feed the cow, pig and hens. Later she milked the cow and cooked all our meals. We were very lucky to have fresh milk and eggs every day and sometimes, home-made sausages too. The local villagers often helped us out and even the cat managed to kill a hare double her size and drag it home so her kittens had fresh meat and we had roast hare for dinner. That summer there was a plague of flies. My uncle offered me a small coin for every 100 flies I could catch. A neighbouring village kept bees and we went there to sample the honey. The flies were worse there and in trying to flap them away, I got some honey in my hair and the flies landed thickly on my head. I finally gave up the struggle and washed my hair thoroughly.

My uncle, the Parish priest, was very run-down and suffered from numerous boils so I often helped him with his dressings. He had an excellent ear for music and couldn't stand anyone going off-key or off-tune. One Mass, the organist made a few mistakes in his playing and I was told to go up to him and tell him to improve his playing. This, of course, upset the organist and he would not talk to my uncle for several weeks. As a result, I had to take over some of his duties in preparing the church for Mass, especially the Easter services.

For my bed at my uncle's house, I had to arrange 8 chairs together in pairs in the living room. If the priest had visitors, they often talked till late preventing me going to bed. This had become a bit annoying by the spring, when I loved to get up early and go for a walk or cycle ride. Sometimes I passed the trenches, some Russian and some German, dug in the First World War when the area changed hands several times. Many soldiers had lost their lives there. I used to help my uncle, the parish priest, with many of the church duties, travelling with him to give Holy Communion to the sick, and preparing the church for the different services. I was once invited to help at a wedding in another village and I enjoyed dancing with all the pretty girls until late. We slept in the stable loft and returned to Wiszenki the next day by horse and cart.

On the eve of St Peter's and St Paul's day, 29th June, I prepared the church for the next day's service and sorted out my better clothes. However, the events of that night made it impossible to go to church the following day. This was the very last time I saw my uncle and grandmother alive.

# CHAPTER 3: JOURNEY TO SIBERIA

## 29/06/1940 – 15/07/1940 (AGE 14)

### *JERZY DĄBROWSKI*

A very loud and insistent banging at the door very early in the morning woke us all up in terror. A Soviet detachment of soldiers armed with rifles had come to arrest us at 2 am on the 29th June, the feast day of St Peter and St Paul. They had commandeered a peasant's horse and cart to take my father, my brother and myself for 'a little ride'. At first they told us we were to be taken back home to our house in western Poland; then we were advised that we would not be going 'very far' but this actually resulted in a 'short' journey of 3,250 miles to Siberia!

We later learnt that every ethnic Polish citizen whose home was in the part of Poland now occupied by the Soviets, as well as all who were well-educated, rich or who had held a position of importance before the war, with their whole families, were to be sent to Siberia. This also included refugees who had fled from their home towns when the Germans invaded Poland. The Soviets wanted to make sure that there would be no-one left who had potential leadership qualities. Their thinking was that those people with a minimal education would be less likely to cause trouble, and would be easier to convert to communist ideals. People of all ages, from the new-born to old folk in their nineties, were taken away. They were told to forget Poland because it didn't exist any more, and to make their home in the place the Soviet Union had selected for them.

We were given two hours to pack our belongings, but there wasn't much one could put in a haversack –

we had left our home in Skarżysko-Kamienna with very little. However, my grandmother and uncle gave us towels, pillows, warm clothing, seven loaves of freshly baked bread and other food. We tried to save the bread for emergencies but on the journey it went mouldy so, with heavy hearts, we threw it away.

Our 'luxurious' transport, a peasant's farm cart pulled by a horse that was barely alive, delivered us to the nearest railway station at Rozyszcze: here, with many others in the same situation, we were unceremoniously loaded into cattle trucks, about 32 people to each truck. The doors were locked and bolted so no-one could escape. Inside the truck there were two large shelves, one on each side. Eight people could be accommodated on each shelf, and another eight below each. A gap was left in the middle so people could move around. It seemed very crowded. We three were lucky to be on a top shelf which meant we had a little ventilation opening through which we could see the world. There was no headroom so we had to get down onto the floor to stretch. This was difficult, especially for the elderly, because there were no ladders. At the 'back door' there was a 'toilet', a circular hole through to the outside with some sort of contraption for a seat. To preserve modesty, it was agreed that every time someone used the toilet, someone else would hold up a blanket. This all contributed to a mass loss of appetite!

Our truck, with a couple of others, was taken to the major railway station in Kowel which, for many centuries, had been the location of a large Jewish settlement. The name came from a Slavonic name for blacksmith. The town had been part of the Russian Empire for over a hundred years. The Jewish settlement increased in size during the war since many Jews from German-occupied west Poland took refuge here. Many of the trains carrying deportees, including Jews, to Siberia started their long journey here in Kowel, where we joined about 50 other trucks, making a very long train. For the first few days, our truck was in the middle of the train, which was just about bearable. Later, our truck happened to be the last in the line and, because the trucks were badly joined together, we were thrown quite violently from side to side, making it impossible to stand up. This was particularly bad when travelling fast down the Ural Mountains.

The day following our departure from Kowel, we crossed the ancient border between Poland and Soviet Russia which made us feel very sad. After three days of travelling, the train stopped in the middle of nowhere; there was a long fence of barbed wire on either side. For the first time the doors were opened and we were allowed to disembark, carefully watched by numerous armed guards. The sounds and stench we all produced as, now without embarrassment, we squatted beside the barbed wire to 'do our business', was indescribable! Later the same day, the train stopped at the main station in Homel (Gomel). Here for the first time we were given food: this consisted of some kind of thick groats similar to millet porridge called 'penchak'. We were allowed to collect boiling water to make tea or soup: this was a standard service on major Soviet stations because the water was undrinkable otherwise. But the majority of their stations had no food or water at all.

Through our little ventilation hole we could read the names of the stations we passed through; these included Bryansk, Orel, Sasawo, Saransk, Pietropavlovsk, Omsk, Novosibirsk, Taiga, Tomsk and finally Asino, where our train journey ended on 13th July 1940. I wrote this poem:

**Ode to Fatherland Poland**

*You have not perished and are still alive*
*You, the Polish Nation, still exists*
*Polish hearts beat in our breasts*
*And the day of freedom is getting nearer!*
*We will defeat our detestable enemy*
*And rebuild the country*

*And you will be free again*
*Because we are still alive!*

*Hitler and his Krauts will perish*
*Together with Goebbels and Ribbentrop*
*Who the power of the German nation*
*Led completely astray.*
*And you, beloved Fatherland*
*Will again be free and famous*
*And you will fully regain*
*Your ancient power.*

*Once again a man will be found*
*Who will fully rebuild you*
*And the brave army will be reborn*
*That will defend you well.*
*Nobody will ever dare to part us*
*You will remain for ever with us.*
*We will always love you dearly*
*And be good sons to you.*

*We shall never abandon you*
*And will always bravely defend You,*
*We will ensure that you remain free*
*And will chase the Krauts away.*
*We will try to make you most powerful*
*Of all the nations in the world*
*And will make certain that your power*
*Will last through long years of eternity.*

*We'll make your enemies tremble*
*Before your great majesty*
*And your people will live in harmony*

*And love one another like brothers.*
*We will make sure there will never be a traitor*
*In your government or parliament*
*So nobody will ever dare*
*To rob you of any of your land.*

*Holy Mother of God will remain*
*The Queen of Your crown,*
*And you, Poland, will be great*
*From one sea to another.*

Tomsk is in central Russia, in the basin of the Ob River which bisects the town and floods it. Extensive swamps in the flat, monotonous landscape make agriculture difficult, although rye, oats and potatoes grow well. Timber-working is the main occupation as almost the entire area is taiga, or swampy coniferous forest, dominated by pine, fir, larch, and birch trees. Asino, a city in the south east of the Tomsk Oblast (province), is located near the Chulym, an important logging river, and is the largest wood-processing centre in western Siberia. It has a railroad spur that connects with the Trans-Siberian Railroad.

At Asino, we were all loaded onto open lorries and taken to the landing stage of the River Chulym, a 1,300 mile long tributary of the River Ob. The lower courses were navigable and here, approximately 1,500 of us were all crammed onto two river boats for the 2-day journey up the river. The River Chulym flowed across a very flat area and therefore had a great number of bends, horseshoe lakes and meanders. The water was deeper on the outer shore of each bend where the bank was high and steep, and very shallow on the inside of the bends where it formed wide beaches. The boats had to change from one side of the river to the other to remain in the deep water. There were so many of us on the boat that it was difficult for anyone to squeeze past to join the endless queue for the toilets. At night we couldn't even find enough space to sit down to sleep.

Finally, in the evening of 15th July, we arrived at our destination; the boats docked along a steep bank on the left and we had to climb up with all our worldly possessions; again, this was difficult for the elderly and the sick. We were then loaded onto primitive horse-drawn carts for the 2½ mile journey to a small settlement. A few days later we travelled another two miles to the main settlement of Sibiryakowskiy Lesozagotovitielniy Uchastok, which means ' Forestry Preparation Unit of Sibiryak' (the name of the nearby village). We had finally arrived, twelve miles from the small administrative town of Tegul'det. The journey had taken more than two weeks.

We were all allocated a space in one of the various log-built houses. At first, the three of us had to share a very large room with a number of other men. Later we were given a small room, about 10 feet by 10 feet, in a building that had four such rooms. The day after our arrival, we were all collected up and taken into the large communal hall to be reminded that we had to forget about the now 'non-existent' Poland - 'Here you shall live'! We were given a lecture on how we should serve our 'glorious' new country, the Soviet Union, by working as hard as we could. Many times in this hall we were told that Poland was no more and that we must no longer be misled by religious teachings as there is no God!

**The Settlement**

The settlement, where we were supposed to spend the rest of our lives, was built on a raised log platform surrounded by the Taiga Forest which was full of marshlands. An elevated timber causeway linked it to the smaller settlement we'd visited and to the River Chulym. This causeway was essential during the spring floods when the river become many miles wide and almost reached our settlement. The causeway was constructed with logs, ten feet long and more than two feet in diameter. They were laid in one to four layers at right angles to the direction of traffic, each interspersed with a layer of thinner logs laid at right angles to the main logs. On top of these layers of logs was a final layer of medium logs, about one foot in diameter, split in half lengthways so that the top surface was flat, and laid in the direction of traffic. On both sides of this roadway there were split logs laid on edge, half projecting above the flat surface and held in place by upright wooden pegs fixed to the top layer of the main logs. These were to prevent the wheels of carts from falling off the causeway. The carriageway itself was about seven feet wide and there were regular passing places where a vehicle could leave the 'road' to allow another vehicle to pass through, and then it would return to the causeway further on.

All the buildings, like typical log cabins, were constructed with round logs a little less than a foot in diameter. The bottom of each was flattened to fit better on top of the log below. The ends of the logs and all cross walls were interlocked, and then straw mixed with wet clay was used to caulk the logs and keep out draughts. The roofs were covered by timber boards sawn by hand on the settlement. All the windows had double sashes with a four-inch wide gap in between, and were able to be opened from the top for ventilation.

The largest building by far was two storeys high and contained a communal hall, a 'library', a 'restaurant' and several residential rooms. The hall itself was large enough to accommodate all the residents when we were called together to listen as some high ranking NKVD officer (later known as the KGB) explained our duties towards the 'Glorious Soviet Union', our new fatherland.

In the communal hall there was a radio receiver which provided us with news of what was happening in the outside world. Of course, everything transmitted was censored so that our minds could not be misled by any foreign propaganda! The hall always seemed to be open, allowing children to play inside when the weather was inclement. Sometimes dances were held there but these were not well-attended. The library contained mainly prescribed communist material although there were some books of literary value such as Tolstoy's 'War and Peace' and 'Tashkent, City of Bread' but they were all written in Russian. With my father's help, I learned the language fairly quickly and so was able to read these books. All the other buildings were only a single storey high. The biggest of these housed the local administration, and the next in size was used as a workshop for repairing our 'valonki', the thick felt boots worn in the winter, and our articles of clothing, especially the 'fufayki',(fufaika) the padded jackets and trousers. Another building contained the communal laundry and still another was used as a barber shop.

In several places there were toilet blocks, either for men and women separately, or divided by a partition for the use of both sexes. Often these outdoor toilet blocks were used as unofficial social meeting places where we could more freely exchange our views on any subject. There were no indoor toilets because there was no running water. Each toilet block was free-standing and contained a long wooden seat that had from four to six circular holes. This seat was normally too dirty to sit on so people had to squat on the top. Below there were holes, two metres deep, accessible from the outside so that their contents could be emptied. During the winter, the toilets froze solid; pinnacles of waste matter would project up to 12 inches above the seat making the toilet impossible to use until someone chopped them down and removed them, in barrels on a cart, to outside the camp. It so happened that water for the restaurant and other communal buildings was carried in similar barrels, so no-one could guess their contents, except by the smell as they passed.

There was only one well on the settlement, which was used for all the communal buildings and by all the residents, who had to queue every time. It was about thirty metres deep and never froze; however, in the winter, any spillage used to freeze on the inside of the well completely stopping the bucket from being used. A man had to stand in the bucket and be lowered by two strong men so that he could chip off the ice with an axe and allow the bucket to pass through and down to the water.

On one side of the settlement at Sibyriak there were houses for Russian villagers, the Kulaks, who had been settled there permanently. Slightly further away were the homes of the members of the NKVD and their families. Beyond these there was a small, electric power station which somehow made electricity from burning wood that had been cut into suitably sized pieces by female labourers, as this was considered to be light work. The power station supplied electricity for the strong spotlights on the watchtowers of the fort next to us, which was a prison for political prisoners. Adjoining the fort were barracks for the soldiers who guarded these prisoners.

Every morning these poor, starving prisoners were led away by armed guards to their place of work in the forest. Food was their only payment for their hard work, and it came in three different cauldrons of different quality food. The better they performed, the better the food they received. We did not realise, at first, that our lives would be as similar and just as expendable as theirs.

# IN THE SPOTLIGHT: DEPORTATION – ARRESTS AND CATTLE TRUCKS

## LINDA GALLAGHER

All the documented stories about the Polish deportations to Siberia have remarkable similarities; the arrest at gun point, the journey of thousands of miles in cattle trucks, and the struggle to survive at the destination. And yet, every individual's story of their journey and life in Siberia is different, and of course, only the survivors were able to tell their recollections. Many people died on that brutal journey and many more would die in the camp or settlement. The soldiers of the Soviet Army, and the NKVD (the secret police) seemed to have been trained to show no compassion for their victims; their attitude and their disinclination to give out any information was standard in every story.

In his own narrative, my father seems to just skim over the facts of the horror, the emotional devastation, the hard work, the deprivation and death. He was only 14-15 years old and his memories were probably coloured by his youth and his naturally optimistic nature.

**Deportations**

There were approximately 30,000 penal colonies in Siberia most of which were originally built for exiled Polish patriots during the 18th century partition of Poland. Then Russians from the communist uprisings of 1905 and 1917 and victims of Stalin's 'Great Purge' of 1936-38 were also exiled there; before the start of WW2 there were already about 1.5 million people living in Siberia. The Poles had known of the camps and had lived in dread of them for a long time.

At the beginning of WW2, the Soviets invaded Poland then deported between 1.25 and 1.7 million Poles, including Jews, families and children to these slave labour camps. The first deportation was the most distressing; it was still winter and no-one was prepared. By the spring and summer, it was warmer and people had now been warned. Despite all this, the Polish people never lost their faith in God nor their deep devotion to Polish Catholicism.

**The Knock on the Door**
First of all, without any warning, there would be a furious knocking at the door in the middle of the night, accompanied by urgent shouting to 'Hurry and open up'. The household, deeply asleep, would thus be confused and frightened when woken so violently. Terrified, the man of the house would open the door to four or five soldiers in improvised uniforms with red armbands, or to the NKVD in blue uniforms with peaked caps and red stripes down their trouser legs. Showing alleged search warrants which the semi-literate soldiers probably couldn't read, these intruders would push their way in, aiming their bayonets at the man's head or hitting him to make him more emotional and unresisting. Sometimes the family dog was shot to produce compliance. The soldiers would shout orders constantly: everyone had to get dressed while they watched and no-one was allowed to eat. All the men and boys had to line themselves up against a wall, while the women and girls were told pack for a long journey and be ready within an hour or so. They were to take all the warm clothes and bedding they could carry, plenty of food and water, cooking utensils, kettles and small agricultural implements. Some women managed to pack a sewing machine, having been told it would be useful where they were going; and they often included their photo albums for sentimental reasons.

Meanwhile, the soldiers would rush round the

house, ransacking each room in their search for weapons, and stealing whatever they could lay their hands on, especially watches. Occasionally a soldier would seem to have a degree of kindness or civility about him, but most just saw it as a job to be done. If the frightened victims asked where they were going, the soldiers would tell lies to make them come peacefully. Some were told they were going to be repatriated in German-occupied west Poland; others were told they were going to stay in Warsaw for a while, or were going on a short holiday.

Often, as they finally left the house, the inhabitants would be confronted with those local Ukrainians who had betrayed them and who were now waiting to take over their home. The prisoners would be hustled onto army trucks, horse-drawn carts or even dung carts, all forcibly stolen from the locals, while some were made to walk. They were taken to the nearest railway station where their luggage was just dumped in a heap.

Thousands of distressed people were gathered on the station platforms, all trying to find their family and possessions and keep them together. There was a cacophony of screaming and crying as families were split up. The Russian guards separated them into groups of maybe 30, 40 or even up to 70, and forced them into cattle trucks, luggage first. With much grief and fear, the old and frail were helped up the very high step into the wagons. Then each truck was locked with a metal bar securing the doors.

## The Journey in the Cattle-trucks

For the first few days, even up to a week, the cattle-trucks would remain stationary in a siding with the people locked inside, because priority on the tracks was given to the movements of the Red Army. This wait was also intended to disorientate the captives and break their spirits. Local people would try to give them food but were deterred by the guards. Some captives shared out the food they had managed to bring but many died of hunger and thirst even before the train moved off.

The journey to Siberia would last for two to six weeks, each local train slowly joining up with more wagons from different towns before travelling to a bigger station like Kowel on the Trans-Siberian railway. A typical transport had 60 wagons, which would include one for the guards and four for heavier baggage and equipment. The guards rarely provided water, wouldn't answer any questions and ignored any demands. They were supposed to provide the deportees with one hot meal and 800 grams of bread per person a day but that rarely happened.

It was dark inside the filthy, deep-red cattle trucks which smelled strongly of the previous 'cargo'. At each end were one or two shelves, and the gap between them on the floor was stacked with luggage. To try to make the truck more 'comfortable', 8-10 people would be assigned a sleeping space on each shelf, keeping their luggage and bedding with them. More luggage was put under the lowest shelf and some was left in the gap in the middle as makeshift seating. During the day, people sat at the edge of the shelves with their legs dangling, but some trucks were so crowded there was only standing or squatting room for those in the middle. The shelves were rather crowded at night and everyone had to turn over at the same time. If someone didn't turn, usually because they had died, everyone had to roll back until the morning when the body could be removed. The top shelves were difficult to get on to without steps. Once up, there was little headroom and no space to stretch out. The nearest 'sleeper' could see a little of the barren or forested landscape through a high ventilation grate. Cinders and black smoke from the engine were blown through the grate into the wagon and the lookout would freeze with the cold, but was still able to give a report of the journey.

Conditions in the truck were appalling. Some of the ladies would try to clean the trucks with old sacking left there. A 'rota' for sweeping and tidying the wagon would perhaps be organised but lethargy usually set in fairly quickly. There was a small, cast iron stove in the centre of the truck, which was totally inadequate for either 'cooking' or heating, especially in the glacial winter when hair or skin would freeze to the wall and some of the deportees froze to death in their beds. The worst problem was sanitation. In some wagons there was a 'toilet' bucket which had to be emptied through the high grating, while most trucks just had a hole in the floor by the 'back door', which was covered by two planks at right angles to each other. This seat-less, squatting 'toilet' had a short gutter open to the outside rails that the cold came up through. A blanket would be held up or nailed up to preserve privacy but using this contraption was particularly difficult for women, several of whom died from burst bladders. The queue for the 'toilet' was everlasting, and the smell was horrific. Only a tiny amount of water was available for the daily washing of faces and hands, and after a very short time, the people themselves started to smell. Soon everyone was dirty, had lice and fleas, and itched. Colds and tummy problems such as dysentery became rife, and the most vulnerable died of pneumonia, hypothermia or starvation.

Women wept, children cried, and the constant rattle of the swaying wagons meant there was always a lot of noise. In the summer, the corrugated metal roof got so hot that the truck's inside temperature became unbearable. The dust and dirt, the heat or cold, the hunger and thirst, exhaustion, the odours, the lack of personal space and the inactivity caused many a bad temper to flare. The men struggled, particularly if they had been smokers, because there was no tobacco. Gradually, however, people got more apathetic and just prickly rather than angry. They spent their time having low-key political discussions, playing cards or trying to read. The more stuff they had managed to pack, the better were their chances of survival. Any dead bodies, even those of babies and children, were thrown out without ceremony into the snow or the marshland beyond the railway line by the Russian guards.

## Stops and Starts

Russia is such a huge country that, even in normal times, travellers would spend a lot of time waiting at stations for unreliable connecting trains. Now, the locked-in deportees had to endure long waits, usually in sidings, so that Soviet troop trains, which travelled mainly by day, could use the tracks while the deportees travelled mainly at night. As the trains crossed over the Polish border into Russia, the deportees often sang the Polish National Anthem, especially the lines 'Poland has not yet perished / Whilst we are still alive,' or the Patriotic song 'Nie Rzucim Ziemi' which means 'We will not forsake the land'.

Once in Russia, the trains would make daily stops for food and water, usually at remote towns or villages. Traditionally, the friendly local peasants, who were very poor but clean and tidy, would approach the train to give or sell food that was often unpalatable to the Poles. They had dark bread, small cucumbers, rough cheese, untreated milk, and maybe some apples. Often the guards would thrust the peasants away with their bayonet butts, knocking the gifts to the ground and treading on them. Occasionally, at a rare village stop, a vat of watery cabbage and potato soup with maybe a bit of unidentifiable 'meat', was put into each truck by the guards. Fresh bread was thrown onto the floor or caught in a blanket but, by then, everyone was so hungry that they didn't care. Some deportees desperately pushed scrunched up bits of paper with their names and addresses on out of the grating and over the heads of the guards for the locals to find, in the hope that they would contact their loved ones and tell them what was happening. Surprisingly, a few notes did succeed in reaching their destination.

Once the Ural mountains had been passed, most of the stops would occur in the middle of nowhere, half a mile or so from the nearest hamlet or station. The train would come to a halt with a great grinding of wheels and sharply applied brakes. The captives, who were hammering on the doors begging to be let out, would suddenly be released into the fresh air although after the darkness, at first it was too bright to see their surroundings which were usually nothing more than a barren landscape or walls of dark forest. People were allowed to walk to stretch their legs and 'do their business' in public at the side of the tracks. Some folk, in the cold months, melted snow for water in the pans they had brought or collected wood for the stoves. Everyone stayed near their wagon for fear they would be left behind.

Local water was unsafe to drink so it was the custom in Russia for most railway stations to provide large cauldrons of boiled water (*kipyatok*) which warmed the travellers up as well as quenching their thirst. However, because the queues at the station for the water and the public toilets were interminable, when the train was ready to move again, the guards would just grab their captives wherever they were, and drag them back to their truck. Sometimes people got left behind if they hadn't returned to their wagon fast enough and then their families hoped and prayed that they would be allowed to get on the next train.

Occasionally the train would stop at a railway station that had a water tower to fill the engine. In the summer, people would sometimes be allowed to strip off to bathe in the water tower, and children could play under a shower. If it was a sunny day, the people may be filmed for propaganda purposes. The delight on their faces at being temporarily released and being able to breathe fresh air, was misinterpreted deliberately by the Soviets, who on their films showed how everyone was so happy to be travelling to Russia, laughing and greeting each other in joy. There was never a chance to escape. No one knew how long a stop was going to be for the Russians kept the deportees in suspense. If anyone tried to run off, the soldiers, with flares and guns, would search the nearby bleak forests and countryside. No escapee could survive either being alone in the wild, or being shot.

**The End of the Journey**

Finally the end of the train journey would come. Amid a great clanging of keys and swearing, all the cattle trucks were opened and with the 'help' of the guards, the luggage was chucked out of the train. There was great confusion as the deportees fought to regain their possessions and find their family. They were often so exhausted that they couldn't eat any hot food that might be on offer, and many just slept or died where they had been dumped.

All the Poles needed to get, somehow, from the train to their assigned settlements. For some groups, large, heavy trucks were provided, each of which had two enormous cylinders; these were filled with wood which was burnt to make the wood gas on which they ran. The deportees often had to get off and collect wood on the way. For others, there were sleighs and carts pulled by starving horses. This was an extremely cold method of transportation in the winter, and the exiles had to use all their bedding to keep warm. Some people just had to walk while their luggage was carried for them by the carts or sleighs.

Sometimes prisoners were dropped off besides a broad river and had to wait for steam boats to arrive. Often they would have to spend the night sleeping on the soft riverbank or on a wooden jetty. Youngsters who thought they could easily swim across the river were shocked almost to death by its icy coldness, even in the summer. The barge-like boats, usually used for hauling potatoes, smelt liked rot. When they arrived, people were crammed forcibly into the holds in their hundreds for a journey of two or three days following the slow meanders of the river. The only 'toilets' were over the side from the deck, and in the evenings, clouds of mosquitoes would arrive, whizzing and biting, making people itchy and miserable. The mornings brought mists full of the scent of pine from the vast forests, but there was no sound; no birds, no cattle, no houses and no change for hour after hour.

The most desperate groups of deportees were those who were just left stranded somewhere in the forest and told to build their own settlement from scratch, without any proper equipment. However, the majority would arrive at settlements previously built by labourers – log barracks now full of cockroaches, fleas and lice and very little in the way of necessities. There was no way of escape for anyone. There was no perimeter wire because there was nowhere to run to. There were no paths through the thick forests so it was inevitable they would get lost, and the land had unseen stretches of bogs and quagmires to sink into without trace. Apart from all this, and the freezing temperatures, there were bears and wolves in the forests. There was no transport and no outside communication. They were hundreds of miles from human habitation of any size, while any local peasants they did happen to see could possibly be Soviet informers.

This was to be their new, permanent way of life – the Poles were told they would never return to bourgeois Poland. 'Zdes zhit budete' - 'Here you shall live'.

The average life span in Siberia rarely exceeded one winter and less than 10% of the captives would survive the 20 months of exile. Once freed during the amnesty, due to lack of resources or good health, few would ever return to Poland or to any civilisation, although a percentage did manage to meet up with Anders' Army. These deportations were ethnic cleansing on a large scale; the prisoners' only 'crime' was being Polish.

# CHAPTER 4: 'HERE YOU SHALL LIVE'

## 16/07/1940 – 02/10/1941 (AGE 14-15½)

### *JERZY DĄBROWSKI*

During the winter, when the temperatures were extreme and there was no wind, the whole forest looked enchanting, as in a fairy story; it was indescribably beautiful.

Apparently 1940-41 was the coldest winter ever recorded in Russia and Europe for over a hundred years. The average temperature that year was very low, between – 20°C and – 40°C; on occasions it dropped down to – 57°C (– 71°F or 103° of frost). Without wind, the smoke from all the chimneys in the settlement went perfectly straight upwards forming columns approximately 200 metres high and then it spread out horizontally into a *'baldachin'*, like a ceremonial canopy. Everything looked so perfect but if anyone was foolish enough to touch anything made of metal, their skin would tear off and remain there. The river froze solid in October, when the only link with the outside world was provided by a postman on horseback. He somehow managed to get to us once or twice a week by travelling on the frozen river as if it were the road.

Our houses were reasonably warm because each one had a stove built with air-dried bricks, on which there were two boiling rings. Our building had four rooms and the corridor serving them was about six feet wide, allowing some firewood to be stored there. All the stoves in the rooms had access doors so that wood could be fed into them from the corridor. Somehow we managed to obtain some wooden boards with which my father and brother constructed a double bunk bed for us boys and a single bed for our father by fixing the boards to proper bed heads he'd made. We had no mattresses or springs but made ourselves a little more comfortable by placing dry straw on the boards and covering it all with old blankets. We were able to eat our food on the table my father built from boards which he placed on cross-legged supports. For seats, we used empty soya flour cans turned upside down.

Half of such a can was used as a chamber pot by my father as he was not so young and the outside toilets were too far away for him to get to in the middle of the night. We younger ones used to race to them in the dark, sometimes only in our underwear even if the temperature was below − 40°C. This, of course, was too cold for germs so nothing bad ever happened to us!

I was still only 14 years old so I was not forced to work except for performing the duties of a 'housewife'. I darned our socks; I looked after our 'home'; I did the meagre 'shopping' which sometimes meant queueing all night in case some better foodstuff became available early the next day; I cooked when there was something to put into the pot; and I provided fuel for the stove. This meant going into the forest and looking for a *sukhostoy*' (deadwood) tree which was dry and free-standing. Using the half of a saw that we owned, I could fell it single-handedly, and then I would cut it up into manageable lengths to transport home. During that first winter, I constructed a kind of sleigh which made it easier to drag the wood along. At home, I cut the logs into smaller pieces with an axe so that they would fit into the stove.

Our accommodation was shared with many other creatures including fleas, bedbugs, cockroaches and mice. To prevent bedbugs and fleas from sleeping with us as well, we moved the beds away from the walls and stood each leg in a can of water; but the little 'darlings' were too clever for us and used to rain down on us from the ceiling. On the credit side, however, the bedbugs and fleas helped us keep warm as our frequent scratching helped the blood circulation, although we lost a lot of sleep. And trying to catch the mice and cockroaches provided us with the exercise we so badly needed. The mice were nearly the size of rats and had a habit of hiding in the stored firewood in the corridor. I used to catch them with my bare hands then swing them by their tails against a tree: I felt a little pity for them until one of them took its revenge by climbing up its own tail and sinking its teeth into my finger!

In the so-called 'restaurant', we could only purchase cabbage soup, barley and rice. Although the prices may have seemed reasonable by western standards, we could hardly afford to buy them with the paltry 'earnings' my father and brother brought back. All our money was needed to purchase essential food like bread, potatoes and soya flour and whatever else was available from the local shop. I do not ever remember seeing any kind of meat for sale. Bread was rationed to a maximum of one kilogramme a day for every worker and 400 grams for everyone who couldn't work because of age (too young or too old) or ill health. The bread was always soggy and under-baked, which helped the bakers achieve their daily 'norm' by weight. Every workman was allowed to buy bread in proportion to his work performance that day. When he achieved 100% of his 'norm' he could purchase one kilo of bread and his full ration of other products. If he achieved less, his rations were proportionally reduced. There was also a very nice, light, white bread especially baked for the NKVD or for those who had managed to get a difficult-to-obtain doctor's certificate.

Apart from the bread, our main food was provided by 5 kg cans of soya flour with which we made a kind of soup by adding barley, or potatoes that we were able to buy in the local village of Sibiriak. The villagers stored these potatoes in holes in the ground, then covered them with straw and soil to protect them from the frost, but this wasn't always successful. Having only a little cash, we paid for them by giving away items we had brought with us from Poland.

Many people became little more than walking skeletons, being slowly starved to death through their meagre rations, often because they were too ill to work and had no items to exchange for food. I think that we, ourselves, were very lucky in having relatives still in Poland who were able to send us monthly food parcels which also contained warm clothing, soap and many useful items. We could not have survived without these. When a parcel arrived we were notified by the NKVD's office and we had to go there while they inspected the contents and confiscated anything they didn't approve of. We soon learned that by making the inspector a present of some of the items, he let us keep the rest.

Apart from the clothing which we had brought from Poland, or was sent to us in parcels, we were issued with padded jackets and padded trousers for the winter. All the workers were given hats with either padded or fur ear-flaps. I was too young to work so I had to make my own headgear out of scraps of fur. I even managed to convert my shorts into trousers by hand-sewing odd bits of material to extend the legs. We were provided with thick gloves for our hands; some had the thumb separated and some had the thumb and the forefinger separated, depending on the type of work they were needed for. To keep our lower legs and feet warm we were issued with felt boots known as 'velonki'. As a minor I was given a second-hand pair which had worn out and had already been resoled with thick rubber to keep the wearer's feet warm. We didn't really need any waterproof footwear because the winter snow was very dry. The velonki were deliberately several sizes too large so that we could wrap our legs and feet in rags before putting them on. In the summertime, we made our own sandals using the bark of birch trees as soles and oddments of leather as straps. This footwear was suitable only where the ground was higher near the buildings, for the lower areas of the settlement were marshy.

We had to do our own laundry by the river, or at

'home' using hot water heated in half a soya can. Soap was very difficult to obtain but any parcels that arrived from relatives, always contained soap which we shared with a very kind lady who occasionally washed some of our clothes with her own family's things. There was just one professional barber for the whole settlement and he happened to be a young Jew with a lively sense of humour. We all had to join the long queue for a shave or haircut, but the NKVD and the soldiers were allowed to go ahead of us. One day, a very young soldier came to be shaved but there was no evidence of visible whiskers on his chin. The barber obliged but shaved him with the blunt side of the razor. On completion, the soldier checked his chin with his hand and being satisfied with such a gentle shave, thanked the barber and left. We all had great difficulty suppressing our laughter until he left then we all exploded!

The 'hospital' had very few beds and a couple of barely qualified staff. Medication was scarce too. The local 'dentist' was in actual fact only a dental technician who used a 'prehistoric' drill for fillings and had no injections or other facilities for pain relief. I went there once to remove some roots from teeth that had badly rotted due to the lack of decent toothpaste, and to the scarcity of vitamins in our diet. The technician struggled for over half an hour to remove these roots with old-fashioned pliers and no painkillers. He badly damaged my gums and the blood just poured out of my mouth. Generally I can stand a high degree of pain but this was a most unpleasant experience although it did not put me off going to the dentist once back in civilisation.

Of the people in the settlement, 75% were Jews who'd probably been in hiding from the Germans. We had many friends amongst them and found them to be generous and helpful, like the joiner who made my father's coffin and the man who repaired my valonki for next to nothing. One has to respect them, grudgingly though, for making their own people a priority. Some of the richer Jews often partly paid for the bread ration and food products for those Jews who were struggling. Those working in administration often tried to make sure other Jews got easier or more profitable work. My father worked at the local baths he'd helped design and erect until he was replaced by a Jew and sent to work as a labourer instead. And when there was a queue at the food shop, they would let numerous of their friends into the line ahead of the other people which sometimes resulted in the food running out before all had taken their turn, even if they had waited for many hours. Their doctor was also more inclined to admit other Jews into the hospital, and when my father lay dying there, a group of them made a lot of noise, which really affected me. However, most of them were easy to get on with and I suppose even Polish people can be inconsiderate of others!

We discovered that some of the local Russian villagers had a good sense of humour. Two of their favourite jokes were:

*Q. Why do the caps worn by the army have a pointed peak on the top?*
*A. To provide the lice and fleas with a place to hold their meetings!*

*Q. Into how many groups can you divide the citizens of the Soviet Union?*
*A. Three groups: those who have already spent time in the prisons or labour camps, those who are doing so at present, and those who will be doing so in the future!*

However, life in the settlement was extremely harsh, the work was labour intensive and the food minimal and of such poor quality that many of us were starving. Our clothing wore out and the weather was extreme. In desperation, one day in August that first year, we all decided to go on strike, something unheard of in the Soviet Union! The guards were very confused and did not know what to do with us. Eventually they sent two companies of soldiers who collected us all up into the open and surrounded us. The senior NKVD officer gave us a 'fatherly' lecture, saying we were sabotaging the country and behaving like hooligans. The following day, a majority of the strikers, including the ringleaders, were taken away and spread out among various prisons, other labour camps, or salt-mines. That was the end of the strike.

# IN THE SPOTLIGHT: ARRIVAL AND CONDITIONS IN THE SETTLEMENT

## LINDA GALLAGHER

In the whole of Communist Russia intellectual thought was banned; the Soviet leaders distrusted and hated the intelligentsia and consequently, there was a mental malnutrition in their country too. Creativity, constructive ideas and research were forbidden, and during WW2, the number of Polish prisoners with higher education who were deported to the forced labour camps in Siberia increased more than five times.

The people arriving in Siberia from Poland were totally unprepared for their new life. The psychological stresses of being forcibly evicted from their homes, losing their family and possessions and their subsequent isolation from the rest of the world, all without warning, brought immense trauma. The horrors of the journey, followed by the daily fight for food, warmth and survival; the hard work plus the anxiety of not knowing whether the future would just be more of the same, brought feelings of desolation and despair to many, especially when told their own country no longer existed. Again, my father seems to gloss over the intensely difficult conditions people were forced to live under, and yet his buoyant personality, even as a young teenager, shines through.

**Settling Down to their new life**
As soon as they arrived at the settlement, the deportees had to attend an assembly in the Communal Hall where the Commandant lectured them, emphasising that 'Poland no longer exists'. They were to live here the rest of their lives, for the glory of Russia. Then rules were

laid down and accommodation allocated; the prisoners were only given a short time to sort out their living accommodation and luggage before being expected to work.

Part of the old Russian Gulag prison system, these smaller logging camps, or 'settlements', were each designed to take about 500 deportees. Surrounded by dense forest, the majority of the buildings in these small complexes were constructed from logs and were single storey. Apart from the Communal Hall, there were dormitory cabins, a canteen with a kitchen, a shop, a library and a barbershop. The Commandant's Office was in the centre and around the edges of the site were the well, the saw-pit, the sanitation block, a drying room and maybe stables and a blacksmith if horses were used. Sometimes there was also a bath house; two cubicles each with two shelves made from planks, sauna-style, made space for up to 12 people at a time. The settlement may sound idyllic but everything was rough and dirty, and infested with cockroaches, lice and fleas. Rats and mice lived in the log piles and even the cigarettes, hand-made from old newspaper and the chopped up spines of tobacco plants, smelt atrocious.

During the first day or two, the exhausted travellers first had to prepare their own living space. They were housed in *'posiolki'*, or pre-built cabins where the logs overlapped at the corners and were secured by wooden dowel pegs. The gaps between the logs were plugged with dry moss then covered with clay while the inside walls of the cabins, were covered in clay then whitewashed. The passage-ways were just wide enough for stacking wood. Each cabin had between two and four bedrooms about 10-15 feet (4.5 metres) square, furnished only with beds or bed-frames in insufficient numbers so had to be shared out. An old brick or iron stove, often broken, sat in the middle of the room. Wide cracks between the floorboards were filled with dried clay that quickly turned to dust. Small grimy windows in ill-fitting frames packed with moss, provided a little light. There were no electric fittings, no running water and barely enough kerosene to keep the lamps lit.

In the winter, ice infiltrated the cabin every night, creeping up the walls to around three feet high. The panes of glass iced over to an inch (2.5 cm) thick so visibility was reduced further. The logs for the stove were constantly wet as the ice on them froze then melted, making the cabin damp. The wood had to be chopped really small and the fires were started using silver birch bark as kindling because matches were hard to come by.

Slowly, over time, the rooms would be made more habitable. Cleaning was the first chore, but this was very difficult without any mops, buckets or cleaning materials. Twigs collected from the forest were bound with creepers to make sweeping brushes. Mattresses were made from old straw and people had to learn to make their own tables and chairs from the discarded planks around the sawmill. Any tools to be found were usually broken, and there was a severe shortage of nails, which generally were drawn out from old pieces of timber and ruined cabins. Clay from the river banks had to be spread regularly over the cabin walls because lice crawled out of them. Soap, which would help get rid of the lice, was in short supply, and clothes were damaged during their regular delousing by a central machine. Toilets were generally communal and dirty, and there was no toilet paper so leaves were often used. A deep well, which seldom froze, was provided somewhere in the compound but walking to it on a sheet of ice in winter was treacherous.

**Clothing and Food**

The weather was often very severe and the clothes and shoes brought from Poland were totally inadequate; many people only had the things they were arrested in. Once dressed in the morning, the exiles soon discovered that by splashing themselves with water, an icy 'armour' would form on their coats, which insulated their bodies and kept them warmer. They also learnt to wrap their feet in rags then cover them with snow which they would then melt by holding them near the stove. They would then move away and the snow would immediately re-freeze and harden the wet rags creating a protective layer against the cold. These were 'ice-shoes'!

In some camps, as their original clothes wore out, the people were provided with *'telogreika'*, which were previously-used Red Army uniforms consisting of a *'fufaika'* (padded jacket), *'vatnik'* (padded trousers), *shushanka* (an ear-flapped fur hat), *'velonki'* (felt snow-proof boots) and thick gloves. Of course the random availability and distribution took no notice of suitability or size so the prisoners had to sort that out themselves by bartering and swapping items.

Food and its lack dominated everyone's thinking; this was a deliberate tactic by the Soviets to control the prisoners and encourage them to work hard. Designated cooks made food for the whole camp population. They worked 16 hour days fetching water, cutting wood for the fires and scrubbing the floors, as well as making the bread and soup. Daily, each person was 'sold' 800-1000 grams or so of dark bread, deliberately left soggy so it would weigh more, and soup made of burnt flour, cornmeal, potatoes, barley and, rarely, meat scraps. Occasionally, meatballs or small fish like pickled herring could be bought extra, and potato peelings could be scavenged. No-one was allowed to fish in the river, but roots, berries and mushrooms to supplement their diet were to be found in the forests. Some Polish people even bartered their belongings with local peasant farmers in exchange for home-grown tomatoes or potatoes. People had to queue for their food each day – stockpiling was not allowed. This was a nightmare because the time of the evening meal would change daily to keep the people unsettled; they had to stay alert or miss it.

## The guards

At each camp, the guards, under the Commandant, had absolute power over the people, and could dictate the rules for everything, including work quotas, punishments, and food distribution. They deliberately stifled what was noblest in people such as creativity or the expression of compassion. Meetings of any sort were prohibited in the camps, although there was often a secret nocturnal flitting from cabin to cabin to exchange news and opinions. For the prisoners, there was no social hierarchy based on any previous status in society – they were all treated equally badly. Any request made by an inmate was always initially vetoed, or granted then withdrawn. Everything the guards did had a 'rational' reason and there was no arguing if they just changed their minds.

Despite this, the lowest 'caste' in the minds of guards and prisoners alike, were the *'dokhodyagi'*, the living dead or nearly dead, those who were beyond starving and beyond saving, who had extreme vitamin deficiency, dysentery, illness, loosened teeth, sores and night blindness. They became demented and raving, and unable to work, they descended into madness and death.

## Christmas

For Polish Roman Catholics, Christmas is a one of the most important celebrations of the Church Calendar, but it was impossible to celebrate in Siberia. By tradition, St Nicolas, the Polish equivalent of Father Christmas, would arrive on December 6th and leave gifts under children's pillows or in stockings. Christmas itself would then commence with the sighting, generally by a child, of the first star in the sky on Christmas Eve. This vigil is called *'Wigilia'* and is usually followed by a banquet. Hay or straw would be spread beneath the table or tablecloth to remember that the new-born Jesus was laid in a manger. Then the 'Christmas Angel' would arrive, bringing more presents for everyone! This festivity is followed by midnight mass at the local parish church.

A Christmas custom unique to Poland is the breaking of the *'opłatek'* which are thin wafers, blessed by a priest, in which a 'holy' picture is impressed. The wafers are shared around the table at the banquet, everyone breaking off a piece, and then on Christmas day they are taken from house to house and shared with other relatives and friends, to show their unity in Christ.

In Siberia, the Polish people found it very difficult to keep their Christmas traditions alive as it was impossible to do either the vigil or serve the banquet. Relatives in Poland would send the wafers in parcels which often did not arrive, or were plundered. Those prisoners with creative leanings did their best to save scraps of textiles or other scarce materials with which to furtively make gifts, and food was secretly scavenged or saved from the tiny daily allocation. Despite all these difficulties, the faith of the Roman Catholic deportees generally remained very strong and a comfort to them in this horrendous situation.

# CHAPTER 5: LABOUR IN THE LOGGING CAMP

16/07/1940 – 02/10/1941 (AGE 14-15½)

## JERZY DĄBROWSKI

In the centre of the settlement there was a large noticeboard showing the results of labour competitions, the 'Socialist Comparison'.

The entire workforce was divided into working 'brigades' of 10-12 people under a *'Brigadier'*, and several brigades formed a larger unit under the command of a *'Dyesyatnik'*, the word being derived from *'dyesyat'* meaning 'Ten'. On the noticeboard, all the brigades were listed in order of their achievements during the previous week, showing how much effort they were making in working for the 'good of the country'. Those at the top of the list were praised by the authority and held up as examples to us all. Those at the bottom were described as 'lazy saboteurs' and were told harshly that they must improve their performance.

Every job had a daily 'norm' that each individual worker had to achieve; but it was really difficult to achieve because every time a worker succeeded in reaching 100% of their norm, it was increased for everyone. On one occasion the senior supervisor announced such an increase to the workers. The horse that pulled the carts had been nick-named 'Norm' by the man in charge of it. On hearing this announcement, the man called out, 'Gee-up, Norm!' which made every one laugh except the supervisor. This resulted in the poor chap having to pay dearly for his exclamation.

Every person in every type of job had a daily norm to achieve, even the local villagers who worked at the camp. The farmer had to deliver a daily quota of milk he produced from every cow he looked after. If he had a pig, he had to produce an annual quota of piglets though how he could be sure of succeeding, no-one knew! If the quota was short, he was expected to purchase the shortfall from another farmer who had plenty, otherwise he would be accused of sabotage and prosecuted. One very hard-working man consistently achieved his norm and he was rewarded with a bicycle. When his health finally failed, and he was no longer able to fulfil his quota, the bicycle was taken away and given to someone else who was currently more deserving.

Most of the people from the settlement worked in the forest and the men were predominantly employed in tree-felling using only hand saws. The trees were 30-50 metres (100-150 feet) tall and quite thick at the base; you had to be very careful that each tree fell in the correct direction or the branches would snag on neighbouring trees. Other gangs of men had to remove the branches from the trees. They then cut the logs into 25 foot lengths which were moved one at a time with the aid of a contraption that had a pair of wheels at the front, while the rear end was dragged along the ground. This was pulled by the horse to the local collection point where they were stacked up. In the winter a short sleigh was used. Later, these logs were transported 3 or 4 at a time on a different piece of apparatus which had two independent pairs of wheels, or two short sleighs in the winter. On this the logs were taken about five miles along the side of the river and were once more stacked up until the Spring when the river melted and they could be lowered into the water.

Once the snow had gone, another gang of men formed large 'booms' by tying logs together end to end with thick ropes made locally. The boom is a large log barrier like a 'bag' made to prevent loose logs floating in the current. Into these booms other logs were lowered until the boom was full of logs. This work was extremely dangerous as the men had to jump from one floating log to another to arrange them properly. Often someone would fall off into the water and be buffeted about by the loose logs making it very difficult to climb up again. When a whole transport was fully organised, it was floated down the river for about 160 miles to the sawmills in Asino. Several men accompanied the timber on a raft which was connected to it. When they needed to stop, they had to drop an enormous eight-foot tall anchor overboard. The journey downriver took about two weeks but the return journey, in a horse and cart, was much quicker.

Back at the settlement in the forest, several specialist jobs were carried out by skilled men and women. Some people made ropes manually out in the open. The ropes were about 100 feet long and 3-4 inches thick, and were used to tie together the floating logs. Two skilled Belorussian men made planks by cutting the logs into boards. Once the bark had been removed, the log was laid on supports and marked with a stretched string covered in soot. The thickness of each plank had to be consistently even.

Once they were 16 years old, boys had to work like the men. Below this age they joined the women for 'lighter' work, such as digging out remaining tree roots, and removing any remaining bits of tree so making a passage for the horses. They also had to stack the logs into piles up to six or seven feet high, using long poles to lever the logs into position at the collection point. There were many other 'light' jobs for the boys and women to do, like removing the bark from logs found floating in the swamps using a tool similar to a garden hoe, while making sure they personally didn't fall beneath them. I did have some experience of all this work and I found it anything but light! In the summer, light work included manufacturing hand-made clay bricks and stacking them in a special way to be air-dried. These were used for building stoves and chimneys. Any adults too weak to work in the forest, were engaged in repairing clothing and *valonki* (felt boots).

My father was a *dyesyatnik*, and my brother Stach (Stanisław), who was four years my senior, was a *brigadier* at first but within a few weeks was also promoted to be a *dyesyatnik*. Among the brigades working under him was the women's brigade which made bricks from wet clay. In April 1941, Stach was unlucky enough to have a slight difference of opinion with one of the communist supervisors and was stripped of his rank and sent to work as a manual labourer in the forest. It was a 3-4 mile daily walk to work and one morning he was 15-20 minutes late. His unfriendly supervisor reported him as a saboteur and as a result he had to walk 12 miles the following day to the court in Tegul'det. After staying there overnight, he appeared before the court who dismissed his case as being of little importance. He walked back to the settlement completely worn out, and this silly episode lost him two days earnings! Later he was transferred to work by the River Chulym, preparing the logs that were to be floated down to Asino.

In the middle of May, once the snow had melted, although I was only just 15, I decided to start working to be able to buy more bread and other food. My first job was to water the vegetables grown for the use of the restaurant. I had to get up early to go to the small stream 100 yards away, then carry the water back in a very large watering can. This activity was repeated until I had finished all the watering before lunch. My other jobs required me to join with the ladies and other boys with their tasks. I also had to use a small axe to make marks on trees that stood in a straight line, so dividing the forest into squares. While doing these jobs, I took a small dog with me for company, but also to warn me of the possible nearness of bears or wolves. On one occasion, I came across a bear's lair, which was apparently empty, but I decided I wouldn't hang around to be greeted by the host; I ran away as fast as my legs could carry me!

There was just one mechanical vehicle on the settlement, a prehistoric tractor that was somehow propelled by burning small cubes of birch wood. These cubes were prepared by women, as light work. They had to cut discs of wood from a log, two inches thick, then chop them into cubes with an axe. To this day I cannot understand how the tractor engine worked, and I only managed to get a ride on it once or twice!

During the summer 1941, I joined my brother and another man marking the trees in the forest to make a grid pattern. This was necessary to assess what trees were to be found in each square so that future felling could be planned. For this work, we used a dumpy level, a long chain for measuring, a compass, a couple of axes for marking the trees and removing the undergrowth, and long, straight twigs we made ourselves along the way, for lining up the sides of the squares better. On one such expedition, after several hours working, we suddenly heard loud screams.

'Look! Look! Humans!'

We turned to see where the shouting was coming from and saw two women, who explained that they had wandered into the forest looking for berries, and couldn't find their way back. The forest was always thicker nearer its borders but the ladies did not know that. They had started walking in the opposite direction, deeper and deeper into the forest. They were lucky to have found us rather than a wolf or a bear. The ladies were soaking wet from walking across the marshes. We let the women stay with us while we finished our quotas, so that we wouldn't be branded as 'saboteurs', then we returned to the settlement altogether. They were exhausted but very grateful to us for bringing them home.

Another time, we three had to travel for three days to reach more distant parts of the forest, which had possibly never been visited by a human being before. Here we had to divide the forest into two-kilometre squares, using the same method as previously described. Apart from the tools detailed above, we also had to carry cooking utensils, soya cans for cooking and smaller cans for eating out of, soya flour for making soup and blankets for the night. We obtained water to cook with and drink from the marshes, straining it through our handkerchiefs to ensure we didn't swallow any undesirable ingredients. The first night, we felled some trees in a circle, leaving the branches undisturbed to prevent wolves being able to come near us when we were asleep. In the centre, we constructed a shelter from loose branches, leaving a small opening. In front of this we built a fire to keep away all intruders, then fell asleep in our 'hut'. When the fire died out in the night, we were visited by a large bear which had climbed over our tree barrier. He smelt our feet but decided they did not smell of honey, and he did not fancy any 'cheese' that night, so he peacefully marched away, leaving wide and very obvious tracks. Bears have a habit of walking from clump to clump of grass so in the morning we followed his tracks deeper into the forest.

The following night we spent near the river in a kind of log shelter without doors and with just open holes for windows. It had three or four sleeping compartments and we could obtain the water we needed from the river. It was altogether a better experience, and the following evening, without any further excitement, we returned reluctantly to the settlement.

# IN THE SPOTLIGHT: SURVIVING AND WORKING IN SIBERIA

## LINDA GALLAGHER

Every day, people exiled to Siberia died in large numbers from the gruelling conditions and sparse medical care. There was surprisingly little general sickness even in the winter because common germs couldn't survive in the cold, dry air, but malnutrition and starvation brought on other illnesses such as tuberculosis, dysentery, and typhoid fever. During the coldest months, people had to wade through the often waist-deep snow in temperatures as low as minus 50°, and in May, when the weather warmed up, large masses of snow, icicles and ice sheets would suddenly slide down the eaves of the buildings without warning, injuring the unwary.

There were also many plagues to cope with. Lice in their hundreds got stuck in the hems and seams of clothing which were then squeezed to make them pop out. Clothes had to be washed in the hand-freezing river, or in scalding water which was used, unsuccessfully, to try to get rid of them. Fleas in their thousands covered the floors but, apparently, they never jumped on the beds. Bedbugs would bite faces at night, leaving a pink rash. In the warmer evenings of spring and summer, millions of non-malarial mosquitoes from the humid river and marsh areas, came to make life even more miserable, biting any exposed skin including eyes and ears. Everyone had to keep themselves completely covered up. Anyone who fancied a short walk outside the camp confines in the warmer weather could very easily get lost in the marshes and trees, and any disturbed insects, such as black gnats, would rise up in swarms around them, fastening themselves on noses, eyelids and ears.

Many people did not survive much more than three months and life expectancy was generally less than a year because the prisoners were literally starved and worked to death. In the winter, shallow graves were dug in the snow, but when it melted, deep graves were dug in the ground and the bodies reburied. Only two people were allowed to attend a funeral.

Depression was rife: with the heavy work load, the lack of food, light and warmth and the absence of hope, everything became meaningless. There was no sense of achievement or progress; there was no leisure time, few real books except Communist propaganda, and no clubs or societies, but only the constant fear of punishment, deprivation, illness and death. The people were told 'You will get used to it or die like dogs'.

## Rules and Rations

Prisoners were never allowed to be alone – there was constant surveillance of all they did, and informers always seemed to get the easier jobs in return for their information. There was some criminal behaviour in the camps, but the women never got molested because there was little opportunity and it was far too cold. There were random fines for many supposed misdeeds in the settlement, which would lead to a reduced food ration. Soviet book-keepers kept accounts of every person's work and behaviour, whether they had achieved their 'norm' and whether deductions in pay could be made for any slight misdemeanour.

Everyone had to work whatever their age or physical condition. Some settlements provided nurseries for the under-twos so that their mothers could work, while the schools provided for children up to 12 years old indoctrinated their students in communist ideology. Older children between the ages of 12 and 15 were expected to do a full day's domestic work, fetching water and firewood, and collecting food by waiting in long queues at the 'shop'. They also had to clean the cabins without equipment, iron clothes without an iron and mend them without thread.

Surprisingly, parcels of food and clothing from relatives in Poland did occasionally arrive at the camps, but when collected, the parcels were usually seen to have been opened to be 'inspected' and the best things stolen by the guards. The packages were closed up again but the receivers were not allowed to reopen them until they were back in their room so that they couldn't complain nor prove theft. Local Russian peasants who lived near the settlements were often very kind and understanding of the plight of the those in the camps, but were unable to help much if at all, because they had so little themselves and were discouraged by the guards.

All food had to be paid for out of the meagre wages; few people earned enough money to buy sufficient food to satisfy their hunger. Each worker who had achieved their full quota or 'norm' was paid five roubles a day. For the others, deductions were made from this amount according to how much of their 'norm' they had actually achieved, or if they had to pay fines for alleged wrong behaviour. At meal times, the exiles were separated into three queues for the three cauldrons. They were fed according to the amount of work they had completed that day. If they had completed over 125% of their 'norm' they were fed from the best cauldron, which had much thicker soup. The next cauldron was for those who had fulfilled 100-125% of their quota, and the third and largest cauldron of inferior quality soup was for the vast majority who had not achieved their almost impossible 'norm'. Those who had worked hard enough to earn the better quality food, or even double rations, from the first cauldron, were usually doomed to die in the near future, anyway, from sheer exhaustion. The old and the ill who couldn't work well, were allowed very little food. The Soviet mantra in the camps was *'Yesli ty ne rabotayesh, ty ne yesh'* which means 'If you don't work, you don't eat'.

### Work in the Settlement

Most of the slave-labour in Siberia was to do with agriculture, mining, construction and timber. The vast area of Siberia has the world's largest deposits of coal, iron, gold, silver and diamonds, and is rich in many other minerals, so mining was very important for the wealth of the USSR. Infra-structure such as roads and railways, canals and towns therefore needed to be built beforehand to bring the products west, so stone quarrying had to be done too. Timber was used extensively for building settlements and dwellings, furniture and boats, and the forests of Siberia, known as the Taiga, were full of many species of tree.

Some of the convoys of cattle trucks ended up in Soviet Kazakhstan, and the deportees were put to work on the agricultural collectives to grow crops, including cotton, and to rear animals. Their 'hosts' were the Kulaks – people who had previously been forcibly 'settled' in the country by the Russians, and over time, had actually managed to make it their home.

The work conditions in each settlement very much depended on the attitude of its Commandant. Producing the 'norm' for that camp was more important than anything else that needed doing for a person's safety or convenience. No one seemed to realise that forced labour, with food as a reward for achievement, was less than half as efficient as free labour. Men, women and children over 15 carried out manual labour that was heavy and often dangerous. Sometimes, the men were sent away for several days to work and then mothers with young children were unable to earn any money to buy food.

### The Workers' Daily Routine

The strict daily routine never varied for the prisoners, although different camps may have had different routines. The guards woke people up at about 5 am by shouting 'Get a move on!' and gave them little time to get ready or eat so the exiles were always on edge. The work-days were each approximately 10-12 hours long. The people were escorted to work by the guards and told they would be shot if they put even one foot out of line as they walked. At mid-day, there would be a short lunch and smoking break when the workers could eat any bread they had saved from their breakfast. If they were lucky, they would sometimes be provided, for free, with a meagre portion of soup brought to them in a cauldron on a cart pulled by an ill-kempt horse. The work day continued till dark when the workers were marched home, starving and near collapse from exhaustion, but before they were allowed to eat or sleep, the camp authorities subjected them to a roll call during which they had to stand for another hour or more until it was confirmed that all was in order.

The winter temperatures often went down to − 40° or more but work never stopped, even at weekends when everyone was told that they had 'volunteered' to work for the glory of Russia. Very rarely, when the temperature was lower still, it was too cold to even go outside so a day off was allowed.

**Logging**

Tree felling was really hard work for the teams of six which usually had four men and two women or older children. The forest area singled out for each day's tree-felling was divided up into long narrow strips by the women or children, then the team-leader, the 'Feller', chose which trees they would cut down. First of all, the team had to gain access to the trunk of the tree by shovelling away the snow which could be several feet deep. Then the men cut down the trees one at a time: a horizontal wedge was cut into the trunk so that the tree would fall in a certain direction, without catching on the branches of other trees. The tree was then sawn down with a heavy two-handled saw, and as it fell, everyone sang out 'Timber' in Russian, and leapt out of the way because the trunk could twist and jump around before reaching the ground. Mishaps and accidents were common. The women chopped off the branches, then stripped them of twigs which were stacked ready to be burnt in the stoves on the settlement in the winter. Sometimes the women were detailed to collect sap from the trees to make rubber.

The 'Cutter' cut the trunk of the tree into logs of a standard length and chained them onto a sledge, thick end first, so that they could be pulled to the river bank ready for stacking. It was difficult to avoid the tree roots that remained in the ground so the women had to dig them up by hand. Horses were sometimes used to help to haul the logs to the river where more women stripped off the bark before the logs were levered into stacks with long sticks. The end of each log was measured and marked with an embossed hammer. Different sized logs had different uses, whether for building homes or ships, or for making furniture.

In summer, when the water melted, the logs could be floated en masse down the fast-flowing river to the towns that had the sawmills. Men had to stand on the logs and use sticks to manoeuvre them away from the banks and each other so that there were no jams, but some men fell off and were crushed between the logs.

The work was relentless but skills learnt in the experience were useful when the 'amnesty' was announced in 1941 and the Poles were free to leave the camps, albeit without transport. Those who had been in logging camps were easily able to build rafts so that the exiles could float down the rivers to the nearest towns that had a railway station connected to the west and freedom.

# CHAPTER 6: BEAUTY AND GRIEF IN THE TAIGA

## 16/07/1940 – 07/1941 (AGE 14-15)

### *JERZY DĄBROWSKI*

Though there were a lot of things that made our lives truly miserable in Siberia, the Taiga forest itself was really beautiful to look at. The winter frosts could make our surroundings seem quite magical and I was so taken by it that after a few months, still only aged 14, I wrote a poem describing how I experienced it. Here it is in a non-rhyming translation:

**An Ode to Taiga**
*Oh immaculate Siberian Taiga*
*Your beauty is impossible to describe*
*You are always so spectacular*
*Beautiful in the evening, beautiful in the morning!*

*Gorgeous trees, old virgin forest*
*Ancient cedars, spruce and firs*
*Beauty lives even in your undergrowth*
*In the great variety of berries and mushrooms.*

*A multitude of singing birds*
*During Summer, Autumn, Spring*
*Glorious wild flowers of many colours*
*Grow here in exquisite abundance.*

*Though when I remember your rivers,*

*Your mosquitoes and thick mud,*
*The great swamps and wild bears*
*Then I lose all my longing ...*

*To live within you permanently*
*And be bitten by those stinging gnats:*
*To walk in fear of your grim bears*
*On journeys through your bogs and marshes.*

Thick snow, up to 6 feet deep in places, would cover the ground, and the snow-covered trees looked like sculptures. Everything was clean and white; it reflected the moonlight so that the long winter nights were as bright as day, which cheered us up. The top layer of snow had a hard crust of ice, usually strong enough to support a man, although if a hapless person broke through that crust, they would have to crawl to the nearest tree in order to regain their feet.

Winter that year lasted for 8 ½ months while spring and autumn were too short to be noticed, passing in a matter of days. The ice on the river started to break up mid-May when warmer water from the south had flowed 600 miles before finally reaching our logging camp. The noise of the ice cracking could be heard many miles away and due to the vast amounts of melting snow, the river would flood enormous areas of the forest almost up to our settlement. Though there was still plenty of snow on the riverbanks, the water was relatively warm and on a few occasions, in my youthful exuberance, I went for a swim. One time I tried to swim in a smaller river nearer to our cabin, but the melting snow caused the water to be freezing cold. Out I jumped very quickly!

As the weather warmed up, I took to swimming more often. After one swim, while still in my swimming trunks, I started picking and eating some large, juicy blackcurrants that were growing in abundance by the river. As I moved along the bank, I removed some branches for easier access only to discover a very active hornets nest! I did not stay to say 'hello' but ran away as fast as I could. The hornets had noticed me and a whole army of them set off in hot pursuit. Luckily the river was nearby and I jumped in and swam underwater as far as I could before coming up for air. I had to repeat this performance two or three times because they would not leave me alone until I was in the middle of the river. I continued to swim to the other bank although the river was 200 yards wide and had a horseshoe bend with a strong current that gradually dragged me half a mile downstream until I finally made land. I had a long walk back to where I had left my clothes!

Then came the summer, which was very hot and humid, allowing every plant to grow at a tremendous rate. There was just enough time to prepare the soil, sow the seeds, ripen the crops and bring the harvest home before the return of winter. In the summer, one could admire the tall Siberian cedars which provided us with tasty nuts, as well as the firs, spruces and birches. There was a large variety of wild flowers which made the surroundings seem so peaceful away from the busy cities. Edible mushrooms and berries grew in abundance: one type of berry, called the '*golubika*' (bog bilberry), was related to the blueberry but the bush grew up to three feet tall and the fruit was as large as cherries.

The downside of the Summer was the arrival of legions of horseflies and mosquitoes, both of which competed for our blood. These creatures were particularly plentiful in the forest marshes where most of the people worked. To protect ourselves against the enemy, we were each given a bag to put over our head. The bag had gauze netting over the face so that we could breathe and see. Sometimes an insect managed to get inside our headgear, and it was a very unpleasant experience trying to get rid of it because we would inevitably allow more to come inside it. In spite of the heat, we also had to wear our long, thick trousers and gloves in the marshlands because the horseflies were able to bite through virtually anything. When walking through the swamp, we always had to jump from one clump of undergrowth to another to remain dry. If we missed the clump, we would get very wet, and so then just took the shortest route for our journey!

I made friends with a local Russian boy of about 10 years of age; he was a very brave boy. He was born looking like a 'thalidomide' baby, having one arm that terminated in a stump like a large finger above the elbow. His other arm was similar but longer. He only had one short leg stump with which he propelled himself, while the seat of his trousers was covered in thick rubber because it generally had to support his weight. And yet he was able to jump from one bench to another in the communal hall because they had no backs! He was also a very gifted artist, managing to hold a pencil or brush with his stumps to produce pictures of high quality, comparable to other notable artists in my opinion. He was friendly but very independent, preferring to try to do everything himself without help.

### My Father, Michał

My father, because he was a building surveyor, was put in charge of all the building work at the beginning of our time in the settlement. He was made a *'dyesyatnik'*, a leader of brigades, while my brother was a brigadier under him. He designed then supervised the erection of a local bathhouse which was constructed on a similar principal to a sauna.

The building contained several rooms, and there was an entrance lobby where you had to pay. From here you entered the changing room and passed all your clothing to an attendant, who then hung it in a disinfecting room that had a temperature of over 200°C, at which heat those lovable creatures who shared our clothes with us, such as lice and fleas, were exterminated! Then you entered a steam room with three wide shelves set at different heights for seating. The higher you sat, the hotter you got. The steam was made by pouring cold water over large preheated stones. Bundles of birch twigs were provided to beat your back to improve blood circulation. After this you went into another room to wash in hot water in metal bowls, before drying off and getting dressed again in your disinfected clothes. This process left you feeling very clean and invigorated. The sad thing was that as soon as you joined a queue or mixed with other people, within minutes you would be re-infested with parasites wanting to inhabit your clothing.

After a few months, the Jewish administration of the bath-house project sacked my father and replaced him with one of their friends. My father was then sent to work manually as a labourer despite being 59 years old and already not in the best of health. This change caused him to deteriorate physically and within a few weeks he had to enter the 'hospital' after being diagnosed ill with jaundice. The men's ward was full of Jewish men who did not seem particularly ill but spent their days joking in high spirits. I found this behaviour very annoying and unforgivable at the time; how could they behave in this way when there was a dying man in the room?

On the 27th of May I felt uneasy, as if something strange was about to happen. For some reason I felt very unwell and went to see the hospital 'doctor' who did not think there was anything wrong with me and sent me away. Soon after, a message reached me that my father was dying and I needed to go to the hospital immediately as my brother was working too far away at the time. In the hospital, I sat beside my father for the last few hours of his life, praying with all my might for his soul. He lay facing the wall, unable to move or talk. Eventually he was in cardiac arrest and turned to look at me with an expression of great pain on his face. He was unable to speak but I felt he was grateful for my presence there and for my prayers. And then he died in my arms. I was 15 years old.

My father's body was covered up by a sheet and then I took his watch with me so that it wouldn't be stolen. All that day the sky had been covered in clouds but just before my father died, the sun appeared for a few minutes, and soon after his death, the sky became cloudy once more.

There was no mortuary in the settlement so when my brother returned, our father's body was brought to our home, laid on his bed and dressed in his best. We spent the night with Polish friends who endeavoured to console us and in the morning, I sat by his body alone for a few hours while my brother obtained a death certificate from the head of the local NKVD and arranged the funeral. While sitting at his bedside, I wrote the following poem. The translation into English loses some of the spirit in which it was originally written, especially when I tried to make the translation rhyme like the original.

**Beside Father's Body**
*My heart is flooded by great sadness*
*My soul is crying out*
*Here lies my beloved Father*
*Unable to move about.*

*Can't you hear, my dear Father*
*My cries, and see my hot tears?*
*I beg you, get up and answer,*
*Return to us still living here.*

*Why does your heart now beat no more?*
*Why are you white and cold?*
*I know! You died; you lost your life*

*Entered God's eternal fold!*

*But you made us into orphans -*
*We're alone! What shall we do?*
*How can we live without parents?*
*God have mercy on us two.*

*Father, hear me! Look around -*
*It's a lovely dawn, the night has gone!*
*Alas you cannot hear my pleading.*
*Let the will of God be done.*

*Already I'm resigned to it -*
*It's God's will your life is ended.*
*God gave and God took away.*
*It happened just as God intended.*

*Though I've lost you, my dear Father,*
*I don't cry. I can't despair*
*But only pray to God in heaven*
*And let you reign with Him up there.*

*Good Lord God, I love you dearly*
*Of all fathers You're the best!*
*From my heart I raise this prayer*
*'Give him, please, eternal rest'.*

*Oh my God, You are the King*
*Here on earth, in heaven too.*
*Count him now among Your saints,*
*That's my only plea to You.*

A friend of my father's, a Jewish joiner, made a proper

coffin rather than the usual box. We were very grateful for this. A grave was dug in the forest outside the settlement near the other graves. Towards the evening, just before he was buried, I went to pay my last respects to my father. I looked at him for the last time and kissed his face. The coffin was sealed and the funeral procession commenced. My father had been popular and well liked by the whole community; practically all the inhabitants of the settlement, Polish, Russian and Jewish took part. A Polish monk, dressed in ordinary clothes (so the NKVD wouldn't realise), said some prayers before the coffin was lowered into the grave which was then filled in. The next day we erected a large cross made of birch logs which could remain standing a long time.

I had a great Russian friend, another local boy who was about 10 years old, 5 years younger than me. For several days he did his best to console me for which I was very grateful as it helped me a lot. He was a gifted young man who could play a balalaika beautifully and with whom I had many stimulating discussions on numerous subjects. There was also a young, local Russian lady, a waitress in the village restaurant, who served us free meals after my father's death. Like the majority of the Russian people around us, once they learned they could trust us, all her family were generous and friendly towards us. In September 1941, when we were leaving Sibiryak, she promised to look after our father's grave for us. I wonder if the birch cross is still standing today?

# IN THE SPOTLIGHT: THE TAIGA FOREST

## LINDA GALLAGHER

Siberia is one of the least-populated landmasses on earth – five million square miles of forestation, wilderness and nothingness. In Russia, the name, Taiga, refers to the swampy, coniferous forests of the northern hemisphere, between the steppes and tundra. It has over a fifth of all the world's forests. The resident bears and wolves rarely come near to human habitations so it is relatively safe.

Temperatures are extreme, from below – 50°C especially in the sub-arctic areas in the winter to + 40°C in the summer. The two winters of the Polish deportations, 1940 and 1941, are recorded as being the coldest of the 20th century; they arrived early so that by mid-September, the snow had already fallen. The forest can be strangely still and silent; in the winter, no birds sing and no animals are to be seen or heard, but once the spring has come, that all changes.

**Spring and Summer**

The snow melts during May, and spring barely has time to make itself felt before the inadequate summer, only 2-3 months long, arrives. The summers have long, hot, dry days and short nights. At dawn, the sky may be covered with pearly pink and pale red colours while the evenings have glorious sunsets – burning gold, crimson and purple skies. The fresh and invigorating morning air is soon filled with the plagues of flies while every evening, mosquitoes in clouds so large that you can't see, descend at dusk.

In summer, the forest is entrancingly beautiful,

despite the swamps hidden in the stretches of flat land, which can suck a person down. A slippery band of mud builds up along the banks of the many broad, meandering rivers and although there are some muddy, rutted tracks, there are very few buildings or farms. Steep-sided mountains are covered with immense, impenetrable forests of tall Siberian cedars, birch, larch and pine which stand up like matchsticks. Mushrooms and berries grow abundantly, sweetly scented flowers bloom, and there are culinary riches to be found, such as fruit, fish, caviar and game. A very sparse rainfall occurs mainly in the summer months and there is just enough time before the return of winter to plant, grow and harvest crops. By late summer, the evenings get cooler and crisper and the beautiful rose-coloured sunrises contrast strongly with the squalor of the settlements.

**Winter**

Winter comes early in Siberia; during the brief autumn, the leaves turn colour, the dawns arrive with lilac rather than pink skies, and as the twilights lengthen, the sun's colours reflect in the rivers like liquid gold and purple. Then there is a sudden alarming drop in temperature, and white-water rapids race in icy river torrents through the valleys before they freeze once more.

Throughout the 7 or 8 months of Siberian winter, there are constant deep snowfalls of 2-3 feet, but also, there are very strong winds called 'Bourans', (or 'Burans') which regularly cause bad snowstorms but without new snowfalls; icy winds blow across the whole tundra area at ground level, forcing clouds of tiny particles of hardened snow up into the air, so reducing visibility to nearly zero. In these blizzards, people have to tie a rope around themselves when out of their cabins, so that they don't get lost.

Once the Amnesty was announced and all the Polish captives were set free, it was very important that they left Siberia quickly before the next severe winter arrived and the rivers froze up again. The Polish people in exile were too frail to survive there any longer.

The Partition of Poland between USSR and Germany 1939 along the Curzon Line

Jerzy's drawing of his cabin at the camp.

Jerzy's Father, Michał, is standing at the back.

Jerzy's Father, Michał

Jerzy's mother, Albina

Jerzy and his father

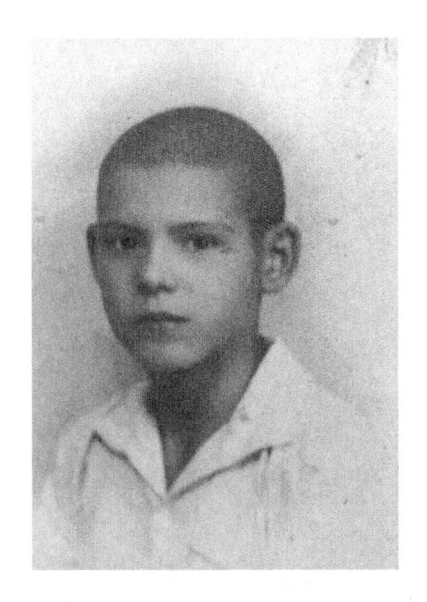

Jerzy

Jerzy and his mother

Jerzy's sister, Halina

Jerzy and Stanisław around 1928

Jerzy, Stach, Albina, Michał

# PART TWO:
# FROM SIBERIA TO PALESTINE

# "AMNESTY AND FREEDOM"

# IN THE BACKGROUND: THE ALLIES

## WHY DID THE SOVIETS JOIN THE ALLIES?

*LINDA GALLAGHER*

**Operation Barbarossa**

The Soviets had occupied East Poland for almost two years from their invasion in September 1939, until Hitler broke the Molotov-Ribbentrop non-aggression pact he'd agreed with Stalin, and betrayed Russia.

With an army of three million Nazi troops, Hitler launched Operation Barbarossa on 22nd June 1941, invading the Soviet Republic along a 1000 mile front and destroying over 1,200 planes, a quarter of the 'Red' Air Force, on the very first day. The Germans' intention was to seize the whole of Poland first of all. Hitler's long-term plan was to resettle 20 million Poles in Western Siberia, Germanise another 3-4 million, and exterminate all who were deemed to be unsuitable, such as Jews, Gypsies, Soviet POWs and anyone else who, for whatever reason, couldn't work.

Hitler then started a further campaign, going deeper into Russia to try to gain Stalingrad. However, the German Army was not prepared for the ferocity of the Russian winter, and took losses of millions of troops. The Soviet Army defeated them in the most violent battle of the whole war, and this defeat changed the course of events in Europe, as Germany started to retreat.

The commencement of Operation Barbarossa was the reason all Germany's enemies decided to unite together in order to conquer the Nazis. Thus it brought the Soviet Red Army into the allied camp to fight against the Germans; but there is no doubt that the Russians would have committed a treachery similar to Barbarossa against Germany if they had thought of it first.

## Sikorski-Maisky Agreement

The same evening that Operation Barbarossa began, the British Prime Minister, Winston Churchill, proposed to the War Cabinet that they should offer Stalin every possible consideration and unconditional aid to battle against the Nazi invasion. General Władysław Sikorski, the Polish Prime Minister exiled in London, was put under a lot of pressure by Churchill to work with Stalin despite his bitter opposition. He was pragmatic enough to realise that this could be the opportunity he needed to free the deported Poles from Siberia and to form a new Polish army to help the Allies.

A month later, on 30th July 1941, Churchill and his Foreign Secretary were both present when General Sikorski and Ivan Maisky, the Russian Ambassador, on behalf of Stalin, signed the Sikorski-Maisky Agreement which enabled the two nations, Poland and Russia, to re-establish diplomatic relations. In order to join the Allies, Stalin first had to state that all previous pacts made with Hitler were now null and void, including the 'secret protocol' to divide Poland up between them. However, this new agreement was criticised by the Polish Government-in-Exile because there was no present or future commitment on behalf of the Soviets to restore Poland's borders, especially those of east Poland annexed by them at the start of the war. Neither did it mention anything about the disappearance of all the Polish military officers.

The Sikorski-Maisky Agreement did, however, ensure that the Polish State itself would be re-established – although maybe not as a completely independent country – and that there would be an 'amnesty' for all the Polish 'Prisoners of War' held in the Soviet Union. Stalin realised he needed many more troops to fight the Nazis and so he even agreed that a new Polish Army could be formed on Soviet soil, which would be subordinate to the Polish Government-in-Exile, and not to the Russians.

This 'amnesty' of the Polish Military was announced on 12$^{th}$ August 1941, but the Poles were very offended at this word because they were not criminals being pardoned. Following this, Stalin personally granted an 'amnesty' to all the Polish nationals and to the citizens of every country annexed by the Red Army, everyone who had been deprived of their freedom and deported to Siberia and the far reaches of Soviet territory – but he did not bother to ensure that this promise was fully carried out.

Thus, Britain and the Allies formed a coalition with the Soviets, and later also persuaded the USA to join the war after Japan tried its own offensive against the west, and blew up Pearl Harbour in December 1941. However, once the agreement was signed, the Soviets repeatedly and deliberately obstructed the activities of the Polish Government-in-Exile which, itself, had had no real say in major decisions regarding their own borders.

The Red Army had been fighting the Germans alone at first before joining the Allies, and so in order to placate Stalin and keep him on board, Churchill and the USA President, Franklin D. Roosevelt, allowed the Soviets to retake and keep Belarus, Ukraine and the east of Poland as part of its territory for now, thus making it easier for Stalin, at a later date, to put the whole of Poland under Soviet control.

### General Anders

Although he was actually Polish, General Władysław Anders had previously served as a Cavalry Officer in the Russian Tsar's army. He had risen to prominence because of his extraordinary military skills, courage, and determination despite being wounded in action many times. When the Red Army invaded Poland in 1939, he was immediately arrested and imprisoned by the Soviets in the infamous Lubyanka prison in

Moscow. Several times during the two years he was there, Anders turned down the offer of a senior military post in the Soviet Army.

General Sikorski favoured General Anders as being the most suitable officer to re-form the Polish Army on Soviet territory. Fortuitously, because he had been imprisoned in Moscow, Anders had not been executed in the Katyn Forest Massacre. He was finally released from Lubyanka on 4th August 1941, aged 49, weak from prison life and the brutal interrogations he had endured. Anders had a very charismatic personality and although he had proved to be a bit of a maverick in the past, he was able to inspire men to follow him. He took up his new command willingly, but only on behalf of the Polish people.

**Forming the Polish II Corps Army**

The new Polish Army had already started to form by the time General Anders took over, but the Soviet secret police, the NKVD, were told to watch him and send in reports. Anders was initially given permission to assemble just 30,000 Polish soldiers, so first of all he set up 20 Army Recruitment and Welfare Centres in European Russia, Siberia and Soviet Asia. These centres would provide identity and travel documents, as well as food and clothing for any soldiers who managed to find them. Thirty-four Soviet trains were put at Anders' disposal and he organised major evacuations of both the military and civilians from certain railway stations in the Siberian Gulag, to help them find these Recruitment Centres and join what would become known as 'Anders' Army'.

The Polish soldiers arrested during the Soviet invasion had been placed in the more centralised labour camps in Ukraine, south Poland and west Russia, where they had suffered two years of horrific, inhumane treatment. These camps were the first to be toured by Anders' Officers sent to locate POWs who had already done active service. At first, 25,000 men were picked but all were emaciated, starving and diseased – in no condition to form an army. Anders was perplexed that there were very few trained officers among them, and no men at all from several camps such as Starobielsk and Kosielsk, where the majority of officers had been taken. Soldiers who had been deported to labour camps even deeper in Siberia, mainly heard about the Recruitment and Welfare Centres by rumour; more than half had already died from their living conditions.

In October 1941, Ander's embryonic army moved to Buzuluk on the Russian border; there it was further agreed with Stalin that the Polish Army could number 40,000 then 96,000 troops. In Buzuluk, only meagre supplies of army uniforms and greatcoats started arriving from Britain and yet, by the end of 1941, the army had grown and two more Infantry Divisions had been added.

There was little provision from the Soviets; no equipment and no clothing or boots for the soldiers, half the promised ambulances and only 10% of the artillery. Also very little food was provided; the Soviet Army had kept most of the supplies for themselves. The Polish soldiers had to train with wooden 'rifles' they had made themselves. It was one of the coldest winters on record and many of the new recruits froze to death at night in their tents because their exhausted bodies had no resilience against the temperatures of – 63°C. At this point in time, none of the Allies had any knowledge of the utter devastation the Polish people had suffered both in captivity and on release.

More Recruitment Centres were set up in several other areas, including at Alma Aty (now called Almaty) in Kazakhstan, and Vrevskoya (now called Almazar) in Uzbekistan, the latter being a camp for army training in engineering. My father and his brother later spent some time in both these places.

The Polish army was moved again in February 1942, to Yangi Yul (now called Yangiyul) near Tashkent in Uzbekistan, where the weather was much warmer. Yangi Yul had been the Soviet Red Army's Summer Training Camp and it had permanent living accommodation for officers, a power station and a firing range. At that time, the Russian troops had lived in tents but had been provided with baths and washrooms. There was even a bakery, restaurants, shops and a hospital. When Anders arrived, however, it was all overgrown and in ruins except for the roads. The camp was reorganised and rebuilt by Anders' Army, and then became the main centre for the administration of the growing numbers of Polish soldiers and civilians who kept arriving from Siberia. Here, another two Infantry Divisions were able to be formed, making five in total.

The Soviets kept interfering in the formation of the Polish Army whose morale was only strengthened by the thought of leaving Russia finally and completely. Stalin wanted the Polish soldiers to be immediately mobilised against the Germans but Anders refused to allow that. The soldiers needed to regain their health and strength after the trauma of the last 20 months, and undertake proper military training first. The agreement had stated that only the army as a whole could be used by the Soviets, not separate divisions that could be lost in the vastness of the field of battle.

Over 400,000 POWs and their dependants, as well as ordinary citizens, had been released in the 'Amnesty', but many thousands died either on the journey or on reaching the camp at Yangi Yul. An increasing number of tents were added to accommodate up to an additional 15,000 refugees, but so many more came that hundreds of people had to sleep in the open. Every single person had to be washed, freed from lice and disinfected, then fed properly and brought back to full health.

**Persia**

Two months after Operation Barbarossa, in August

1941, it seemed to the Allies that the Persians were beginning to align themselves with the Nazis who were now very close to the north of Persia (Iran). Consequently, in order to secure the Allies' access to the Iranian oil and coal fields to protect their own supply lines, and also to limit any German influence in the country, Persia was invaded simultaneously by Russia from the north and Britain from the south.

Persia quickly surrendered and became an Anglo-Soviet protectorate but relationships between the invaders and the Iranians were strained. The Soviets forbade the transfer of rice to the central and south parts of the country causing food shortages where there was already famine and hardship. The Allies together had taken control of the manufacturing industry as well as many forms of transportation including the Trans-Iranian Railway, to help the war effort. Despite these tensions, the hospitable Persians warmly welcomed the Polish evacuees from Soviet territory and helped to process them.

The newly-formed Polish army was evacuated first to Persia, to escape the Soviet obstructions, and then on to Palestine, where it was joined by the Carpathian Rifle Brigade, to be made ready for battle. Thus combined, the 2nd Polish Corps became the third largest fighting force in the west after Britain and America. Anders' Polish army was of great benefit to the Allies during the Italian Battle of Monte Cassino in 1944 when they finally broke through to Rome. With the Polish Air Force, which had also re-formed in Britain, the Polish contribution to the Allied victory was immense.

By 1944, the Soviets had ousted the Germans from Russia, re-conquered all of Poland and then marched west in order to destroy the Nazis in Europe, raping and pillaging as they went in retaliation for the behaviour of the Germans towards them during Operation Barbarossa.

# CHAPTER 7: LEAVING SIBERIA ON LOG RAFTS

## 07/1941 – 03/10/1941 (AGE 15-15½)

*JERZY DĄBROWSKI*

Our 'hosts' had been invaded!

Germany had broken all its promises and had invaded the Soviet Union. This news, which came in late June 1941, raised our spirits as it gave us a glimmer of hope that perhaps we could now leave Siberia and return home to Poland. The Soviet radio continuously broadcast its descriptions of the atrocities committed by the German 'man-eaters' as the Russians liked to call them. Soon, we learned that the Polish Commander-in-Chief, General J. Sikorski, had reached some sort of agreement with the Soviet Dictator, Marshall J. Stalin. Sikorski would organise the Polish Army inside the Soviet Union to help the Russians fight the Germans and Stalin would set all the Polish people in Siberia free. It is difficult to say how many people had been illegally removed from Poland and taken to the Siberian labour camps; at that time, information suggested it could have been anywhere between half a million and four million Polish people, although the truth is probably somewhere in the middle (maybe about 1.5 - 2 million).

The Polish army was organised in several places within the Soviet Union, such as Buzuluk, Yangi Yul, Tatishchevo, and Dzhalal Abad. The Soviet authorities wanted the Polish to fight side-by-side with their 'brothers' in the Red Army, but somehow, the Polish General Anders managed to make an agreement that a large part of the Polish Army should go to the Middle East to fight the Germans there.

People in the labour camps were also given their freedom; we were going to be allowed to leave the logging camp at Sibyriak so that we too could join the Polish forces. Unfortunately, no transport was provided for us to leave. This presented us with a major problem as the nearest railway station was at Asino, some 160 miles away down the River Chulym. We were not aware of any overland roads going there although some of us thought there may be a track on the other side of the river. Also, it was not practical to walk so many miles carrying all our worldly goods – not that we owned much.

It was decided, therefore, that we would build rafts and float on them down the river – after all, this is what we were used to doing. We would have to work fast because the first snow was expected to fall, as usual, in the second half of September. The space on the rafts would be limited to those who did the work of building them, and their families. Some exceptions were made for people who were incapacitated and had no family to work on their behalf. On our raft, we took a lady whose husband had just died, with her daughter and boyfriend who was helping to construct the raft.

Twenty rafts were finally built and joined together in twos to form ten pairs. Each raft itself was a square, with sides of about 8 metres. They were built in three layers, with the largest logs forming a platform at the bottom. The middle layer of thinner logs was laid at 90° and the top layer of thin poles, was laid tightly again at right angles, to form a floor. The bottom two layers were held together with thick ropes, while the top layer was nailed down. In the middle of each raft, boards laid on edge formed a rectangle for a cooking area. At the bottom of the rectangle, a sandpit was built for the cooking fire. Two Y-shaped timber uprights supported a crossbar on which cooking pots and utensils were hung on hooks above the fire. The pots, of course, were just the familiar soya flour tins suspended by a handle of wire threaded through holes in the top.

The rafts were arranged two together in a line ten rafts long. Each of the two rafts at the front and the two at the back had a pair of long oars for steering. A small boat and a length of thick rope were taken aboard to facilitate tying up along the shore for the night. To achieve this, two strong men would have to take one end of the rope and row the boat to the bank, and tie the rope to the nearest large tree or tree stump. The other end of the rope would then be tied to the rearmost raft. In practice, it sometimes took the men several attempts to secure the rope because the job was far from easy. Once achieved, they would be able to bring all the rafts alongside the shore and then a second rope previously secured to the front raft, would be fixed to another tree.

During the day before our scheduled departure, we loaded all our belongings onto the rafts, together with a supply of whatever food we could find, and water for the journey. And then we spent the night on the rafts. There were approximately 276 people on board and there was no space for more. Already long queues were forming for the one toilet cubicle on the rear raft, which charged directly into the river. Many people preferred to continue using the shore for this purpose!

The long-awaited day of departure finally arrived. Early in the morning of the 18th September 1941, we cast off. Fine snow was already beginning to fall. Many of our Russian friends from the villages, as well as those who unfortunately had to be left behind, stood on the shore and waved us goodbye, wishing us a safe journey. It was with much sadness that we left these people with whom we had spent the last 15 months: many had become great friends of ours. However we were pleased to be able to leave that place of suffering and sorrow. A day or two before our departure I had written a poem. Here it is in translation without forcing any English rhymes!

**Farewell Taiga**

*Old Taiga whispers in sadness*
*A joyless murmur of ancient trees*
*A bear growls mournfully*
*A bird sings a sad song.*

*The whole of Taiga's nature*
*Is melting in sorrow*
*Such is old Taiga's farewell*
*To her departing guests -*

*Guests who suffered here greatly*
*Who often shed their tears*
*While from morning to nightfall*
*They sweated at their hard work.*

*They were brought here to suffer*
*From Poland, faraway,*
*Then in hunger and misery*
*Lived here for well over a year.*

*Early death mowed down the lives*
*Of the young as well as the old.*
*My father also perished here*
*And lies at peace in his grave.*

*Now, to you, old Taiga*
*We're saying goodbye for ever*
*And all your mud and swamps*
*We're happily leaving behind.*

*No longer will we be bitten*
*By your mosquitoes in the hot summer*

*And your bedbugs and cockroaches,*
*Your lice, will annoy us no more.*

*We are no longer afraid*
*Of your boggy marshes and swamps*
*Nor do we fear your grim brown bear,*
*Your mosquitoes and your horseflies.*

*So goodbye, you virgin Taiga*
*We're going to distant lands*
*Better for us though yet unknown*
*Beyond mountains and rivers.*

*We will travel far away*
*Through forests and mountain ranges*
*Forever will the walls of distance*
*Separate us from you.*

*Farewell cedar, spruce and fir,*
*Farewell you ever-weeping birch*
*Goodbye Taiga. We will never*
*Remember you with pleasure.*

*Sadly whispers Old Taiga*
*Sadly it melts in sorrow*
*Sadly says goodbye forever*
*To the departing guests.*

During our 160 mile journey down the meandering Chulym River, we had to sleep under the open sky in spite of the fact that the snow was already falling. We used old blankets, rugs and coats to cover ourselves. We tied the rafts up to the bank two or three times every day to enable people to stretch their legs and to use the facilities on shore where there was no queue! To help supplement our diet, many people dug up frozen potatoes from village allotments which had to be eaten raw.

Once we stopped fairly close to a village, and a group, including my brother, went ashore to buy food, paying for it mainly by giving away such of our belongings that still had value. The raft 'management' decided, for some reason, not to wait for their return, despite strong opposition from the family members of those stranded on shore. They just cast off and when the 'shoppers' returned, the rafts were nowhere to be seen. One of the people on shore had observed that there was a wide horseshoe bend in the river further on, and suggested that, by walking cross-country, they would be able to overtake the rafts. As we on the rafts came close to where they were waiting, we saw them all waving their arms frantically to be noticed. We forced the 'management' to tie up the rafts and allow the 'shoppers' back on. There were many heated arguments afterwards but that trick was never played again!

During the two-week journey, a baby was born on one raft, and an elderly Jewish gentleman died on another. Some of his friends prayed over his body, wrapping it in their prayer shawls. Then they weighted his legs and lowered him overboard in a proper sailor's burial. On another occasion, a man fell overboard and was swept underneath the rafts. A couple of men jumped after him into the ice-cold water and successfully pulled him to safety. Further along on our journey, the rafts were forced to go through a newish cut made by the river during the spring floods a year or two before. This narrow section provided a shortcut but the rafts travelled faster than usual and the banks on both sides were very close to the rafts, making us rather anxious for our safety.

A few days later, all the rafts ran aground in shallow water. The only way to continue our journey was to split the whole unit of 20 rafts into individual rafts and then try to rejoin them once we were clear of the river bed. Most of the men had to enter the freezing water and untie the ropes holding the rafts together, freeing each separately. It proved to be impossible to join them all together again as they started to float down the river in small groups of only two or three rafts.

Our particular raft was only joined to one other and we were lucky enough to be able to get hold of one oar to help us steer, as well as a length of rope for tying us to the bank on our frequent stops, because we had no toilet on board! To achieve this, we had to manoeuvre the rafts close to the shore then one man, usually my brother, had to jump off with the end of the rope and try to tie it as quickly as possible to the nearest tree or stump. If he was unsuccessful, he then had to run further ahead and try again. Somehow this part of the journey was far less nerve-wracking without the less-than-helpful 'management'!

After travelling down the river for two whole weeks, we finally arrived at Asino, our destination. We tied up by the sawmills and managed to sell all the timber from the rafts there, which provided us with the finance for further travel. We then walked into the town carrying our luggage; luckily we found some very kind, local people who allowed us to sleep on their living room floors. It was marvellous to sleep on dry land again.

All the other rafts arrived the same day or the following day. We bought train tickets, booking ourselves into a cattle truck which was very similar to the one that had previously taken us away from Poland at the beginning of our odyssey! We obtained food and water for the journey but our resources were only sufficient for us to travel to the city of Pavlodar, on the bank of the great River Irtysh in Kazakhstan, which was considerably further south.

So finally, without regrets, we were able to say goodbye to Siberia! The future, whatever happened, would be a different adventure.

# IN THE SPOTLIGHT: AMNESTY

## 06/1941 – 03/1942

### LINDA GALLAGHER

The news of an 'amnesty' for all the Polish exiles in Siberia filtered through to the settlements in June 1941 but the idea was initially met with much incredulity; this had never happened before. The word 'amnesty' brought great offence to the Poles because they were not criminals being pardoned – there was no crime except on behalf of the Soviets, unless it was deemed a 'crime' to be Polish. The other inmates in the camps looked on the Poles with jealousy and awe, and even hostility.

The Amnesty, one of the terms of the Sikorski-Maisky Agreement, was officially signed off and then proclaimed publicly on 12th August 1941. All the Polish detainees in Soviet Russia, Siberia and Kazakhstan, military and civilian alike, if they had proof they were Polish, were to be released. An announcement was sent to every settlement:

**Announcement**
*The Soviet Government has granted an amnesty to all Polish prisoners and deportees. The amnesty document will serve as the family passport and as a one-way travel permit to the destination of your choice.*

The first snows of the long winter would fall in mid-September, so the ex-prisoners only had a few weeks in which to leave and find their own way back to civilisation. The Russians did not help in any way at all, neither with food, transport nor even maps.

Transportation was in short supply because the Red Army needed it for their own war effort. The starving and exhausted Polish men, women and children had to rely on their own efforts and on each other. The majority, knowing they couldn't return to Poland, wanted to find Anders' Army, the newly reforming Polish Army, and the safety of their own countrymen. The men, especially, wanted to join the army and fight for Poland but no-one seemed to know where it was being formed.

The release of the captives was chaotic and never actually completed. Documents were not sorted out very quickly by the Soviet authorities because there were so many thousands to produce. Directives from the Soviet Government were obeyed or disobeyed by the camp authorities at whim. In some camps, the NKVD wanted to keep the cheap Polish labour in the camps to fulfil the daily 'norms' and so were often obstructive to the more able prisoners. Surprisingly, some of the deportees had only been 'allowed' their freedom from the settlements on condition that they spy on Anders and the forming army and report back to their NKVD handlers. Once they got into Persia, a lot of these people confessed in shame what they had done.

A minority of the freed Polish people decided to stay for a while in their settlements, growing crops, picking berries and mushrooms and making proper plans for their extended stay, but any Polish people left behind either by choice or by their inability to travel, were later forced to become Soviet citizens and to accept Soviet passports. Those who did leave were helped by the generosity of the poor, local Russian peasants who donated what little they could in the way of potatoes, milk and bread. The travellers also had to resort to foraging in the fields and gardens of the collective farms, digging for potatoes or onions which were frequently frozen in the ground, and eating them raw.

Some people begged lifts on carts or lorries; still

others walked, not knowing for how long or how far. Many of those who had been detained in logging camps made rafts on which to float down the rivers. At the borders between Soviet territory and free countries, the NKVD tried to turn the ex-captives away, saying they had only been granted the freedom to travel within the Soviet borders not across them, but most just continued their journey despite being told such lies.

Everyone tried to get to the nearest railway stations where 'Persons of Trust' from the Polish Consulate were detailed to receive the Polish refugees with smiles, food, money, train tickets and most importantly, instructions on how to continue on their journey. Many thousands of people were sent on to Alma Aty (now Almaty) in Kazakhstan, on the border with China and Mongolia, or to Yangi Yul (now Yangiyul) in Uzbekistan to where the new Polish Army was being formed. Their main transport on the railways was in cattle trucks or goods wagons similar to those in which they had been deported, but this time the doors were not locked and they were on their way to freedom, in more comfort and with hope in their hearts.

## Uzbekistan and Kazakhstan

Many of the people arriving in Uzbekistan and Kazakhstan had travelled thousands of miles from all over Siberia, from the Arctic circle in the north, and the Kolyma area in the far east, as well as from the more central regions. Like the soldiers, many of whom had got there first, when they arrived they were skinny and exhausted, ill and penniless. They were dressed in lice-filled rags and had typhus and dysentery. There were those men, with their dependants, who hoped to become soldiers and there were also thousands of civilian men, women and children of all ages.

Some of the liberated Poles froze to death or died from hunger, thirst or illness on their journey to freedom while others barely survived by bartering their personal possessions with local people in exchange for food. Some people had been left behind when they got off the train to get food, only to find it had left without them. Mothers near death gave their babies and children to total strangers in order to give them a chance of surviving. Younger people seemed to cope better with the arduous journey, even though their hearts broke when they had to abandon their very old or frail relatives so that at least some would live. Even on reaching the army camps, many more people died, whether just from the relief of arriving, or because their minds and bodies just couldn't cope with anything more. Locals in Uzbekistan reported that when they opened the doors of the trucks to let the refugees out, dead bodies would just fall to the ground.

At Yangi Yul, Alma Aty, and the other army camps set up to receive them, the numbers of Polish refugees arriving increased daily. Only ex-soldiers could be recruited into the army at first, and so there were over 70,000 displaced people who could not be included. Also, the Soviets had set a limit on the number of Polish Jews who were allowed to join the Polish army, so most had to be turned away.

The Soviets had made minimal provision for the Polish army but none at all for the thousands of civilians camped in the open around the perimeter of the Army bases. In the heat of that summer, hundreds of people died from from infections such as dysentery or typhus, or from their general ill health from starvation and exhaustion; mass graveyards in these countries stand as memorials to these Poles. At first the local Uzbeks and Kazaks didn't understand why so many of them had come to their land – they thought this new army must be German because of the very strange mix of uniforms donated from Europe and America.

General Anders, with wisdom and compassion, enlisted as many people, including women and children, as he possibly could into the Polish Army, to try to save them from starvation by thus obtaining more provisions. However, the Soviet NKVD tried to stop this tactic by sending Polish civilians to Soviet collective farms called 'Kolkhoz', to help harvest the crops until they received their call-up papers. My father and his brother Stanisław were sent to work on cotton farms in Kazakhstan for a few months.

With the constant interference of the Soviets, and their broken promises to provide enough food and equipment, General Anders realised the time had come to leave the USSR completely. He had already struggled with protocol and had fought to turn this military operation into a humanitarian one, in order to save thousands of lives. Now, he made the executive decision to personally take the whole army, and as many civilians as possible out of Soviet territory to freedom in Persia.

# CHAPTER 8: ON THE TRAIN TO KAZAKHSTAN

03/10/1941 – 15/12/1941 (AGE 15½-15¾)

*JERZY DĄBROWSKI*

Our journey south away from Siberia was very stimulating and eventful. We were among 50 people who had booked two goods wagons which were very similar to those that had taken us to Siberia 15 months ago. Each had two wide shelves half-way up the sides to accommodate more people. As we travelled, we sometimes spent a few days in different marshalling yards of the major stations such as Novosibirsk, (the name means 'New Siberia' and under Stalin, became one of the largest Industrial centres and cities of Siberia). If we got out of our wagons, we often had difficulty finding them again as they were moved around, and we had no idea at what time they would continue the journey.

Several times we passed trains going in the opposite direction. These were made up of cattle trucks full of German prisoners-of-war. The men made a pitiful sight, looking pale and half-starved, but somehow I just couldn't feel sorry for them because it was their nation that had brought such grief and suffering to Poland. If Germany hadn't invaded Poland, we would all still be safe and living in freedom at our homes and Russia would, more than likely, have remained within its borders. My father would still be alive and my brother and I would still be continuing our grammar school education.

At Barabinsk on the Trans-Siberian Railway, we spent three days in the huge marshalling yard while our wagons were shunted around from one siding to another. We didn't dare leave the truck to go to the town to buy food for the next stage of the journey in case we couldn't find our wagons again or the train left without us. At another station en route, we were assured that we had two free days so we walked two miles into the town and managed to find the public baths. These was based on a similar principle to the 'baths' in the Siberian settlement, but was considerably larger. The staff at the baths were all women because this was considered to be light work! Again we had to give all our clothes to the female attendant to be disinfected while we went into the steam room, then the wash room, where they filled metal washing bowls with hot water for us. The local Russian men who worked in industry were used to being served by women but we felt a bit strange. The attendants often used to sit on the bench next to naked men, just to have a chat! However, even to my youthful eyes, these ladies were not particularly young and beautiful so the experience wasn't too exciting! After washing ourselves, we went to another room to rinse our bodies with ice-cold water to stimulate the blood circulation, then we collected our clothing and left.

Our next long stop was at the junction station of Tatarsk, where our wagons were to leave the Trans-Siberian line for a branch line to the city of Pavlodar, in Kazakhstan, which is famous for its salt-producing industries. After a two-day wait, our trucks were added to a goods train pulled by a prehistoric locomotive, for the 500 km (320 miles) journey which lasted a whole week. The train travelled at a very sedate speed and frequently stopped in the middle of nowhere. However, each time it stopped, we had enough time to find firewood, light a fire and cook our soup. Someone would notice when the train started to move again; then we knew we had enough time to put out the fire, gather our pots together and get back on board. Sometimes local people sold melons by the side of the railway; the train would slow down enough for us to jump off, buy melons and jump on again before picking up speed once more.

Travelling due south and passing Kupino, Karusk and Slavgorod, we arrived at Kulunda, which was a junction rather than a proper station. Here the train made a long loop of several miles to some secret industrial undertaking and when it returned it was facing the opposite direction. Those who knew about this loop, would leave the train to go shopping, rejoining it when it had returned. We then travelled due west to the terminal station of Pavlodar.

On 15th October 1941, we finally arrived at Pavloda in north-east Kazakhstan. Disembarking, we stacked all our belongings against the railway station fence. Here many of us waited out in the open while my brother, Stanisław, with a group of other people, went into Pavlodar itself to try and find accommodation. My brother succeeded in finding a temporary home for the two of us with the family of a senior Russian army officer. He and his whole family were very helpful to us, and in return I read some of their books aloud to their two small children, which helped me to learn some Russian folk tales and nursery rhymes. This family had a large and seemingly vicious dog which was kept on a running lead across the whole frontage of their property, to keep undesirable intruders away. We both had to be personally introduced to the dog so that he would allow us to pass freely into the house. The dog finally accepted us and even allowed us to pull him aside to allow visitors into the house.

From time to time we went to the market to sell some our belongings in order to buy food. We found a jeweller who was willing to buy our father's Omega watch because it was a quality piece, even though the hands were lost. I preferred to go shopping alone and buy some potato cutlets to satisfy my hunger with the little money I possessed. Fairly soon my brother got a paid job in a factory, making the felt 'valonki' such as we wore in Siberia. I often visited him there and learnt how to make them myself. Felt dust, which made the air thick, was mixed with water then poured into the moulds to form the correct shape. When they were dry, they were taken out of the moulds then thoroughly sanded by hand to obtain a smooth surface.

In Pavlodar, there was already a Polish organisation with an office where they were recruiting people for the Polish army which was being reformed on Soviet land. We went there to fill in some forms after which they helped us to join a contingent going to Uzbekistan where the Polish 5$^{th}$ Division was already being established. We had to have our papers stamped and approved at a Soviet Office but time was not on our side. We were in a hurry and the local bureaucrat was being very unhelpful; his superior was also difficult so we asked to see their top man there. By this time my brother was very annoyed with their attitude and started shouting him and frightened the man: in their communist culture, if you shouted with authority, they thought you must know someone very important. This person went pale, then arranged for our papers to be stamped immediately which allowed us to board the train.

We finally left Pavlodar on the 16$^{th}$ November – we had been there a month. On our way to Uzbekistan, we first had to retrace our journey northwards in the direction of the Trans-Siberian Railway, beyond Kulunda and back to Tatarsk. This time the journey only took two days. We had to wait two or three days in Tatarsk for our connection eastwards to Novosibirsk, sleeping at night on the floor of the station waiting room with a great many other travellers. We had to severely ration our food supplies and snow was already falling. We woke up several times each night and did some exercises to warm ourselves up. We finally boarded the train to Novosibirsk where we had to wait yet again, six days this time, for a further connection to travel south. We slept in the station waiting room at Novosibirsk, which was the biggest I had ever seen. On each wall were 20 feet high portraits of all the Soviet party leaders and it seems like they stared at us day and night in a disapproving and unfriendly way, especially at night as the lights were never switched off! At least there was a form of restaurant here where we could buy some food although it was not cheap. And also, to our joy, there were some flush toilets, the first we had seen since we had left Poland; so many people were waiting for their train connections that the queue for the loos were an hour long!

After six days, the train arrived and we continued our journey through Central Asia, which stretches from the Caspian Sea in the west to China and Mongolia in the east, and from Russia in the north to Afghanistan and Iran in the south. The area includes many countries whose name ends in *'stan'*, (an Iranian word meaning *'land of'*) and encompasses a large part of the Silk Road. We travelled through east Kazakhstan to Uzbekistan, via Barnaul and Semipalatinsk, bypassing the large Lake Balkhash which is one of the largest lakes in Asia, and stopped for the night at the capital of Kazakhstan, Alma Ata. Each compartment of the train had wooden seats with a suspended slatted shelf above for sleeping on. I was lucky to be able to sleep on one while many people had to make themselves comfortable while sitting on the benches below.

Seven days after leaving Novosibirsk, we arrived at Dzhambul in southern Kazakhstan. It was November and snow was already covering the ground. Once again, every night we had to reserve space on the waiting room floor to sleep in temperatures of -10°C. One night we were too late and had to stay outside, sleeping on someone's nicely swept house steps. To keep warm, I slept in my father's long black winter coat and his officer's boots while my brother wore our grandmother's sheepskin coat turned inside out. Luckily we still had our Siberian fur hats. Despite all this we still needed to get up and exercise every half hour to keep from freezing. On another night we were pleased to find a sleeping space inside a passenger carriage which had been left in the sidings.

We spent the days wandering aimlessly around the town looking for food. On our sixth day we noticed a passenger train full of people parked in the sidings. We discovered that they were Polish people on their way to Uzbekistan to join the Polish army being formed there! The train was already really crowded but the passengers made room for Stach and myself and we were so grateful, although every seat was taken and it was difficult to find a sleeping space for the night. However, I found a trunk, three feet long with a barrel-shaped lid, and I managed somehow to sleep quite soundly on it without falling off!

The two-day journey through Chimkent (now Shymkent) finished at Tashkent, the capital of Uzbekistan. Now there was yet another six-day wait for our next train to Dzhalal-Abad in Kyrgyzstan which was part of the old Silk Road. With a group of about 30 other people, we stashed our belongings in one spot in the station yard, sitting next to it in the daytime, and sleeping around it with our heads towards the pile in the night. There were many masterful thieves in Tashkent so when anyone went into the town, several people stayed behind with the luggage. My hair had grown quite a lot since leaving Siberia and one day, when it was my turn to go into town, I managed to get a decent haircut from a proper barber!

We watched many overcrowded passenger trains pass by until finally we were informed our train had arrived. Numerous people were trying to force their way on; Stach left two of our suitcases at the entrance to the carriage for just a few seconds while taking other luggage to the compartment. On his return, he realised someone else had decided to 'take care of them' and we never saw them again. Inside there were many items of clothing and some albums of family photographs which we were very sad to lose, but in the circumstances there was nothing we could do. We had to resign ourselves with making the most of what we had left.

The train took us through the fertile Fergana valley of the great River Syr-Daria, which was surrounded on three sides by mountains. We were close to the highest mountain range in the whole of Russia, the Pamir range in Tajikistan which edges onto the Himalaya, and whose highest peak, at 23,406 feet, was Kommunizma (Now called Ismoil Somoni Peak rather than Communism Peak). We passed through many once-prosperous towns which had been decimated by the Soviets, such as Kokand, Namangan and Andizhan, finally reaching Dzhalal-Abad (now Jalalabad) in Kyrgyzstan on 15th December 1941.

We hoped to be able to join the Polish Army immediately, but to our great disappointment this was not possible as the Soviet powers decided to send everyone, in the first instance, to work in one of their 'kolkhozes' which were collective farms and settlements. Instead of soldiers, Stach and I were to be cotton pickers for the harvest was ready!

# CHAPTER 9: WAITING AROUND IN UZBEKISTAN

15/12/1941 – 03/1942 (AGE 15¾-16)

*JERZY DĄBROWSKI*

I was allowed to ride on top of all the luggage that was piled up, including what remained of ours, on the platform of a local Uzbek's horse-driven cart, because I was still a minor and rather small. The wheels of the cart were approximately six feet high with the platform above, so I had a lovely view of where we were going. Stach, (Stanisław) my brother, being four years older, had to walk for many hours with all the other adults to our destination, Kolkhoz Kirowa, a small Russian collective community named for some small-time communist hero. This village was very close to the regional capital of Suzak which, although having an Uzbek postal address, was actually part of Soviet Kyrgyzstan; a high mountain range separated it from the rest of that republic. The Suzak district included one main town and 123 Kolkhoz villages, or collective farms.

Stach and I, and another man, were allocated accommodation in the barn of a local house which was built in the typical Uzbek style: high boundary walls built of clay formed a rectangle along the street and two sides, while the main house made up the fourth side at the rear of the enclosed yard. The house was built of timber allowing for movement in the event of earthquakes which were common in this area. The house had two compartments, one of which was for living, cooking and sleeping in, while the other was a barn for storing straw and other necessities. Both compartments had unglazed windows with shutters which looked over the yard, and a sturdy door. A large open fire used for warmth and cooking burned continually in the centre of the family's living compartment and at night the family all slept with their feet towards the fire. Above was an opening in the roof to let the smoke escape.

But the barn was to be our new home! Our 'room' had no central fire, but at one end there was an enormous unused fireplace with a fully open chimney, both about six feet wide and two feet deep; you could look up and see the stars through this chimney. At the other end of the barn the straw was stacked. We would sleep on the floor in the space in between but there were no mattresses. Early one morning, while sleeping in the barn, we were woken up by the movement of the floor beneath us and the creaking of the structural timber – this was a frightening experience but at least the building did not collapse during the mild earthquake!

In the yard adjoining the house, there was a high-level open oven for cooking the 'laposhki', a flat circular bread. For fuel, cow dung was collected from the fields and dried in the open air by being pressed to the boundary walls. When this fuel was burnt down to its embers, the bread dough was stuck to the roof of the oven and when they were ready, the bread fell off. Our generous hosts always cooked enough laposhki for their hungry guests to eat too. We also made soup with potatoes, onions and corn cobs, cooked on the fire in the familiar empty tins of soya flour. My brother found an old tin plate on which he was able to make popcorn. We supplemented the fuel for our own fire with some straw, and if our host noticed his supply diminishing, he never commented on it.

We shared our room with many annoying, squeaking sparrows and one day we decided to catch some of them to eat because we hadn't had meat for a long time. We closed the shutters and the door but only caught one sparrow as the rest flew up and away through the chimney. However, we made ten litres of soup with this one tiny bird, potatoes and onions and we ate it all, even sharing the bones; it was the most delicious food we'd had for many months!

Every day, Stach had to collect cotton from the fields and was paid at the end of each session of work, which helped our finances. And each day, I had to go to the local administrative office with Stach's supervisor's statement that recorded how much of his expected 'norm' he had achieved that day. Here we were paid 'in kind' so I was able to get some food from the store in exchange for his work. A Kolkhoz generally kept a share of its produce for itself and paid its workers with this rather than cash. The rest of the crop was supposed to to be sold to the Soviet Union at very low, fixed prices.

On my part, I tried to make some money by sewing sacks made from oddments of fabric I found, some of them textiles used for food storage. I found some old socks and unwound them, rewinding the thread on pieces of wood to make the 'cotton' for sewing. I was very unlucky in this enterprise – no-one wanted to buy my sacks! I took them to the market in Suzak, but again no-one wanted them, although some people saw how hungry I looked and gave me food anyway. My brother tried shoe-repairing but only ever had one customer for his re-soling business.

We went to Suzak several times, usually for shopping or to get cleaned up in the Roman-style communal baths. A 12 feet square pool with ice-cold water was placed between four pillars holding up the roof. Around the pool was a gallery with benches beyond for putting your clothes on and the metal bowl of hot water and soap you were given with which you washed yourself. Once clean, you had to jump into the freezing water to improve your blood circulation to help harden you against the winter weather.

On one occasion, not wanting to complete the long trek back home, my brother and I decided to spend the night in the local Uzbek guest house, known as a 'Tchayhana' (Chaikhana) or teahouse. The tea, a weird-tasting green or black beverage without milk or sugar, was drunk from a shallow porcelain bowl called a 'piyala'. The local men squatted on the floor, drinking this tea throughout the night, with some folk supplementing it by smoking opium. Intoxicated men would then start singing in high-pitched drawling voices to the delight of the other guests. All this took part in a single, long room on one side of which there was an eight-foot wide platform two feet above the floor; this was the 'continuous' sleeping area, where we each slept side by side with our heads towards the wall.

The Uzbeks had some rather nice local customs. If there was a wedding feast going on, passers-by were invited in to eat rice with them because this would assure the newly-weds had luck and prosperity in the years to come. Stach and I were lucky enough to be passing a wedding reception one day, and were welcomed in. The bride was beautifully dressed and all the bridesmaids had their hair done up in 60 little plaits, as was the local practice. Everyone, men and women alike, also wore the highly embroidered skull caps. We were so pleased to be offered food that we wished them lots of luck before going happily on our way again!

After two months, early in February, 1942, the three of us at the kolkhoz finally received our call-up papers to join the Polish Army at Dzhalal-Abad. There was actually nothing for me because I was still not yet sixteen years old. The day before leaving Suzak, my brother had to finalise everything with the local officers in the administrative building and was also paid for the work he had done in the cotton fields. The next morning, the man who had lodged with us in the kolkhoz left very early before we were awake. In addition to his own belongings, he stole our large wall rug which we had been using as a blanket; this was quite a valuable possession. He was hoping to sell it at the next village but luck was not on his side. One of the local Uzbeks in that village recognised the rug as belonging to us, and he had the man arrested. I am not sure what happened to this dishonest person, but it was a lovely surprise to be given back our rug when we passed through that community ourselves.

We walked for several hours carrying our belongings, and finally arrived in Dzhalal-Abab, a small country town serving the surrounding area. It had a number of shops which unfortunately had very little to sell, particularly in the way of food. We were starving so we found a local eating place that sold, as its only hot food, some soup made from a kind of barley. Afterwards, as we explored the town, we discovered that one shop was for the exclusive use of the families of the Communist party members and senior officers: apparently it was always full of merchandise. We disregarded the signs and went into the shop. The serving lady, observing how thin and poorly we both looked, took pity on us. She asked us to go away but to return in a few minutes, once all the other customers had left. When we returned, she served us some inexpensive but good quality food – we were so grateful! Later that day, I was walking alone along one of the main streets when I was stopped by a well-dressed Russian woman whose husband, she said, held an important position in the Communist party. She had seen my feather pillow on the top of my rucksack and insisted I sold it to her. I refused but she persisted for several minutes, even raising her offer, but to no avail. Disappointed and upset she finally left me alone with my pillow.

We found it very difficult to find somewhere to sleep that first night in Dzhalal-Abad, despite looking everywhere. Towards midnight, we walked into a hotel and begged to be allowed to lie down and sleep somewhere there. One of the receptionists agreed we could spend the night on the floor of an external corridor. From here we could see into the rooms through all the half-glazed partitions; every room was overflowing with beds, as many as could be squeezed in, and was fully occupied by people of either gender, all crowded in together. No sooner had we started to drift off to sleep, when a senior member of staff arrived, and in no uncertain terms, told us to get out. So at two o'clock in the morning we had to resume our search for a safe place to sleep. Eventually we came across a Tchayhana, or teahouse, which took guests, and was very similar to the one described earlier in Suzak. Again, many customers squatted on the floor drinking their tea or smoking opium throughout the night, but luckily there were no nocturnal singers. In my innocence, I observed a couple on the sleeping platform seemingly doing exercises beneath a large blanket. I was too young and naive to fully understand what they were doing and no-one else took any notice of it anyway!

The very next morning, my brother, Stanisław, had to report to the recruitment office at the army camp for his medical examination, which he passed. He was admitted to serve in the Polish Army, but although I was almost 16, I was still far too young to even be accepted as a Polish volunteer. The lowest age allowed was 18, so this time I couldn't go with Stach who was 19 years old. However, the officer in charge took me on as one of his batmen, although he already had six or seven such people. If it wasn't for him, I would have been left alone in the Soviet Union when my brother went away with the army. This all happened on Friday 13th February which I consider to be one of the luckiest days of my life.

My first night as a batman was spent in the main barracks, sleeping in one of the three-tiered bunks constructed next to the wall. The next day, I moved in with the kind officer whose rank of Captain was shown by three embroidered stars on each epaulette. He had just been issued with a new uniform that had no stars, and because I had learnt to sew, I neatly embroidered the stars on to his uniform for him which seemed to please him. Along with the other batmen that first day,

I was issued with a First World War American overcoat. I was given the job of messenger, carrying various important papers to other parts of Dzhalal-Abad. At that time, there was an epidemic of typhus in the town and people were dropping like flies, even dying in the streets. I had to get used to stepping over dead bodies on the pavement but I'd already learnt to do that in the Soviet Union where one had had to be prepared for anything. For the first time since leaving Poland, I was able to attend the Roman Catholic Holy Mass and even managed to serve at the altar sometimes. There was a great deal to be grateful for as I now had a roof over my head and regular meals, and what was most important, the opportunity to leave this so called 'Garden of Eden' which was the Soviet Union.

A week later, I was transferred back to Suzak with approximately 20 other young lads aged between 10 and 17. We didn't have to walk this time as we were transported on carts pulled by horses. This group was under the supervision of the NCO but because I had been a Boy Scout in Poland, I was put in charge of them. In Suzak we received some training and did some exercise drills. We had to take our meals at a building on the other side of the town, and we always marched there singing various Polish songs, and looking rather odd in our long American overcoats and Siberian headgear. The locals, on seeing us, would chant 'Look, Look, Little People!' The town had a very different effect on me now, with my new perspective. I had the chance to really look at my surroundings, to notice the type and quality of its buildings and the way the local people dressed.

Within a couple of weeks we had left Suzak to go on to the large Polish camp in Vrevskaya, near Tashkent, Uzbekistan, travelling by train from Dzhalal-Abad. I often seemed to be retracing my steps on this twisting journey to freedom!

# CHAPTER 10: FREEDOM IN THE MIDDLE EAST

## 03/1942 – 05/1942 (AGE 16)

*JERZY DĄBROWSKI*

Alongside several army units, there were already many boys in my age group in the camp at Vrevskaya, and their number kept growing until there were nearly 500 of us. We were divided into platoons of approximately 35 boys. For some reason, the boys in my platoon seemed to trust me enough to choose me to be their leader, even though there were a few older lads. Our accommodation was in a large room in a barn-type building. There were two wide, horizontal shelves on which we slept, one about two feet up, and one about six feet above the ground.

I worked out a fair system for distributing the daily rations amongst my platoon. I divided the fairly dry bread into equal portions on the lower bed, then without looking, I randomly called out the names of the boys while another boy pointed at a portion. With the thick, barley soup ration, someone else read out names while I dished out individual portions with a large ladle. If any soup was left in the bottom, it was given to those who volunteered to do the clearing up afterwards; this proved to be a very popular pastime.

Every day, after the morning parade, we youngsters were allowed to just wander around, in and near the camp. We found a small kiosk that sold jars of pickled onions and other pickled vegetables so we bought some to supplement our diet even though they weren't exactly food. On one of our wanderings, three of us came across an old dilapidated shed. The door was partly open so we went inside. When our eyes got used to the dark, we were almost sick. This building seemed to be a mortuary for poor people – lying on the ground were several naked corpses – skeletons with no flesh, just dried out skin. We retreated rather rapidly and returned to the camp in rather a sombre mood.

We were all undernourished due to the lack of vitamins from the poor quality of the food we'd existed on so far, and our resistance to illness was very low. When an epidemic of typhus hit the camp, many boys had to spend time in the camp hospital. With dysentery also raging, the queues for the few primitive facilities was very long. One sad incident occurred when a small and very weak boy fell through the opening of the toilet into the tank of excrement below, and with great difficulty, we managed to get him out and clean him up. This was not the most pleasant experience I ever had!

Towards the end of March we finally received proper English uniforms, just as we were about to leave the camp for our long-awaited journey of over 1,600 miles to Krasnovodsk, (now called Turkmenbashi), a peninsular on the Caspian Sea in Turkmenistan, then on to Pahlavi in the Middle East. We collected what was left of our possessions and boarded a passenger train for the three-day journey. Being in charge of my platoon, I had to stay awake on duty half the night, to ensure that no undesirable characters boarded our train at the intermediate stations, as well as being on hand if any boy needed help in the night. We crossed the wide River Amu-Darya and passed through places with romantic-sounding names such as Bukhara which is rich in historical sites, and Samarkand, one of the oldest continuously inhabited cities in Central Asia, famous for its beautiful mosques. From the train we could see some amazing mosques and other historical buildings surrounded, unfortunately, by drab, mass-produced houses which were completely out of character with the ancient town centres.

It appears that the Golden Horde of Ghengis Khan and his successors came from this area. In the early part of the 13th century, these hordes conquered Samarkand and invaded Europe, managing to reach as far as Kraków, then the capital of Poland, in 1241. Here, one of their archers shot an arrow through the throat of the bugler playing the hour from the high tower of Our Lady's church in Kraków square, stopping him halfway through his call. The tradition persists to this day, that daily, on the hour, the trumpeter in the tower stops halfway through his playing the bugle. There is a legend in Samarkand that they would only be free from the enemy if a trumpeter from Poland played the whole hourly call in their own marketplace. The Polish Army stationed nearby managed to oblige but it still took nearly half a century for the Uzbeks to be free from the Soviet Union.

After Samarkand, we travelled close to the border of Persia (Iran) with its high mountain ranges in the distance, through Ashgabat, the capital of Turkmenistan, and finally arrived at Krasnovodsk where we were allowed to stretch our legs by walking around the port which shipped oil and coal across the Caspian sea, but we were banned from exploring the adjoining military base. Eventually we boarded a large coal ship bound for Pahlevi (now called Bandar e Anzalin) in Persia, named for the ruling dynasty.

Approximately 6000 of us were squeezed into the ship for the two day journey across the sea, but no-one minded for we were about to leave the Soviet Union forever. For their parting gift, the Soviets gave each of us just one salted herring and some very dry *sukhary* (rusk) bread slices. The water on board was only sufficient for the crew so it ran out after a couple of hours. Should we eat the herring but be thirsty, or not eat it and remain hungry? It was a dilemma but most of us chose the first option.

The ship was not built for passengers so sleeping

space was hard to find, with many people just squatting wherever they could. I was very lucky to find a space on the very top of the coal storage compartment, between some rings used for tying ropes to. This space was far from comfortable but at least I was certain to be very far away from the people who had dysentery and were unable to reach the toilet in time! The toilets were just two enormous barrels which were soon overflowing so people were forced to sit on the deck rails with their backs to the sea! I felt very sorry for the dockers at Pahlevi when the ship arrived, smelly, dirty and totally contaminated for they had to make it seaworthy once again.

It was such a wonderful feeling to disembark from the ship and place our feet on the dry land of a free country. We could hardly believe we were really free ourselves after two and a half years. All our past sufferings suddenly seemed of little importance as we finally cut our ties with the dreadful communist regime of the Soviet world, and could say 'Hello' to the free world, this last day of March in 1942. It felt like a dream and we wondered if we would wake up still in Siberia.

In Pahlevi there was a very welcoming British military camp but the first priority was to feed us. We were each provided with a tablespoon of both margarine and brown sugar which were to be eaten with the bread and tea that was coming, but I was so hungry and it was so long since I had seen these things that I just ate them on their own with great enjoyment. We later had a hot meal and were given a packet of dates each, and so for a short while our hunger was satisfied. After this we went into a tent and had to pile all our belongings ready to be disinfected. Our clothes were to be incinerated, our hair was shaved off and we had a good, old-fashioned all-over wash with a disinfectant soap. This was to ensure no lice or fleas were allowed to survive. For the first time since leaving Poland I felt really clean. Then we collected brand new uniforms, underwear and blankets, ready for our new life.

The only fruit I had eaten since leaving Poland was some water melon in Kazakhstan, so imagine my joy on seeing a Persian vendor selling oranges. I had no money and he only had seven oranges left, so I exchanged them for my good quality Boy Scout knapsack. The vendor disappeared rather fast in case I changed my mind but I was more than satisfied with my purchase. There were some Polish soldiers in the camp and I soon found out that my brother, Stanisław, was among them. He'd heard that I had arrived there too but despite spending a lot of time searching the enormous site, we were unable to find each other, which was immensely disappointing for both of us.

We rested at Pahlevi for two days before being transported in open lorries to Tehran. Each lorry carried about 30 of us for the two day journey. The convoy often stopped in inhabited areas where we would be surrounded by local beggars and vendors selling hard-boiled eggs. For the night we stopped at Qazvin, at a large country house standing in a beautiful garden which was so pleasant and peaceful to walk in. The next day, our journey took us through the narrow range of the high Elburz mountains that curve along the southern edge of the Caspian Sea like a sheer wall. The highest peak is Mount Damavand, reaching over 18 thousand feet (5.77 metres). In Iranian mythology, these mountains were a remote resting place of the heroes and gods. The roads were very narrow with many bends, tunnels and sheer drops of several thousand feet to the trees below which looked like matchsticks. The Persian drivers, who were obviously used to it, drove the lorries at speed, often narrowly missing oncoming traffic. It was frightening for those of us who were sitting at the side of the drop in those open-topped lorries; we often couldn't see where the road went and it gave us the impression at times that we were flying in an aeroplane! Luckily, we only lost one lorry on the whole journey.

That evening we arrived in Tehran and were accommodated in an enormous hanger at the aerodrome. We were organised into four companies of about 120 boys in each, with the youngest being in the first company and the oldest in the fourth. As a sixteen year old, I was put into the fourth company. Each company had an officer in charge who split the group into three platoons each under an NCO, which were each then divided up into three sections, making a total of 36 sections. Being quite small, I was invited to be a section leader of all the shortest boys in the company!

We laid out our belongings in the hanger, two long straight lines per company and no mattresses. During daylight we had our usual parades and received any instructions. For our main meals, we had to march in sections to some buildings about a mile away in Tehran where the British Army fed us. Other food stuff like bread and packets of dates, were delivered to the hanger. We had finally started receiving some money so were able to buy groceries from vendors who sold mainly fruit quite near to the hanger. We had to put guards in place so that the vendors didn't come too close: officially we were supposed to chase them away but they just moved a short distance then returned. We actually developed a game with them. When they were chased away, they would leave a piece of fruit as a 'gift' to the guards who then picked it up and stayed away for a while, giving them the chance to sell their wares to other boys. Then the guards returned to be seen to be doing their duty of chasing the sellers away, and so the game would continue.

This aerodrome was the principal airport for Iran so we were able to watch the planes land and take off, which gave us all an interest. Near our hanger there were a number of pre-war planes, twin-engined and twin-winged. We were allowed to inspect them but were forbidden to actually leave the airport individually in case we got lost. On Sundays, Roman Catholic church services were held out in the open and I often managed to be chosen to serve at the altar. Once

I was very proud to serve when Mass was celebrated by two archbishops and a Polish Bishop, Fr J Gawlina who was in charge of all the clergy within the Polish forces abroad.

The Shah of Persia took a lot of interest in us boys and invited several of us to his palace but I wasn't among the lucky ones. He also adopted several boys whose parents were both no longer alive. Many of us made friends with the soldiers of the British Forces who found it very difficult to pronounce our names. They overcame this by giving us nicknames. For instance, one boy whose surname was Niepokulczycki was given the name 'Popeye'!

All the most able-bodied people of military age, including cadets, were to be transferred to Palestine to join the Carpathian Rifle Brigade which had already formed there. The time for our departure from Tehran arrived, and we left on 30th April 1942, in the same sort of open lorries that brought us there. We stopped in the same town, Qazvin, in the same large country house, overnight, and then continued our journey through fertile valleys and various mountain ranges and rivers. The second night we spent at Hamadan and the third near Kermanshah (also called Bakhtaran), passing close to the famous rock tomb of King Darius who is mentioned in the Bible. Years later I had to draw this tomb while studying architecture. We spent one noteworthy night in the mountains on the border with Iraq. My section was on duty and we had to peel a similar sized mountain of potatoes (so it felt) for the whole convoy! In the morning we once again celebrated Mass in the open air; after this my friends nicknamed me Dominic after St Dominic and this name stuck with me until I left the Polish Air Force in Britain in October 1946.

The last day of this particular part of our journey, the 5th of May, took us through Baghdad, the capital of Iraq. We were amazed to see their famous Mosque with its blue dome. After crossing the great rivers Euphrates and Tigris, we arrived at the military airfield at Habbaniyah, in Iraq. This camp, our home for the next fortnight, was on the shore of a beautiful lake of the same name.

# IN THE SPOTLIGHT: ACROSS THE CASPIAN SEA TO PERSIA

## 03/1942 – 09/1942

*LINDA GALLAGHER*

A vast number of Polish refugees, civilians as well as ex-soldiers, all in really bad physical and mental condition, managed to reach Tashkent in Uzbekistan, or one of the other Polish Army Registration Centres. General Anders, who had set up several of these centres in Soviet Asia, soon realised that he couldn't form a viable Polish army with these people who had been in exile in Siberia until they were healthy again.

The Soviet authorities, although supposedly now on the side of the Allies, continued to deliberately create severe situations on their own territory hoping that starvation and epidemics would complete the process of eliminating the Poles as a nation on what they deemed to be their territory. They provided very small amounts of food, clothing and equipment to the army camps, which was to be allocated only to military personnel. This situation is what prompted Anders' decision to transfer the whole army and all the civilians to Persia (Iran), which was held by the Allies, in order to save more lives. Although many soldiers and citizens had already died, the morale of the army was strengthened by the thought of finally leaving the USSR.

The Soviets and the Polish-Government-in-Exile said they would only agree to evacuate the military – not the civilians – to help with the war, and to guard the oil fields in Persia, but Anders was stubborn and ignored this rule. He enlisted as many people as he possibly could into the army – not just younger men, but also older citizens, women and even older children. He managed to transport them, and also a majority of other refugees, to Krasnovodsk in Turkmenistan, the main port on the Caspian Sea from where ships could be requisitioned for Persia. He knew that this might be his one and only opportunity to save the lives of these suffering Polish citizens, and eventually he got reluctant permission from Stalin to proceed.

My father and his brother Stanisław had been legitimately recruited into the Army relatively early, and therefore were now in a slightly better physical condition than the crowds of civilians who had arrived later and who now travelled with them. Warm clothing, regular meals and rudimentary training were beginning to help them heal.

### At the port of Krasnovodsk

Thousands more refugees poured into Krasnovodsk, having somehow made their own way there from other areas of Siberia; they begged to be included in the evacuations. Many of them arrived by rail, only to be told by officials – who pretended to be Polish – to get off the train about three kilometres from the port, and congregate in a field. Here, they were told they would have to walk the last few kilometres and were only allowed to carry hand-luggage. They had to leave all their personal possessions which they would no longer need, in the field. They were told that the NKVD would be searching them for contraband at the port, so for now, they were to put their valuables and documents into the sacks the 'officials' were carrying, and their possessions would be returned to them later.

However, when the weary travellers finally got to Krasnovodk, there were no NKVD officials and no searches, neither were their possessions returned to them. Those bogus officials had lied; this was a tragic scam as so many people lost the personal and sentimental luggage they had carried everywhere with them for the last two years or so.

Krasnovodsk, a major industrial fishing port, sits on a peninsular jutting out into the Caspian Sea. Coal, oil and wood were regularly carried to and from Pahlavi (now Bandar e Anzali) in Persia, taking two or three days to cross the 250 miles of sea to the Middle East. While they waited to be organised, the crowds of refugees camped out on the sand-dunes on the outskirts of the town. They were incredibly weak after up to two years of maltreatment and starvation, followed by this long trek to freedom. Their hunger was terrible – there was so little bread that the one soggy loaf a day they had received in Siberia now seemed like luxury.

**Evacuation**

Anders had requisitioned as many large ships and smaller boats as he could, and arranged what unfortunately became only two main evacuations. Priority for the first evacuation was to be given to the military, including pilots, engineers, mechanics and wireless operators, who would be sent on to Britain to be trained. Military administrators, who were required to set up more army bases in Iran, were prioritised next, along with sick civilians and children who may not survive unless sent quickly.

The first evacuation took place from March 24$^{th}$ until 2$^{nd}$ April 1942; my father was on one of these first ships to leave Soviet soil. The people had to queue for a long time before reaching the gangplank where their names were ticked off by both a Polish Officer and a NKVD officer, but records show this was all done in a hurry and none too accurately. In total, about 44,000 military personnel and 11,000 civilians and children were shipped to Persia on oil and coal ships, and smaller boats. Some say that approximately 6,000 people were carried on each of the large industrial ships. Each vessel was grossly overcrowded, had no food or water, and no toilet facilities – people sat on the ship's railings to relieve themselves over the sides. The prevalence of sickness and dysentery meant the decks of the ships were awash and many people died, their bodies being thrown overboard with little more than a prayer. There was barely a place to sit and so others just fell overboard from the overcrowding. The evacuees put up with these new horrors because they knew this was only a temporary situation, and the hope of freedom was infinitely preferable to staying in the Soviet Union.

However, after that first evacuation, Polish-Soviet diplomatic relations deteriorated and the NKVD in Krasnovodsk started to arrest Polish Officials. The second evacuation took place between August 10$^{th}$ and 1$^{st}$ September 1942, and consisted of about 43,000 military personnel and 25,000 civilians. However, the Soviets did not allow a lot of the Polish army equipment, stores and uniforms to be taken on the boats, making the case that since the Russians had 'provided' them, they were now entitled to keep them.

It is estimated that Anders managed to get at least 116,000 refugees (some evidence suggests it could be double this number) over the sea to Persia and freedom but this number represents only 8-10% of all the Poles released from Siberia at the 'amnesty'.

Further evacuations of the Polish Military and citizens to Persia were banned by the Soviets after the discovery of the Katyn Forest Massacre by the Germans in April 1943. The number of Poles who were thus left stranded in the USSR, far exceeded the number who had been safely evacuated. Many disappeared without trace or died; some were forced to take on Soviet citizenship and were sent by the NKVD back to the Kolkhozy in Kazakhstan to work on the collective farms, while others managed eventually to return to post-war Poland where they lived in fear of the Communists, had survivors' guilt and were unable to talk about their experiences.

### Welcome to Persia

Pahlavi, where the evacuees were put ashore, was the biggest port on the Caspian Sea. It was a beautiful town, with a lagoon, white beaches and palm trees. Although they would actually be the 'guests' of the British occupiers of Persia rather than of Iran itself, Pahlavi was the Poles' beacon of hope and freedom.

The larger ships were too big to dock so the evacuees were taken off in groups by smaller steam ships. British Officers, together with Iranian Officials and the International Red Cross, had set up reception centres, and as they watched the first boats squeeze into the port, they had little idea what to expect – how many people there would be or what condition they would be in. They were alarmed to discover that they would be receiving about 25,000 Polish people a day, many of whom were ill, and that there were many civilians, women and children among the numbers, for whom they were totally unprepared.

Starving and totally bewildered on landing, some frail Polish people, unable to cope any longer, just lay down on the sand and died. Others knelt and kissed the ground or prayed, or wept for joy, while the more active rushed to barter or buy food and fresh fruit; some ate too much too quickly and became extremely ill. Some wandered around in a daze, searching for their lost ones and holding tightly to their meagre possessions.

The British Forces gradually processed the arrivals. When it was realised that over 40% of them had typhus which spread exponentially in these conditions, the reception area was separated into two spaces by a barbed wire fence, for those with infectious diseases and those without. All clothes were taken away and burnt, disinfectant spray tunnels were walked through and hot water showers were insisted upon. Heads were shaved to get rid of lice, but many people were too traumatised to go through this additional indignity after all they'd been through. Many women took to wearing headscarves to hide their baldness. Truckloads of civilian clothing had been sent from America by the Red Cross and once clean, each person was given fresh clothes and blankets and then directed to their new living quarters.

Along the shores of the lagoon near the town, the Iranian army had set up a 'city' of some 2000 tents which stretched for several miles and included bathhouses, laundries and bakeries as well as a hospital. Empty houses were requisitioned but the provision was still inadequate. The type of food provided seemed to make matters worse for those who were used only to eating hard bread. Fatty soup, lamb and corned beef played havoc with their systems and a large number died from overeating the rich food which their bodies could not tolerate.

The Persians seemed to find a mutual affinity with the Polish people and were very kind and generous both to the soldiers and to the refugees. A spontaneous custom sprang up; Polish soldiers would respectfully salute Persian officers on the streets, showing their gratitude and the friendliness of their relationship.

**Illness**

The hospital set up in Pahlavi only had 10 doctors and 25 nurses to start with. It was so full of those ill with typhus and dysentery, malaria, ulcers, skin conditions, and exhaustion, that no more could get in even though there were thousands of really sick Poles. Nearly 3,000 people died within a few months of arriving and were buried here and in towns nearby. The Armenian Cemetery in Pahlavi is full of identical tombstones etched with the unfamiliar Polish names and the single year of death – 1942 – which speaks of the great tragedy.

After spending several days in quarantine in enormous warehouses, government buildings, community centres, or in the tents erected along the beach, the refugees were sent on to Tehran. Again, many died on the journey or on arrival, and within weeks there were over a thousand tombs in the Polish Graveyard in Tehran alone. Iran itself was unable to help every single refugee, and now, with the German army threatening the Caucasus (the area between the Caspian Sea and the Black Sea), many civilians and children were sent from Tehran to countries willing to accept them, such as South Africa, Uganda, Kenya, India, and New Zealand.

The Polish military were to join the British High Command in the Middle East, and so were sent from Pahlavi, via Iraq, for training in Palestine. Now that they were no longer under Soviet influence, some of the Jewish soldiers left Anders' Army in Palestine, and joined the embryonic Zionist militant group who were the main body pushing for Israel to become a nation again with its own land. The Polish Army itself, once trained, proved very competent and useful in Battle of Monte Cassino in Italy. After the war, the majority of displaced Poles who had fought with General Anders settled in Great Britain.

# CHAPTER 11: ARRIVING IN THE 'PROMISED LAND'

## 05/1942 – 06/1943 (AGE 16-17¼)

### JERZY DĄBROWSKI

We were overjoyed to learn that RAF Habbaniyah had several swimming pools. We were very tired and extremely dusty when we first arrived there because the weather, that last day of travelling through Central Iraq, had been really hot (about 50°C or 120°F). This immense base, built on the banks of the Euphrates River, was a very green place, because water taken from the river enabled it to have flowerbeds, lawns and gardens. It was just like a town, having cinemas and theatres, sports stadiums and its own power station. As well as fuel and bomb stores, there was also an RAF hospital.

Lake Habbaniyah was being used as a refuelling point for flying boats travelling from the UK to India. It was so close to our camp that we all decided to have a good sleep that first night then go for a long swim in the morning. Dressed in our swimming trunks and waving our towels, we raced down to the lake but to our horror it was no longer there! During the torrid night, so much water had evaporated that the shore was now half a mile from the camp. We ran on and reached the lake only to find it was so shallow, it only reached up to our knees, despite walking several hundred yards into it. At least we had a bath of sorts and returned ready for breakfast. The next days were even hotter; we had to get up really early so that all our tasks for the day were finished by 10am. Except for using the toilet, we had to stay in the shade of our tents from then until

4pm unless we were on duty to collect meals for everyone from the kitchen tent. Those six hours were spent dressed in very light clothing and lying in our tents. Drinking water, warm and not very tasty, was brought to the camp in tankers then emptied into large containers 4 feet high and 15 feet long, made with animal skins. It too evaporated quickly so had to be topped up continually.

The weather became more bearable after about two and a half weeks, so once again we loaded all our possessions onto the lorries for the last 540 mile leg of our journey to Palestine, the 'Promised Land' in more ways than one. Practically all of this journey was through the desert; the days were still quite warm but we slept for two very cold nights under the clear skies. There was no defined road so the convoys of lorries often travelled side by side, sometimes up to ten abreast. Once the desert ended, we continued our journey on Palestinian buses which were far more comfortable. It was so marvellous to see green, orange groves and palm trees on our way. By the evening, we had reached our final destination at Bashshit camp, near the town of Gedera in Palestine. It was luxury! There were showers and flushing toilets, tarmacked roads and orange groves, as well as Polish sausage and scrambled eggs. The ground proved to be very sandy and we had to drive the tent pegs deep into the ground. A female unit had arrived at a similar time, and their tent was placed close to ours. In the middle of the night we were awoken by loud screams as their tent had apparently decided to collapse onto its sleeping occupants. It took quite a while to free all the ladies and help them re-erect it.

After a few days, I was moved to the tent of the Commanding Officer of our company, which he shared with his sergeant, the 'Chief of Staff'. My new duty was to be the company messenger, and to help divide the food and bread between the different sections. I made many new friends this way because there was always food left over. The youngest boys didn't eat as much as we older boys so I freely distributed what was unused.

Soon after our arrival here, I learned that my brother Stanisław was in the military hospital near Richon-le-Zion, with a bad case of bursitis on the knee. It just so happened that a Polish General was visiting our camp that day and on his return journey he would pass very close to the hospital so I was able to beg a lift. It was wonderful to see my brother again and to share all that happened to each other since February in the three months we'd been apart. I spent the night with him in the barracks there then caught buses back to my base. I visited him a couple more times, sometimes thumbing a lift from civilian or Arab lorries. Stach had an operation then was moved for rehabilitation to a camp on the Mediterranean Sea, at Natanya. I continued to visit him several times, staying overnight so that in the mornings we could swim in the sea from the sandy beach there.

The Polish Army in Camp Bashshit was properly organised and undertook training in the mountainous areas to get the troops used to the terrain so that they would be prepared when they went on to Italy. Towards the end of the summer, a School of Communications was opened in our camp and a special company of suitable students was formed. I was selected not only to join this group, but also to be section leader once again. Because of this advantageous position, I was allowed to move to a tent with some others on the fringe of the camp, a place where I was less likely to be called on to volunteer for various duties. The less 'romantic' advantage was that we were often visited by scorpions and black widow spiders, who liked the fact that we slept only on a blanket on the ground as there were no beds. Each bed space was raised up on a pile of sand, thus forming a water channel around to drain rainwater off.

One morning I happened to disturb a scorpion that was sleeping peacefully inside my shirt. To show its disapproval it decided to sting me in the thumb. I am not really cruel by nature but this time, I stamped on it hard with my army boot, thus ending its miserable life! My thumb swelled up very fast and I raced to the camp doctor who pacified me and treated the sting with permanganate of potash in hot water, which soon reduced the swelling. I was stung again a few times but I had now learned the antidote. I soon lost my love for these creatures for on many occasions I discovered a scorpion asleep under my pillow. The other boys and I used to capture these sleepy animals by tying a cotton loop to their tail and frying them alive, upside down over the fire. No doubt, these days we would be prosecuted for cruelty to animals. We once managed to catch both a black widow spider and a scorpion and we put them on a piece of wood which we floated in a large puddle to see which would win the battle they fought.

I thought of myself as being a reasonably brave person, so when two boys ran around the camp shouting that a 'monster' was inside a two feet wide culvert under the road, I crawled inside and 'chased' the monster slowly backwards away from me towards the other end. This 'monster' proved to be a four-foot long iguana which the boys captured and took to the camp. I couldn't help noticing that the creature's feet were just like a baby's hands, both in size and appearance. The boys later killed the poor animal and in the middle of the night started throwing it around their tent. Those who had been asleep were woken up in horror. They made so much noise that they also woke the army sergeant who gave the boys a nice 'fatherly' chat in the early morning then made them do extra exercises of the 'Run, walk, duckwalk, lie down' type. Discipline was restored.

Four of us older boys were selected to perform some patriotic Polish songs on a stage for a group of visiting VIPs. We had our rifles with bayonets at the ready with which to accentuate certain passages in the poems. My bayonet wasn't properly fixed and at the moment in the performance when we had to thrust it forwards, it flew off the rifle and landed at the feet of the most important guest. Although shaken, embarrassed and ashamed, I did manage to finish that performance. Later I had to recite a long piece of poetry alone for which I received a standing ovation. The crowd had great sympathy for me after what had happened!

As well as the School of Communications, other schools were starting up; a Primary school for the youngest children, a Mechanics school, a 'School of the 'Air' for younger secondary school aged children, which was conducted by radio, and a Cadets School to which I was now transferred, having completed a year of Grammar School before the war. Altogether 26 different schools were set up and eventually they began to leave the camp for different destinations, mainly in Egypt and the near Middle East. The first school to leave was the School of Communications and I was chosen to make a farewell speech for them on the day of their departure. For the amusement of all, I wrote a rhyming poem to read out but I was very sad to part from so many of my colleagues.

The Cadets School was a Grammar School with military training which was supposed to help us train as Officers later. After several weeks, the school was transferred to Qastina, an RAF station in Palestine, where we were accommodated initially in tents. Here, one day, we were all given some boxing gloves so we could learn this noble and gentle art. My best friend, who was six inches taller than me, started to practise sparring with me inside the tent. He stood against the end of a metal bed while I stood in the doorway. I threw a punch at him and he ducked, lost his balance and fell on the bed which then collapsed. He was helplessly spread-eagled there when one of the other occupants of the tent entered and saw me with a raised fist above my friend. Everyone collapsed in laughter! The boy spread the story of my seeming achievement around the camp so I was treated with great respect from those bigger than me from then on.

Later in the Autumn, a third class was opened at my school, which was to allow some more gifted pupils to do a shortened course which incorporated both the second and third years together. I was lucky enough to be selected. We were transferred to a large room in the barracks which was divided into two levels by a shelf. I found out that my bed would be on the shelf. The entrance to this building was via a cowboy-style veranda. Our long coats were hung on the wall, with our well-polished boots and gaiters placed neatly below. This gave the impression that people were hiding behind the coats. Although we were studying very hard, we still enjoyed playing tricks. One night we balanced a cup of cold cocoa on the top of the door in such a way that the next person entering the room would get soaked. Unfortunately, the staff sergeant came in to check we were all asleep. In anger at receiving the cocoa treatment, he put the lights on and asked who was responsible for this prank. We all pointed towards where our coats were hanging and he strode over to separate them, saying 'I've got you!' He soon realised he'd been taken for a ride and left without speaking. The next morning he took his revenge by giving us the full extended treatment of the 'Run, walk, duckwalk, lie down' exercise.

A fourth class was soon started at my school which was equivalent to the British Grammar School 5th form 'O' level class. Thirteen pupils were invited to join this class including me, but I found the work very difficult to keep up with on this concentrated course and had to resit the exams in several subjects.

General Wladysław Sikorski was the Commander-in-Chief of all the Polish Forces abroad. He led the Polish Government-in-exile during the war. When he visited our barracks in early Spring, 1943, our company, being composed of the oldest boys, was chosen as usual, to be the Company of Honour. We had to dress incredibly smartly, whitening our belts and gaiters with a snow-white cream while our ironed uniforms were spotless. Sikorski inspected the lines, looking into everyone's eyes and giving them confidence that he was the man who would lead us to a free Poland. However, a few months later we learned with great sorrow of his death in an air accident near Gibraltar, by the Spanish coast in early July 1943. There have been a lot of conspiracy theories about this air-crash.

Polish General Władisław Anders, the organiser of our military units in the Soviet Union, also came to see us. I'm sure that it was thanks to his efforts that Stanisław and I were able to leave that unhappy country. Anders was trying to establish proper training for officers because he had realised that very few experienced officers had actually survived Siberia to join the army he had formed. Bishop Józef Gawlina, the military Bishop of the Armed Forces, paid us a visit too. He was in charge of all the clergy serving with the Polish Forces abroad. He was a bitter enemy of both Nazism and Communism and spent his years travelling throughout Europe and the Middle East pleading for support and aid for Poland and the other Eastern European nations. I still have a photograph of myself talking to him while some other boys are standing nearby. When other important British personnel came to the camp, we had to sing to them the song 'It's a long way to Tipperary'. I just couldn't understand all the words.

During Easter time that year, I was among those selected to be part of a Guard of Honour, with rifles, on Good Friday and Easter Saturday at the Tomb of Christ in the Church of the Holy Sepulchre in Jerusalem. Two cadets had to stand there at attention in two hour shifts, at all times, day and night. The guardroom was in a nearby building from which the new guards had to march to the Church, then back again for four hours rest before their next duty. The following year, although I wasn't chosen for this duty again, I did have the chance to take part in the Good Friday procession through Via

Dolorosa to Calvary, supposedly following in the footsteps of Jesus.

# IN THE SPOTLIGHT: THE KATYN MASSACRES

## 05/03/1940, 13/04/1943

*LINDA GALLAGHER*

**History of the Massacres**

At the beginning of the Second World War, when the Soviets invaded the east of Poland, they arrested as many Polish Military Officers and civilian intelligentsia that they could find, in order to prevent the resurgence of an independent Poland in the future.

Starting on March 5th, 1940, Admirals, Generals, Colonels, and Majors, as well as civilians such as chaplains, lawyers, teachers, and judges were arrested because they were deemed to be counter-revolutionary spies and an obstacle to Stalin's future plans for Poland.

Lavrentiy Beria, the Chief of the NKVD (The People's Commissariat of Internal Affairs – or Secret Police), had suggested to Stalin that executing them all was the best option and this idea was then approved by the Soviet Politburo. All the captives were first taken to prisons where they were interrogated and tortured to make them confess to being anti-Soviet. Then some were taken to labour camps such as Kozelsk and Starobelsk for a short period, but eventually they were all delivered to the Kalinin or Kharkov Prisons in the Soviet West.

After the Russian Revolution of 1917, a large Villa had been built near Smolensk in Russia as a Rest Home for Officials of the Political Police. The Polish prisoners were taken to this Villa at night in groups of about 250 men; they were shot one at a time in the basement and then their bodies were thrown into mass graves.

Russian guns were not made for such heavy and continuous service so German guns and bullets, part of an arsenal built up prior to the beginning of the war, were used.

### The Discovery of the Katyn Massacres

Since the German invasion of Russia in 1941, a German unit had been billeted in the Villa at Smolensk. One day in April 1943, a German Officer walking near the Katyn Forest found some bones that had been dug up by wolves or feral dogs. He realised that they were human bones. Captive Polish railway labourers working nearby confirmed that they had heard local rumours of mass burials of Polish Officers in the vicinity. A local Russian peasant led the German Officer into the woods to the place the bones may have come from and the area was quickly excavated. The Germans unearthed over 4,500 corpses there, buried in seven or eight mass graves in the Katyn Forest. Most of them wore Polish Officer Uniforms and every single one had had his hands tied behind his back either with wire or rope, and had been killed by one shot to the back of the head. The bodies were stacked in layers then covered with soil, but they could almost all be identified because their uniform pockets, which hadn't been emptied, contained documents and letters whose final dates were in April 1940, three years previously.

### Propaganda and Politics

The Germans decided to use their discovery of the mass graves in the forest to drive a wedge between the Allies. They launched a massive propaganda campaign and blamed first the Jews, and then, in order to discredit the Red Army, they blamed the Russians, for the massacre. In retaliation, because of the German bullets, the Soviets insisted that these prisoners must have been murdered by the Germans when they had launched Operation Barbarossa and had invaded Russia. It was suggested that the Germans had come across the Soviet labour camps where the Polish Officers were held and killed them all.

Well before these bodies were found, the relationship between the Polish Government-in-exile and Stalin had already deteriorated. In January 1943, Stalin had revoked the Amnesty for Polish Citizens, and the Soviets had closed all their borders. By March, all the Poles who remained anywhere on Russian territory were forced to become Soviet citizens. The gruesome discovery in the Katyn Forest then caused a rapid cooling of the relationship between the Allies, who needed to appease Stalin and keep him on board in the battle against the Nazis, and the Polish people, who had been through so much and did not trust the Soviets.

**Investigation**

General Sikorski, the Polish Prime Minister-in-Exile, referred the matter to the International Committee of the Red Cross in Geneva, who started an investigation to find out the truth about who had massacred these Polish officers and citizens. A commission of twelve neutral, international medical officials was put together and after a long investigation, they decided that it was a Soviet atrocity. Dating of artefacts proved that the officers had been killed in 1940 by the Russians at the beginning of the war and not three years later by the Germans. When challenged by the commission, Stalin accused Sikorski of committing a hostile act of betrayal by collaborating with the Germans, and immediately broke off all diplomatic relations with Poland's government in London. Further, he stopped all future evacuations across the Caspian Sea of the Poles still in Soviet-held lands.

The British Government, led by Prime Minister Winston Churchill, put the Polish Government-in-exile under enormous pressure not to state publicly what the Poles knew to be the truth, but to blame the Germans instead, because they didn't want to upset Stalin. The

Allies had been very impressed by the Red Army's performance on the Eastern Front and as it was the biggest army of all the Allies, it was needed to fight the Nazis throughout Europe. Apparently, Stalin had to be appeased at all costs and Churchill assured him that no investigation would take place. The British did not want to believe that the Russians, who had been their allies in the First World War also, could be so evil as to massacre all these officers, and chose instead to believe their lies. At that time, they had no idea of all the horrors that Stalin had already inflicted on his own countrymen, nor of the hundreds of thousands of Poles deported to the Siberian Gulag.

Stalin launched a great propaganda campaign against the Polish people, and also started to insult and undermine General Anders who had been questioning the Russians as to what had happened to the 15,000 Polish Military Officers who had not been released from Siberia to join the re-organisation of the Polish Army. The Soviets told him lies, intimating that somehow they had all escaped to Manchuria in N E China.

Britain did not stand up for Poland or the Polish people, but actually found it easier to negotiate with Stalin without General Sikorski's input. Why upset the new Soviet Alliance just for the sake of the Poles? This attitude of the British persisted throughout the war. The Poles themselves were now beginning to feel politically marginalised and isolated, despite the fact that WW2 had started because Poland was invaded by the Nazis.

**Other Mass Graves**

Nearly 50 years later, at least five other mass graves were discovered in places such as Miednoj, (Mednoye in Russia, where the Kalinin prison was) and Kharkov (Piatykhatky, in Ukraine) where children had been found to be playing with dozens of Polish Army buttons. It is estimated that over 28 days in April 1940, at least 22,000 Polish people were murdered or 'purged', and maybe as many as 30,000, although there may be still more mass graves as yet undiscovered. The generic name, 'The Katyn Massacres' usually relates to all these different atrocities.

Poland had been deprived of its leaders, military and civilian, yet this has never been considered to be a war crime and no-one was ever made responsible, because the Soviets had never actually declared war on Poland.

**The Truth**

The Soviet explanation that the Germans had probably committed this atrocity, despite the fact that the Germans themselves had been the ones to discover the mass graves, was generally accepted by the American, British and Polish Governments. This was the case from after the war right until March 1989 when communism collapsed and the Soviet Union, under Mikhail Gorbachev who had promised through 'Perestroika' to be open and honest about Soviet Politics, allowed a non-communist coalition government to come to power in Poland. This government officially shifted the blame for the Katyn Massacres from the Germans onto the Soviet Secret Police.

In 1990, Gorbachev, himself, admitted that the NKVD was responsible for the massacre; he surrendered key documents, proving that the NKVD had been responsible for both the atrocity and its cover-up, to the next Russian President, Boris Yeltsin. In 1992, Yeltsin handed these papers in person to the Polish President, Lech Wałesa who released them to the world.

Finally in 2010, the Russian Government, under Putin, symbolically and formally admitted their guilt, declaring that Joseph Stalin had ordered the executions in one of the worst mass murders in history. Putin also urged reconciliation and healing between the nations.

# IN THE SPOTLIGHT: DEATH OF SIKORSKI, THE POLISH PRIME MINISTER

## 04/07/1943

*LINDA GALLAGHER*

General Sikorski, the Polish Prime Minister-in-exile, was also the Commander-in-Chief of the Polish Army. During one of his inspections of the Polish Forces in the Middle East, a conflict grew between him and General Anders about the fact that Sikorski wanted to continue the process of normalising diplomatic relations with Stalin, as suggested by the British and Americans, but Anders did not agree. Sikorski clearly needed to find out what Anders' opinions were and his reasons. Anders, himself, was well aware of Stalin's ambitions regarding the future of Poland but no-one took him seriously. He violently objected to this 'normalisation' because he, personally, had seen and dealt with the results of the devastating Soviet treatment of the Polish Nationals. Sikorski hadn't witnessed this atrocity at all and may not even have known about it.

**Plane Crash**

On July 4th 1943, less than three months after the Katyn Massacre discovery, Sikorski was killed in an air accident. His plane, an RAF B24 Liberator II, took off from Gibraltar but crashed almost immediately into the sea, killing him and his daughter, his chief of staff and seven other officials. There had been 16 people on the plane but only the pilot survived – he was the only one wearing a life-jacket.

After take-off, instead of levelling off at the appropriate height, the aircraft continued to climb, putting great strain on the joystick, which then jammed. Unable to alter the angle of flight, the engines stalled, and the plane lost power. An initial investigation confirmed it was most probably an accident – it is possible a piece of luggage was found to have slid under the elevator controls or ailerons of the aircraft as it took off.

Some of the bodies, including Sikorski's, were recovered by divers but five of the bodies, including Sikorski's daughter, were never found. All injuries were found to be consistent with an air crash. When the aircraft itself was recovered from the seabed, it was found to be carrying large amounts of contraband like whiskey, cigarettes and fur coats.

However, because of the timing, conspiracies of sabotage were rife; blame was put on the Germans, the Soviets, and even the British, who wanted to stop any Katyn Forest investigation and keep Stalin sweet. There were suggestions it had happened because Sikorski refused to accept Stalin's claim that the Katyn Massacre had been carried out by the Germans. Other people suggested that he had been colluding with Stalin to try to improve Polish-Soviet relations. Sikorski's death was certainly convenient for the allies, while the Germans used it for propaganda purposes.

**Conspiracy**

Some Russians were actually at the airport in Gibraltar at the same time as the Polish Prime Minister. Sikorski's plane had been parked in a remote spot and guarded by a British Platoon with fixed bayonets, because, inconveniently, the Soviet Ambassador to Britain, Ivan Maisky, was due at the airport too. These top men couldn't be allowed to meet because of the breakdown of the diplomatic relationship between Poland and Russia. However, for some reason, Maisky's plane had been parked near to Sikorski's. The Polish Prime

Minister was therefore hustled off the Rock of Gibraltar that morning until Maisky had departed, and it was deemed safe for him to return.

Apparently, in the Spanish heat, one of the British guards had fainted and was dragged into the shade under a wing of Sikorski's aeroplane, and someone had placed his army knapsack in a small, open hatch at the rear of the fuselage. This had been forgotten about but it has been suggested that this bag slid forward and jammed the joystick mechanism. Also, an abandoned mailbag, for which no explanation was ever offered, was found on the ground in the place where the plane had been parked.

In 2013, a further investigation into Sikorski's death concluded that there was a possible mechanical failure but there was no evidence of wrong-doing; sabotage could be neither confirmed nor denied. But the question remained – how come the Czech pilot was the only one wearing a life-jacket? So as not to tempt fate, pilots rarely put them on before take-off. He wouldn't have had time to put it on in the few seconds he had before the crash.

Relations between Poland and Russia were not improved after a further tragedy occurred in 2010. A plane travelling in thick fog from Warsaw, carrying Polish President Lech Kaczynski, his wife, and high-ranking Polish Government officials and clergy, crashed nose-first into trees near Smolensk, killing a total of 96 people instantly. They were there to commemorate the 70th anniversary of the Katyn Massacre. Again there was no substantial evidence of sabotage, although the landing navigational lights on the approach were not effective enough and the radar was unstable, but conspiracy theories did circulate once more.

# CHAPTER 12: PALESTINE – EXPLORATION AND EDUCATION

## 14/06/1943 – 08/1944 (AGE 17¼-18½)

### *JERZY DĄBROWSKI*

To everyone who had ever heard of us, my company of Cadets, the 5th Company, was recognised as the best to be in. There was to be a Grand Military Parade in Cairo, Egypt, to celebrate the victory of the armed forces over Germany the previous autumn, at the Battle of El Alamein. My company were always very well turned out, and pretty perfect in our drill formations and so we were chosen to represent the Polish Army at this important parade.

Cairo was surrounded by a score of tented military camps and the local people didn't much like the riotous behaviour of the soldiers in the evenings. We had already spent a few days in Mena 6 Camp near the pyramids, in the shade of the Mena Hotel, where Sir Winston Churchill stayed on several occasions on his war-time trips to Egypt. The day of the parade, June 14th 1943, was extremely hot. We had to wait several hours in the courtyard of an imposing building for our slot in the parade. The ages of the cadets ranged from 12 – 17 years old. Our time came and we started marching, our rifles on our shoulders. After a mile or so, General Henry Wilson, appropriately nick-named 'Jumbo Wilson', who had been appointed Commander-in-Chief of the British troops in the Middle East in February 1943, was in his place ready to take the salute. Different bands played marches for their own countries, at different speeds to suit their marching, but there was no Polish band so we marched to the beat of the band ahead of us, thankfully at a reasonable pace. Altogether we marched over three miles and our shoulders began to ache from the rifles. A friendly and grateful Egyptian patted one very tired small boy on the back, making him bend over, but he kept marching. From the top of a 14 storey building, another well-wisher threw down rice for 'good luck' but the grains stung our bare arms.

In our free time we were allowed to visit the Great Pyramids. We climbed to the very top of them, and also had the chance to go into the very centre of the largest of them all, the pyramid Cheops. A new entrance to the sarcophagus of this pyramid had had to be made a little way up the front face, because many of the huge stones had been removed over the years to build the Salah El Din Citadel which was one of the world's greatest monuments to mediaeval warfare. The stones were also used to build the largest mosque in Cairo which we visited. Another time, we visited the world-famous zoological gardens and the interesting waxworks, and we crossed the Nile to the City of the Dead, a strange place where the houses were supposed to look like the houses once lived in by those buried, yet had no roofs. Relatives were still leaving food in the doorways of their 'houses' so many beggars lived there and benefited from these offerings.

We travelled by tram to and around Cairo. These trams had two or three carriages joined together, with continuous running-boards down each side, which the locals stood on to avoid paying their fare. The trams travelled so slowly that one could buy food, souvenirs or even clothing from vendors on the way. For many miles along both sides of the Nile, the land was very green and fertile. Beyond the great maze of canals were vast deserts. On our return from Cairo to Palestine by train, we went over several branches of the River Nile and finally crossed the Suez Canal on a swing bridge, arriving in Gaza from where we were transferred to our camp, Gedera, by road.

I had to share a tent with nine other boys, two of whom regularly woke us all up by returning to the tent late at night. We played tricks on these two to try and change their behaviour. We would swap their beds around, or just the bed covers, or just their possessions to confuse them. We filled their water flasks and suspended them, lidless, with strings above their beds. The other ends of the string were held by people in the furthest beds, who would gently tip the bottles until water dripped on the faces of the late-comers. Eventually they'd had enough and started to get back to the tent earlier!

Several Polish civilian families had travelled with us from Siberia, and they were accommodated in old monastery buildings set in an orange grove on the outskirts of Jaffa. I used to stay with one particular family over the weekends. I was allowed to pick and eat as many oranges as I wished. There was a large water tank in the grounds and I often climbed its solid walls to swim in its cool waters. I learnt to somersault into its depths! My 'boxing' friend, mentioned previously, lived nearby in Rehovot with his family who had come with us. They invited me to stay several times. On one occasion, while waiting in the cinema queue, we saw a beautiful eclipse of the sun by the moon, which caused darkness and a very cold wind until the sun reappeared.

Weekend passes allowed us to visit many of the larger and more interesting towns such as Tel-Aviv, Haifa and Jerusalem. We also explored the area a lot during the summer holidays. We could travel either on the Jewish or Arab buses, or thumb a lift on a lorry to save money. On the way from Tel-Aviv to Jerusalem one day, we stopped to see some pre-historic underground cave dwellings by the side of the road. Another time we were invited into a monastery by monks who told us the history of their monastery and let us taste their excellent wine. A trip to the Dead Sea meant a long climb up the winding road from

Jerusalem, then the equally long descent to below sea level. That day was extremely hot and I decided to strip off and dive in. The water was so heavy with minerals that it threw me out again with smarting eyes, burnt lips and a terrible taste in my mouth.

I visited Jerusalem many times, and saw the Church of the Holy Sepulchre, with it's Tomb of Christ and Golgotha, the famous Al Aksa Mosque, the Wailing Wall with its rocking, black-hatted, praying Jews, and the Garden of Gethsemane. I saw the pretty basilica built over the place from where Mary, the Mother of Jesus spent her last moments on earth. We visited the room where the last supper was said to have been held above King David's tomb too. The narrow lanes of the Arab quarters were usually deserted but a small Arab boy once managed to persuade me to buy a newspaper. After giving him the money, I opened the paper to read it but discovered it was only half of a front page. The boy, of course, had vanished! The Old Town of Jerusalem was also full of tiny narrow lanes and alleyways. The shop-fronts were open and the vendors did their best to persuade you to come and buy something. Many free-lance souvenir sellers called out from their seats on the ground, eager to barter with you.

During that same summer, a group of us visited Bethlehem to see the Church of the Nativity and then at Christmas, 1943 I travelled with my friends from Ein Karem to Bethlehem to attend the Midnight Mass at that church. Many people from many nations had gathered there to hear Mass said in their own language. The turn for the Poles came at 2.00 am and we packed the church to capacity. The experience of hearing Holy Mass in Polish in the Church of the Nativity in Bethlehem at Christmas was an experience never to be forgotten.

A unit of Boy Scouts was organised at the camp and I decided to join as I had been in the Scouts before the war. We all enjoyed taking part in the organised activities and games. At Ein Karem, near Jerusalem, where St John the Baptist was said to have been born, Polish girls were also being organised into a Girl Guide Company. They invited us all over for a social evening which we really enjoyed as our camp was only boys. Food and conversations were very pleasant indeed and we hoped to visit the girls again soon.

After completing the fourth class and obtaining our Lower Matriculation Certificates, we cadets were given the chance to leave school and join a short Officer Training course. Several of my friends took advantage of this opportunity but sadly a number of them lost their lives in the battle for Monte Quassino (Cassino) in Italy. I had wanted to join this course, but during one visit to Rehovot, my friend's father, a Lieutenant Colonel who was a military judge for the Polish Forces, took me aside and gave me a long fatherly talk about why I should remain in the cadets' school where I had the chance to complete the final two years for the Certificate of Full Matriculation in one year. He said that I had plenty of time to get killed but that the nations would need educated people to help rebuild the war-devastated countries. I listened to his advice and finally agreed with it; I am so grateful to him that I remained alive.

In the summer of 1943, we were moved from Gedera to Camp Barbara near Gaza, where I stayed until I left Cadet School in August 1944. Thousands of young cadets, over the age of 6 years old up to 18, were trained and educated here ready for the day when they would join their seniors as men fighting for the liberation of their country and could choose which branch of the Polish military they preferred. Here in Camp Barbara, we were again accommodated in tents, but to add a little spice to our lives, we had to put up with a plague of mosquitoes instead of scorpions. The netting made breathing difficult in the heat, and while most of the little blood-suckers stayed outside the net, occasionally one or two managed to get in and annoy our ears with its high-pitched buzzing! There were also large, inquisitive centipedes who had venom packed at the end of each leg. They had an unfriendly habit of sticking their legs into human flesh, making it swell painfully. We had to admire the coolness of one of the cadets when a centipede came to investigate inside the leg of his shorts. Eventually it reappeared and the boy shook the intruder to the ground and stamped on it!

The following Autumn, eleven of us 'boys' started our last 'Lycée' year of cadet school, to complete two years of study concentrated into just one. All the lecturers were given nicknames, including one we named Professor Quasimodo' after the hunchback of Notre-Dame. Our Latin professor was an officer who loved talking about his pet subject, masonry. We could engage him in this topic for a whole lesson at a time, but when the bell rang, he would always apologise and then give us a lot of Latin words to learn for next time! A few of us, who had been friends in Siberia, went on an outing to see the Opera 'Carmen' in Tel-Aviv. This inspired some of the cadets to stage the Polish Opera 'Halka'. I became fed up with the practising by the future Pavarottis in my tent. The opera performed well even though, to my surprise, the principal girl part was sung by an older woman, who happened to be one of the organisers!

We had a great adventure on April Fool's day in 1944. My whole company of 120 members woke very early and formed ourselves into a column four persons wide. Then in a very orderly fashion, without saying anything to our officers, NCOs or boys from other companies, we marched away to the shores of the Mediterranean Sea some four or five miles distant. As we cleared the Camp Barbara, we started singing military songs to help us keep in step. We stayed in formation the whole way, receiving many admiring glances from the inhabitants of the small villages we passed. We marched close to the ancient ruins of Ashkelon before eventually arriving at the beach. We had taken enough food and drink for the whole day, and because the beach was deserted, we stripped off and swam stark naked. We played various beach games and really enjoyed ourselves, but all good things have to come to an end. After several hours we resumed our four-man wide formation and marched in an orderly fashion all the way back, with songs on our lips.

In the meantime, the powers that be were very worried about what could have happened to a whole company of 120 cadets. How could they vanish without trace, without witnesses? When we arrived back at the camp, there was a reception committee of our officers and NCOs. We had to disband then reform ourselves into the more usual three lines on the parade ground. The Company Commander advised us he was far from amused by our All Fools Day trick and gave us an enlightening talk as to how we were expected to behave. He was of the opinion that we had far too much energy, so he sent us to go and collect all the rifles and return to the parade ground. I happened to be on duty that evening with another cadet, and so we had to issue every one of those 120 rifles from the stores. All the other boys had to perform several exercises with the rifles as punishment, but after a short time they were allowed to disperse. We two on duty then had to collect up all those rifles, check them thoroughly and return them to the stores. We were quite worn out doing this job after a long and tiring day. The other cadets were allowed an evening meal but ours was brought up to the store room. I took the first duty in the night, waking the other boy a few hours later so that I could have a well-deserved kip. Despite all this, I considered this whole adventure to have been well worthwhile!

In the late Spring of 1944, when I was 18 years old, all other activities for the eleven of us had to give way to swotting for our Full Matriculation Exams which would take place in July for the very first time in the cadets camp. Frequently we stayed up till 2.00am trying to cram as much knowledge into our heads as was humanly possible. There were 600 other cadets at the school in that camp and they were all affected by our preparation because we used to unwind by singing loudly and walking arm-in-arm as we went back to our tents early in the morning.

During this last year I improved so much in Maths and Physics with Chemistry that I got very good marks. For the exam, I had to choose one of these subjects so I chose Maths, but the actual exam was far more difficult than I had expected and I only achieved a satisfactory mark. There was a variety of other subjects to study and pass and so I chose English rather than Latin. I was rather proud of myself that I had completed five years of school study in only two years and still managed to obtain my Full Matriculation Certificate with good marks all round, catching up on the three years I'd lost in Siberia and travelling to this point. After passing our exams, we were given three to four weeks to relax. It was such an anti-climax that I could neither read nor write for a few months. I couldn't even correspond with my own brother who, at the age of 22 years old, was now a fighter pilot based in the UK.

Stach became rather worried about me and he demanded I write to him. I finally obliged and wrote to inform him that I was coming to England to join him in the Polish Air Force!

# CHAPTER 13: SAILING TO BRITAIN

## 08/1944 – 12/1944 (AGE 18½)

### JERZY DĄBROWSKI

Before we departed, we were given a magnificent send-off on the Parade Ground by the remaining companies and by all the NCOs. The Commanding Officers of all the schools of the Polish Young Soldiers Battalion, the Cadets School and our own Company were present, and we were privileged to have the Chairman of the Polish Examination Board with us that day. We were so excited to be finally leaving Palestine to join the Polish Air Force in Britain. This decision had been our first choice but we still felt sad to be leaving behind so many of our younger friends and colleagues, as well as the many helpful lecturers with whom we had spent the last few years. Apart from the eleven of us who had joined the Lycée (Grammar School) for our Full Matriculation, there were another 120 boys our age who were leaving, having received their Lower Matriculation Certificates. Many of them had been in my class in 1942, before I was promoted to the accelerated class.

The day of our departure, towards the end of August 1944, finally arrived. We left the camp in lorries for our journey to Gaza from where we would board our train to Egypt. On the way, we passed the same RAF stations as in the Spring of 1943 when we had been going to Cairo to take part in the Grand Military Parade of the Allies. When we got off the train, we were transported, in lorries yet again, to a camp at Al Qassasin, Egypt. Although we had all signed up to join the Polish Air Force in Britain, the army personnel in this camp had organised a shortened Officers' Course for us with the intention of keeping us there, to serve in the army. During our six-week stay, we learnt a lot about the art of leadership, and about all kinds of weapons and ammunition including the use of live grenades.

One of the corporals wasn't too bright – he believed that everything written in the manual should be carried out to the letter. Once he asked our group what metal the barrel of a rifle was made of. We gave him various replies, such as gun-metal, steel or brass but he said every answer we gave was wrong. He told us that the manual stated that the barrel was made of 'the following metal'…..We all had to accept his statement! So many times we didn't understand what he was talking about and he used to say, 'This is not a university. Here you have to think….'

Apart from this concentrated training, we were taken in lorries two or three times a week to the town of Ismailia and thence along the shores of the Bitter Lake to the Suez Canal for a swim. The bottom of the canal was full of sea stars – a type of starfish – and other prickly sea creatures, so we had to dive straight into the water and not paddle. Several times, with others brave enough, I swam across the Suez Canal, stating I had 'swum from Africa to Asia' which wasn't quite true. On the way back to Al Qassisin Camp, we were sometimes able to shop in Ismailia and I bought my brother a good quality watch with money he had given me for this purpose.

The Polish Air Force finally laid claim to us and on the 3rd October we were transferred to a transitional camp near Suez to await our transport to Great Britain. There was a very nice NAAFI club where we were able to buy food and drink: for the very first time in my life I was able to eat 'Fish and Chips', a typical English meal! I was disgusted to see that it was served in newspaper and eaten with your fingers – uncivilised and unhygienic. But I liked it so much that I bought it on many occasions.

Many military and naval bases had been set up near Suez by the British for defence purposes. In this camp we did daily exercises, and marched together for our swim. Those of us who had passed our Full Matriculation Exam were given the responsibility of being platoon leaders, deputy leaders or section leaders. Being a little on the short side, I was made platoon leader of all the shortest boys again! I had to lead this platoon on marches for food or to the place where we swam.

Early in the morning, a week later, we were taken by lorries to Port Said. After a while, several motorboats transported us to the ship, S.S. Strathmore which had been requisitioned as a troop carrier for the duration of the war. It had been launched in 1935 by the Duchess of York (later, the Queen Mother), one of the daughters of the Earl of Strathmore. The ship was lying at anchor some distance from the shore. Our company was accommodated in the 'bowels of the ship', just above the water-line, the lowest level of all the decks used to transport personnel to England. A large room for our use was full of hammocks, three tiers high. I was allocated one at the top of the tier so despite being rather lacking in height, I had to climb over two lower hammocks to get up there.

We left Suez in late evening, once it was dark, so that no German planes could possibly notice us. Early next morning we passed the places where we used to go swimming while at Qassasin, and later we passed through Ismailia and El Qantara. All the road and rail swing bridges had been opened for us to pass through unhindered. Finally, the next night, we arrived at Port Said in Egypt, where we stayed for nearly two days. During daylight, young Arab boys would swim in the narrow strip of water between our ship and the shore, begging us to throw coins to them which they dived down to retrieve with their mouths. Surprisingly, they only seemed to like the more valuable coins!

We left Port Said in the dark, and the ship's course took us well away from the shore of the Mediterranean Sea. Soon we were joined by a multitude of other ships including several warships; they were mainly Corvettes, which were small war ships like frigates. Convoys were formed of approximately 60 ships organised into several columns with up to about five ships in each column. Attacking 'U-boats' could quickly be fired upon by the warships in a convoy, whereas single ships were in far more danger. Among the ships of our convoy was the Polish passenger ship, M.S. Batory, which we were proud to watch. It was an ocean liner of the Polish Merchant Fleet and was named after Stefan Batory, the 16th King of Poland. During the war, it was used as a troop carrier under the British Admiralty,.

Being a platoon leader, I wore a red and white band on my arm and was allowed to walk around almost every area of the ship except for the crew quarters and the top two decks which were occupied by civilians. To supplement our food, a few of us used to go to the shop on the ship but the only food product for sale were tins of condensed milk. Somehow we could get through a whole can at one sitting without being sick. To our surprise and disappointment, after several days they ran out of this commodity!

Our convey kept well away from the coast of Africa in order not to be spotted by anyone who could pass information to the Germans. For the same reason, we passed Malta and the Straits of Gibraltar in the night. During the day I often went up on the open deck so I could enjoy looking at all the ships in our convoy including the M.S. Batory. The Mediterranean was a deep blue colour and its waves were short but steep. Many times I watched Corvettes having their decks washed by the waves or seeming to dive right into them; this filled me with admiration for their crews. As we entered the Atlantic Ocean, the sea turned to lead-grey and the waves became long and rather flat. When we were in a trough, the view of the other ships was completely blocked by the large waves, but when we were on the ridge of a wave, we could see the whole huge convoy. Sometimes I stood on the deck at the very front of the ship which, when climbing a big wave, went up and up, then when descending from the wave, went a long way down. My tummy seemed to follow this movement but at a slower pace which made me feel very strange! I felt sorry for some of the boys who were not allowed to leave our quarters, especially those who were sea-sick. I was lucky to have the freedom to roam around and I did not seem to suffer.

At meal times we sat at tables which were fixed to the floor. They had raised edges all round to prevent plates sliding off. As the ship climbed or descended a wave, the plates would travel across the table even as we were eating. It was funny to watch someone trying to immerse their spoon into a bowl of soup as it slid away from him.

From the Atlantic we entered the Irish Sea, with its beautiful green waters. No wonder it was called the 'Emerald Sea'! After nearly two weeks of travelling by ship, we entered the Port of Liverpool, UK, on October 22$^{nd}$ 1944. It was so lovely, after more than five years since we left our home in Poland, to be able to see European houses with tiled roofs, European trees and a little bit of green grass once more. In fact, at that time, we thought Liverpool was a beautiful place indeed! The town was a vital port during the war and was Britain's lifeline for the maritime trade; consequently, it was the target of several bombing raids by the Germans, who concentrated on disrupting the Merchant Navy, sinking more than 2000 merchant ships and killing more than 4000 people. At first, only essential work had been done to repair the damage caused by the blitz, so when I arrived there, I was greeted by miles and miles of bombed-out buildings everywhere. Yet I could still say it was beautiful!

We spent two more days on the S.S. Strathmore, before being allowed to disembark. The ship stayed on the anchor and changed direction with the tide, so Liverpool was on our left, then on our right – a strange feeling! Below the ship there was a multitude of tugs moving busily to and fro. They all had red and white flags signalling that they had a pilot on board. Unaware of this tradition, we all thought they were Polish boats as the Polish flag is the same colour. We started to call out to the boats in Polish but the English crew just smiled and waved at us.

At last, on 24th October 1944, we disembarked and were greeted by the lovely smiles of the Women's Voluntary Service as they offered us all a typically English cup of tea. It is amazing how welcome this made us feel, even though we were unable to communicate our gratitude. We stretched our legs on solid ground for the first time in two weeks, then boarded a train bound for Blackpool.

Blackpool had been a favourite British holiday resort since Victorian days, but in 1939 the RAF took it over. 18,000 Polish Troops and Polish Air Force personnel arrived there in large numbers, and initial RAF training took place in its Winter Gardens and Empress Ballrooms. To cater for all these people, the town council opened the Pleasure Beaches throughout the winter as well as the summer, and every evening, the Tower Ballroom and the Winter Gardens were packed out with dancers. The Vickers Armstrong factory which built Wellington bombers was also located in RAF Blackpool.

On arrival, we were split into small groups to be accommodated in various of the immense number of boarding houses and hotels. Our group was billeted in Chapel Street which ran at right angles to the sea. The advantage of this was that we could see the sea and could easily find our way back if we got a bit lost in our wandering. The disadvantage came to light when strong winds blew sand from the beach along the full length of our street, bringing back memories of our time in the Iraqi desert, especially when our eyes were full of sand.

Within the next few days, all our tropical army kit was replaced with the warmer RAF uniform, which was far more suitable for the colder British climate. We would march proudly through the streets of Blackpool to the buildings where we had lectures or Parade Ground Drills. Two or three times a week we marched along the sea-front to the famous Derby Baths which had a 16-foot deep diving pool. Although the underground pressure was enormous, I enjoyed showing off by diving from the top board to recover coins thrown by the other boys.

Due to the war, there was a shortage of workmen in the town and we had to help out by delivering sacks of coal to various households. Most of our free time was spent wandering around the town, especially the Blackpool Tower complex with its beautiful ballroom, aquarium, amusements and of course, trips to the top of the tower. Sometimes we visited the Winter Gardens, and there I used to go to watch a Variety Show in the theatre which cost only one shilling and sixpence (7½ p) for the best seats! We enjoyed going to the amusements on the three piers, visiting the Waxworks, and walking past all the Gypsy Smith Fortune Telling booths.

Unfortunately, I did not have very much money to spend in Blackpool. We were allocated three shillings (15p) a day but I had a personal fortune of nearly £4 which I had saved up somehow. To supplement our diet, we would buy a big portion of Fish and Chips which was only 9d (4p), or visit the local cafes. There was one cafe I did not fancy at all. The sign on the window advertised 'HOT DOGS' and 'PIES'. In Polish, the word 'Pies' (pronounced differently) means 'dog' and I thought they'd written that for the benefit of the Polish airmen in the town. However I never even wanted to try to eat dogs, hot or cold and I couldn't understand how the English enjoyed them!

My brother, Stach, knew Blackpool well because he'd been there many times already. He came to visit me, and we went to the Tower Ballroom where his current girlfriend tried to teach me to dance. I really enjoyed the experience and she didn't complain too much when I crushed her toes or kicked other dancers accidentally. It was wonderful to spend two whole days with Stach as we had so much to tell each other. After four or five weeks of this luxurious life, we had to leave Blackpool; we were posted to an RAF Bomber Command Station in Faldingworth, Lincolnshire, to join the Polish Bomber 300 Squadron.

Jerzy's drawing of the road construction in the settlement.

Jerzy's drawing of the log raft construction.

Stach & Jerzy, the day they split up

Meeting again in Palestine

First camp in Palestine, Jerzy in the centre

Jerzy in the UK

Jerzy in the UK

Wedding to Gwen, Feb 1950

The happy couple

Stanisław (Stach)    Stach's girlfriend Pammy

Stach's diary

Stach and his de Havilland Vampire in Egypt

Stach's last picture

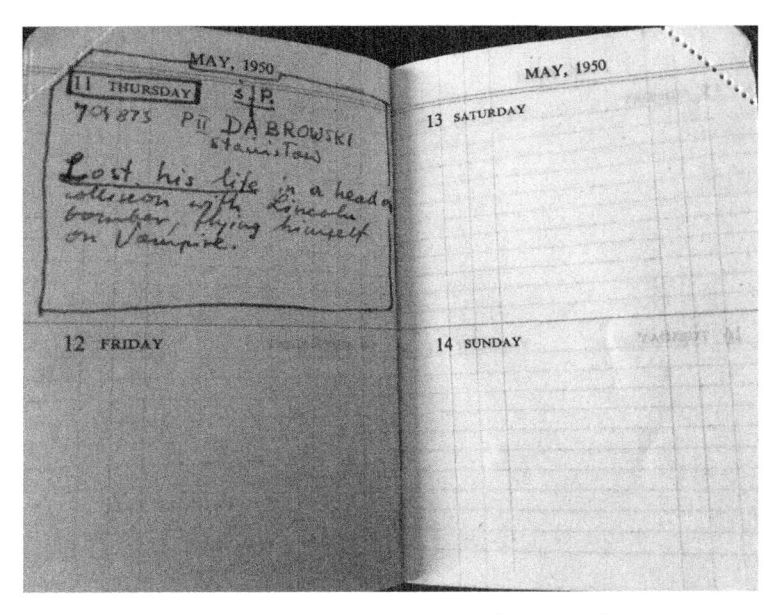

Stach's diary, Jerzy recorded his death in it

Stach's tombstone in Egypt

# PART THREE: FROM PALESTINE TO BRITAIN

# "A NEW START"

# IN THE BACKGROUND: THE POLES

## WHAT HAPPENED TO THE POLISH PEOPLE?

*LINDA GALLAGHER*

**The Hidden Holocaust**

The horrific crimes carried out by the Russians during WW2 still aren't well known even now. The fact is, around 1.7 million Polish men, women and children were forcibly deported from their homeland on cattle trucks to the labour camps of Siberia ostensibly for the rest of their lives; more than half of them died there and of those set free in the 'amnesty' just 18 months later, fewer than 10% made it safely to the west. Thousands of Poles ended up staying in Siberia because they did not have the means to leave. Nothing is known about what ultimately happened to them.

Under German occupation, for the ordinary citizens everyday life in Poland was just as intolerable. They lived in daily fear of being executed for little or no reason: even children could be shot for being out in the street or for just for being Polish. Rations for the Poles were far less than for the Germans (just over a quarter), and black-market trading for food and essentials became the focus of survival. The Nazi strategy was to pauperise the Polish people first by lowering wages and raising prices just for them, then gradually annihilate the whole Polish nation, after using the able-bodied as slave labour. Jerzy's mother, Albina, didn't survive the privations of the occupation and no-one knows what horrors she and her daughter, Halina, endured.

For many years, few Polish people could speak

about what had happened to them. Many felt that no-one would really understand how traumatic their experience had been on a national or personal level. This was the 'hidden holocaust' in that as many Polish citizens as Jews were killed by the Germans and Russians together. The strength of the Jewish lobby, especially after the discovery of the concentration camps at the end of the war, and the disclosures during the Nuremberg Trials in 1946, ensured that the wholesale annihilation of the Jews was reported and recorded in so much detail that it became public knowledge – today, most people are aware of that story. But, the devastating suffering of the Poles during the war has not been publicly known; that genocide has generally been ignored for Stalin's sake because the Allies needed the Russians on board in order to conquer the Nazis, but also, it was subsumed beneath the stories of the Jewish holocaust.

### The Yalta Agreement Sellout

During the war, the Polish Armed Forces remained completely loyal to the Polish Government-in-Exile. This army had grown to become the third largest army to fight the Germans under British High Command, and it fought valiantly for the freedom of all Europe, excepting its own country – the Polish Army had no loyalty at all to the Soviet Union and the puppet government installed in Poland by the Soviets once the Nazis were in retreat. The Polish Forces and civilians had hoped to be able to return to a democratic, non-communist Poland after the war but that wasn't to be.

The Yalta Conference of February 1945 was a meeting of the heads of government of America, Britain and Russia, to shape a post-war plan for peace, but the Polish Government-in-Exile hadn't been invited. The Poles angrily denounced the outcome of this conference, the Yalta Agreement, which 'gave' East Poland to the Soviet Union in order to keep Stalin on-side. Stalin had emphasised that he needed this portion of Poland to defend the USSR because hostile nations had, historically, travelled through this area to attack Russia.

As a 'consolation', Poland was given land that had previously belonged to Germany so, geographically, the whole of Poland, while keeping the same size of territory, shifted 150 miles to the west. There was just one bonus: the land lost to the USSR consisted of fairly primitive and undeveloped rural districts whereas the land acquired from Germany, the regions of Silesia and Pomerania, was rich in coal and iron, had efficient modern road and railway networks and a large number of cities and seaports, so Poland's economic and manufacturing prospects for the future were actually increased.

However, the decisions made by the 'Big Three', Roosevelt, Churchill and Stalin, at Yalta meant that Poland would not be independent, but was in the same position, or worse, regarding the Soviet Union as if the war had never happened.

**Betrayed by the Allies**

The Second World War officially ended in May 1945, and in July of that year, the British government ceased to formally recognise the democratic Polish Government-in-Exile in accordance with decisions made secretly at the Yalta Conference. It had been decided that Poland itself would, politically, now be part of Russia's new 'sphere of influence' in Europe, and therefore Britain would only approve the communist-dominated Provisional Government of National Unity in Poland.

The Polish Allied Forces under British Command, were then formally disbanded, but they refused to stand down, and this expression of defiance became extremely symbolic. Named the 'Polish Problem', it threatened to embarrass the British who had entered the war at the beginning on behalf of Polish independence. The Polish troops, always totally loyal to General Anders, now began to talk of mutiny. They wanted to engage in another war until Poland would finally be completely liberated from the Soviet regime, and regain its independence, but the British did not want to engage in any more hostilities. Tens of thousands of Poles became bitter and disillusioned – the handing over of Poland to the Soviets was a humiliating betrayal by the allies. In addition, the number of Poles who had been deported to Siberia as slave labour was an embarrassment to the British now that the Soviets were apparently 'friends'.

To try to solve the problem, the British decided to remove General Anders from his command of the Polish Forces, and dispose of him completely. He had already been stripped of his Polish citizenship and military rank by the provisional Soviet government in Poland. This act by the British meant that all the Polish military personnel in the UK suddenly found they had lost their official status. The Polish Forces were then strongly encouraged to go back to Poland and rebuild their own country, but over 80% of the Polish troops, the majority of whom were still in Italy having fought at the Battle for Monte Cassino, had already experienced life under the communist regime in Siberia, and refused. The communist government in Poland seemed keen for them to return, but the Poles had strong reasons to believe that they would be accused of anti-Soviet activities and either executed or deported to Siberia once again.

The last thing the Soviets actually wanted was a victorious Polish Army on Soviet soil hindering the communist takeover of Poland. The vast majority of Polish troops rejected the Soviet government and chose to live in the liberated countries in the west while continuing the struggle for an independent Poland. About 250,000 military personnel remained in Britain after the war, and many were later joined by their families and dependents from wherever they had finished up when the war ended. Even so, they endeavoured to maintain their Polish language, culture and traditions in their new country.

The Polish people had hoped for a Poland that was truly free and independent, and that dream only finally started to become a reality in 1989 with the fall of the Berlin Wall.

**Sidelined at The London Victory celebrations of 1946**

The Victory Celebrations held on June 8th 1946 after both Nazi Germany and Imperialist Japan were finally defeated, were for the glory of the British Commonwealth, the British Empire and the Allied Forces. The plans for the celebrations consisted simply of a day-time Military Parade through London, followed by a night-time fireworks display. Most British Allies were to take part, including USA, France, Holland and Greece, for example, but none of the Polish Forces were invited; this was despite the fact that, at the beginning, WW2 had been all about defending Poland.

The British government, now with Clement Atlee as Prime Minister, finally invited the Soviet-backed government in Poland to send a 'flag party' to represent Poland among the Allies in the parade, but did not initially welcome any representation from the Polish Forces that had fought under the British High Command. Winston Churchill, as leader of the Opposition, with some of his prominent MPs as well as many figures in the British RAF, made strong protestations against this decision which was definitely seen as an affront to the Polish war effort as well as an immoral concession to Stalin and the Soviets.

The democratic Polish Forces, themselves, did not believe the Soviet puppet government either could or should represent them. It negated the whole reason for the war, which they thought should have preserved their nation and their borders, but had now become the final part of a massive betrayal.

After many complaints, 25 Polish pilots who had fought in the Battle of Britain were reluctantly invited by the British government to march alongside other foreign detachments as part of the RAF, but not with the Allies. The British Government said this was a necessary compromise because of the current political difficulties, but the idea was rejected by the Poles. After yet more public criticism, the British Foreign Minister sent last-minute invitations to the Chiefs of Staff of the Polish Army, Navy and Air Forces as well as to individual generals, but they all refused to participate because several other branches of the Polish Forces had been omitted. The Soviet Government in Poland also chose not to send a 'flag' delegation because it was offended by the fact that the Polish Pilots had been invited.

In the end, the Victory Parade in London took place without any Polish Representatives marching with the Allied Forces. While Britain celebrated, the Poles asked, 'What victory?'

# CHAPTER 14: FALDINGWORTH BOMBER COMMAND

## 12/1944 – 04/1945 (AGE 18½-19)

### JERZY DĄBROWSKI

RAF Faldingworth, near Lincoln, was originally planned to be a decoy airfield with mock-ups of Whitley Bombers randomly parked around the area. It was a Class A airfield for the Polish 300 Bomber and Fighter Squadron, and had three new runways, hard standing for 36 aircraft, and accommodation for 2,000 personnel, both male and female. Just before we arrived, it became the home of Avro Lancasters whose first mission had been to bomb the French railway system, and railway yards in order to delay any German troop movements. The brave determination of the Polish crews flying over 500 operations and sorties was well documented, and only 30 aircraft were lost.

The group of eleven of us who had passed our Full Matriculation together, were detailed to get ourselves to RAF Faldingworth. We all stayed together as we travelled by train, with changes at Manchester, Sheffield and Lincoln. It was very late at night when we finally arrived at the railway station of Market Rasen, a small town in Lincolnshire, which was famous for its racecourse. It was the closest one to our destination about five miles away but there was no transport at hand to take us to our aerodrome. Finally, early the next morning, after numerous phone calls to RAF Faldingworth and an interminable wait, some covered lorries with half-awake drivers arrived.

We all overslept and missed breakfast, but had to attend a 'Warm Welcome' during which the unsympathetic Staff Sergeant gave us a stiff talk on carrying out our duties at the station in all circumstances. Then his heart slightly softened when he realised we'd had a very tiring journey and he arranged a late breakfast for us. After breakfast we had to report to a Warrant Officer responsible for allocating duties to new arrivals. He had gained his rank the hard way, through long service, and did not seem to like people who were better educated than himself. When he realised we had all completed a Grammar School education and had our Full Matriculation Certificates, he decided we needed to give our brains a rest and so allocated the worst jobs on the RAF Bomber Command station to us. There was quite a hierarchy there even among the officers. The elite were the Officers who had been trained in Military Academies, and then the NCOs, the not-so-elite Non-Commissioned Officers who had been promoted through the Ranks. It appears this Warrant Officer thought that if we were eligible to become officers, then we needed to have first hand experience of all the jobs available, so we were detailed to clean the crew room, the Officers' and NCO's messes (dining rooms) including the toilets, and spread salt and sand on the runways when required.

When our Lancaster Bombers returned from a night mission to destroy various German installations, there was often a ground fog covering the aerodrome and our duty was to position special oil lamps that had long spouts and a wick, at equal intervals along both sides of the 2,000 yards long main runway. Just before the bombers were due to return, we had to light the lamps; with the heat they produced, they usually succeeded in dispersing the fog as the water droplets in the air dissipated. The lamps looked a bit like Aladdin's magic lamp and I tried rubbing one to see if a genii would come out, but all that appeared was the aforementioned Warrant Officer who told me off for wasting time!

On Christmas Eve, we kept up a certain Polish custom.

By tradition on that day, all the servants in big houses in Poland had to be served by their employers. Many airmen of all ranks sat at long tables in the NCO's mess room and we were served with our Christmas meal by all the officers. After the meal we all sang Christmas Carols but somehow, St. Nicolas, the Polish Santa Claus, didn't manage to find us and so we didn't receive any presents!

That first winter in UK was very severe and the snow lay very thick everywhere. All the 2,000 personnel at the base had to take wooden shovels to try and clear the mountains of snow from the main runway but there was so much that the idea was abandoned.

A few weeks into the New Year, 1945, I asked the Station Adjutant if he could arrange for me to have several copies of my Matriculation Certificates. He was pleased to oblige, and also asked me how my colleagues and I were getting on carrying out the work on the station. I described to him in detail what we had been doing; he was of the opinion that these jobs were not suitable for us and promised to have a word with the Station Commanding Officer. The very next morning we were all moved to other jobs where we were allowed to use our brains! I was seconded to the Flying Control where our duty-roster had a three day cycle which worked like this: 20 hours on duty, then 24 hours off duty; 4 hours on duty then 20 hours off duty. There were times, however, when we were short of available people for the duties either through sickness or because someone was on leave. Then we had to be 24 hours on duty and 24 hours off duty while our food was delivered to us direct from the kitchens.

I was shown how to record, on a blackboard, the details of every plane leaving the station – the name of the pilot, his time of departure, his expected time of return, and the code letter of each aircraft. I also had to write the times and details of all arrivals. Our aeroplanes normally took off for their bombing sessions late in the evening and returned early in the morning, being away for between 4 and 12 hours. The code for our squadron was *'White Lie'* and the code for the station was *'Rimmer'*. Early in the morning, it was so good to hear the aeroplanes reporting their return with their own code: *'White Lie B Baker to Rimmer, over'*. Knowing, for instance, that a particular plane had returned safely, we then directed its pilot by radio to whichever of the three runways he was to land on.

Sometimes one or more planes failed to return, and then with great sadness, we had to mark them on the blackboard as *'Missing'*. It was even worse if we knew the members of the crew personally, but this was war and we had to accept it. Once, one of our planes returned with only one engine out of four working, and the pilot had to land it diagonally to maintain its balance. Immediately on touching ground, the pilot swung off the runway and finished up on the grass, damaging one of its wings. The pilot later told us he had lost two engines over the continent and the other over the English Channel, but for him, the honourable thing to do was not to abandon his plane, but bring it back to base.

Our station, Faldingworth, had the capital letters FH marked at the ends of each runway for recognition. Nearby was another RAF Station, Fiskerton, which had the recognition letters FN. From the air the two looked similar. One time, one of our planes reported its return and we talked it down. The pilot said he had landed safely but we couldn't see any planes on our runways. A few minutes later we received a telephone call from RAF Fiskerton, advising us that they had one of our planes. We were all relieved that the plane had been found and it was later returned to Faldingworth, but the pilot and navigator had very red faces for the next day or two!

There were times when planes from other stations had to land at our aerodrome, including American *Boeing B17 Flying Fortresses* and *Liberators*. This gave us the chance to view these aircraft at close quarters. *The*

*Flying Fortess,* a four-engined heavy bomber, was used primarily in WW2 by the American Air Force for strategic daylight bombing raids on German industrial and military targets. Also, some of the smaller aircraft, like the twin-engined Oxfords, were frequent visitors to our base; these often carried the 'Top Brass' to and from our station.

Shortly after my arrival at RAF Faldingworth, I found a bicycle pump, so of course I had to buy a second-hand bicycle to go with it. Others bought bikes too and very soon we were expert cyclists. In fact we were so skilled, we were able to pass each other going in opposite directions on very narrow pathways without falling off, even when carrying passengers on the cross-bars. Late one evening, a group of us were returning from Market Rasen in the dark without any lights on our bicycles. We were stopped by a police trap hidden in the shadows at the side of the road. This resulted in us all having to appear in the local court a few weeks later. No-one would accept our explanation that we were Polish, had just arrived in the country and did not know the language nor the traffic regulations. We were all fined five shillings each (25p) and so we now had police records.

Several things happened at RAF Faldingworth that almost cost me my life. For instance, on my way to Flying Control, I had to pass the lorry depot where several lorries were parked side by side. One day, there was an enormous puddle and in order to avoid it, I started to cycle in the very narrow gap between the puddle and the back of a lorry which unbeknown to me had started reversing, knocking me into the air and into the centre of the puddle. I screamed as loud as I could and the driver heard me and stopped just in time so that I wasn't also run over.

At the beginning of 1945, some German Junkers 52 Bombers managed to penetrate British air space and paid us an unfriendly visit. They dropped bombs all over the place, some on which landed on the runaway, but no planes were damaged and no people were hurt. I was on duty when I noticed that one of those planes flew straight at Flying Control. Three bombs landed in a straight line causing little damage, but thank goodness there was no fourth bomb as that would have landed on Flying Control and I would have been obliterated!

Early in 1945, I went to visit my brother Stach in Crieff, a market town in Scotland, where he was on an officer's course. I travelled by train and enjoyed seeing the stunning scenery of Perthshire. I had to change trains twice on the way, but on the last leg, I caught a bus from Perth to Crieff and fell asleep, very nearly missing my stop. My brother, with the others on the course, was accommodated in a very large Hotel called *The Hydro* which had been requisitioned by the RAF, on the outskirts of the town. The *Hydro*, situated near mountains, was built in Victorian times to bring about 'water cures' for the rich. The residents in the town seemed to be very indignant that scarce supplies of food were being diverted for the Poles' exclusive use in the hotel.

We spent two days walking around the town and hiking in the surrounding hills. On the third day we went to Glasgow, and spent a very pleasant evening in the dance hall, and the following day we visited the famous castle in Edinburgh before I returned to RAF Faldingworth.

In our free time, a group of us would cycle around the pretty local villages or to towns near the RAF Station, such as Market Rasen and Brigg. Once in Market Rasen, for the first time in my life I saw a typical English funfair with roundabouts, side shows and food booths. We spent some time there with a group of the local girls, one of whom lived in a small village where later I visited her on several occasions. Her father, trying to impress me, took both of us for a ride around his farm in his car, which he hardly ever used because petrol was so scarce. One of my friends gave me the address of a young lady in Stoke-on-Trent who wanted to correspond with a Polish airman. We started writing to each other and the next time I was on leave, I went to visit her and her family. She and her two sisters took me to see the local beauty spots including the well-known Trentham Park with its boating lake. I stayed overnight in Stoke town centre, at a Toc H Club, which had facilities for servicemen. Toc H is an international Christian movement seeking to help others and promote Christianity. The name is an abbreviation of *'Talbot House'*. The word 'Toc' signified the letter 'T' in the First World War signals spelling alphabet, and 'H' obviously was for 'House'. It was named in memory of the death, during WW1, of the son of Edward Talbot, the then Bishop of Winchester.

During the day, while all the girls were working, I used to go boating on a different lake in Hanley Park. On the bus one day, I got talking to a plain-clothes policeman who arranged for me to visit one of the famous porcelain works in Longton. Here I was shown around every department, which was very interesting indeed. I just had to admire the skill of the artists who hand-painted decorations on each item, including porcelain figures.

When I had first joined the Polish Air Force, I was given the opportunity to choose what kind of work I would like to do. Being too short-sighted, I was not eligible to become a member of an aircrew, so I decided to select Wireless Mechanics and Radar. Around Easter Time, in early April 1945, an order came through transferring me for training in these aircraft trades at RAF Locking near Weston Super Mare in Somerset. It was huge and at its peak, it sometimes had 6,000 men on parade at the same time. This base had the very important No.5 School of Technical Training, which had opened just before the war started to provide training for the RAF and Fleet Air Arm in subjects such as Engines,

Airframes, Flight Mechanics, Parachute Packing and Air Gunnery. It was also the home of the No.1 Radio School which trained regular servicemen, like me, in the Radio and Radar trades.

# CHAPTER 15: WIRELESS, RADAR AND RESETTLEMENT

## 04/1945 – 24/10/1947 (AGE 19-21)

### JERZY DĄBROWSKI

My squadron leader, who was in charge of Flying Control at Faldingworth, was very unhappy when I first informed him that I was transferring to RAF Locking to learn about wireless and radar, because he had plans for me. He showed his immense disapproval by ordering me to bring all my kit to be inspected before my departure. My Nissen hut was well over half a mile away and it would have been very difficult for me to bring everything on my bicycle, or even carry it if I walked. He eventually calmed down and, with the intervention of a Flight Lieutenant who said he would do the inspection, agreed that my kit could be inspected at my quarters. Of course everything was in order.

I travelled to RAF Locking in Weston Super Mare, Somerset, together with a group of other airmen, mainly my old colleagues from the Cadets School. This time we were accommodated in proper timber-built barracks placed close together. Our beds were neatly spaced and the floor was beautifully shiny. We soon learnt it was our duty to polish the floor every morning before breakfast! We were woken very early to the strains of one of the most popular contemporary songs of the day, *'They call him Pablo and they know he is a dreamer'* blasting out of the loudspeakers. We had to tie felt squares on our feet and 'dance' on the floor to the music. Within a few minutes, the NCO on duty would check we were all up, dressed and dancing, and only then we were allowed to wash and shave before being marched to the dining hall for breakfast.

After morning parade, we marched, yet again, to one of the hangers for our lessons in *'The Theory and Practice of Wireless Mechanics'*. Our manuals were made by a duplicator, where the English versions had been translated into Polish and included hand-drawn diagrams of the various electrical circuits. Our evenings were free so we could relax in the club room, listening to music or playing cards, or we could wander into Weston-super-Mare, making sure we didn't miss the last bus back.

At the beginning of May, I had to go to the station Sick Bay to have an operation on an ingrowing toenail on my big toe. In order to remove the nail and part of the root, they gave me an injection to put me to sleep; I didn't wake up until the following afternoon, feeling very weak and ill. Apparently the injection hadn't agreed with me and I had to spend several more days in the Sick Bay because of it. The nurses were all very pleasant and those of us in Sick Bay were visited from time to time by some local people so it wasn't too bad. Only a couple of things annoyed me there – being woken daily by the more able patients tidying the ward and polishing the floor, and the sound of a neighbouring patient sharpening his shaving contraption!

On VE day, (Victory in Europe day, May 8th) I was still in sick bay but the news cheered me up a lot. Germany had unconditionally surrendered and the Allies had formally accepted the surrender. When I finally returned to my barracks, it seems my full bottle of Eau de Cologne, hidden in the bottom of my kit bag, had been found and drunk in celebration of the event by my 'friends' who sought to assure me it had evaporated!

Every one was given an extra day's leave so I added mine to my next free weekend and decided to go to Southampton. We all had to fill in a form stating where we would be staying, so not knowing anyone there, I used a map and carefully invented a fictitious address. However, once in Southampton, I registered at the YMCA hostel for Servicemen, and then went to check whether the address I'd made up actually existed. To my surprise, I found that the two houses either side of the address I'd given were still standing, but 'my' house had been bombed flat, and cleared. Of course, I did feel sad for the people who had lived there and understood that many people in the UK had also lost their homes.

Our financial resources were rather scarce and we were often unable to hitch a lift anywhere, so most of our travel was done on public transport. Now, as summer approached and the weather warmed up, I started going to the open-air swimming pool in Weston-super-Mare. I loved diving from the highest board and I proudly learnt to do double somersaults.

The war was now over and there was little need to train any more radar mechanics so early in the summer we were transferred yet again, this time to RAF Cammeringham, to the north of Lincoln, to complete our *Wireless Mechanics* course which could well be useful in future civilian life. This station had been used by RAF Bomber Command and the Polish Air Force as an overflow airfield and a training unit. The No. 301 Polish Bomber Squadron and the No. 305 Polish Bomber Squadron, both used for flying Vickers Wellingtons, had been based here during the war.

RAF Cammerington was no longer operational because the condition of its grass runways had deteriorated too much, and so we were able to use all the buildings, including Flying Control, for our lessons. For the Polish air crews as well as for us, these included preparation for demobilisation and citizenship by teaching skills useful for employment. We were accommodated in Nissen huts that had a free standing stove in the middle to provide heating in cold weather. The nearby fields were full of edible mushrooms known to us Poles but not acknowledged by the

English. We used them to cook a delicious mushroom soup, and often added potatoes, to supplement our diet. The potatoes were obtained from nearby farms where we volunteered to help the farmers with picking them. The tractor digging the potatoes up drove too fast for us and yet we were supposed to collect every potato that was uncovered Soon we all had backache but we did receive a small payment for this incredibly hard work.

Apart from the *Theory of Wireless Mechanics* course, we carried out various practical experiments and soon learnt how to play practical jokes on each other. We discovered that if we loaded a condenser (capacitor) using a 500 volt hand dynamo, and placed it in a conspicuous place, anyone touching it would receive a mild electric shock! We tried having two of us holding one dynamo terminal each while a third person operated it. The two of us would then try to shake hands simultaneously with an unsuspecting passer-by, giving him a shock. These pranks amused the perpetrators immensely but the recipients were not always so delighted!

Once I received an enormous 5,000 volt shock from a high frequency alternating current. There was a very large, glass transmitting valve with a hatch door for servicing and usually, when this was opened, the electricity automatically cut off. I opened this hatch and put my head inside in order to see better what I needed to do but my ear somehow went into the disconnecting aperture, reconnecting the electricity supply. In other circumstances this high voltage could have killed me, but because the current was of a very high frequency, it only burnt my ear and the shock caused me to knock my head on the top of the hatch opening. I would not recommend this experiment to anyone!

Each RAF Station had its own NAAFI Club, the Navy, Army and Air Force Institute which was founded by the government in 1920 to help the lower ranks of servicemen. Commissioned Officers were not usually allowed access to these Clubs because their own elite 'messes' provided everything they needed. If they happened to enter the Club, it was deemed to be a massive intrusion. The NAAFI Club would have shops and laundrettes, canteens, bars and restaurants, and even places to relax, dance or watch a film. Occasionally ENSA (The Entertainments National Service Association which operated as part of the NAAFI) would put on a variety show. We discovered that the next nearest RAF station at Scampton, under five miles away, put on better films than ours, but the best, most up-to-date films were shown in the public cinemas of Lincoln.

In our spare time we often went exploring on bicycles, and so one of our colleagues bought himself a bike that had a dynamo attached to the rear wheel. We made a bet with him that he would not be able to lie on his back, holding the bicycle upside down, and pedal for half an hour making the dynamo operate the front light all the while. In the meantime, some of us went to the guard room and reported to the officer that our friend had gone crazy. Within minutes, two RAF police arrived to take care of their 'patient' who suddenly had a lot of explaining to do. Eventually it was all cleared up and, with the exception of the victim, we all had a great laugh but we couldn't understand why he wasn't on speaking terms with us for several days!

My bicycle continued to be unlucky. On my way to a dance in Lincoln one day, I was cycling at speed down a very steep circular road that bypassed the city centre when I noticed a car parked on the inside of the bend. For a split second I turned my head to check behind before overtaking but as I turned my head back, my handlebar just touched the parked car and I went flying over the top of it. I landed in front of it on my face and hands, leaving my bicycle at the rear. I picked myself up and went to a chemist to be patched up because I had grazed my forehead, nose and hands quite badly. That evening I still went dancing but it was difficult to explain the condition of my face to my dancing partners. They all decided I'd been in a fight.

We cycled to many of our neighbouring towns including Lincoln, Brigg and Gainsborough, or just around local villages. In Gainsborough, 13 miles away, there was a lady who had a dancing school and we started visiting her regularly in order to improve our dancing skills. I found Lincoln to be a very interesting city. It had numerous historical buildings and a famous cathedral. I managed to climb the 365 steps up the tower to enjoy the wonderful views of the neighbouring countryside from the top. The cathedral itself sits on top of a hill and is visible for miles around, so was a very useful guide in our explorations around the area.

I had to travel by bus or train to more distant towns. One trip, I stayed in the Salvation Army Hostel for servicemen in Boston where I saw the large and historic street fair. Several times, I spent a couple of days in Chesterfield, staying at the White Swan Hotel close to the famous parish church with a crooked spire. Sometimes I met up with my brother's girlfriend who had corresponded with me while I was in Palestine, to help me with my English. I once cycled, with her family, to Matlock Bath which was very hilly and we often had to dismount from our bikes. Some weekends were spent in Scunthorpe or Hull where I stayed in Young Peoples' Institutes which, as well as accommodation, provided entertainment for the forces like dancing, variety shows and musical evenings. In Hull, a dance hall called the 'New Yorker Ballroom' had an enormous mirror along the length of one wall making the room seem twice the size: even with all my expertise, I nearly danced 'through' this mirror.

Whenever we went on leave, we were issued with a Railway Travel Warrant which stated the nearest station to our chosen destination, although we were allowed to break our journey. Of course, I usually applied for a warrant to a very distant station then broke my journey several times to visit other places en route. For instance, I once had a warrant to Pembroke, so I stopped at Newport and then found I had to sleep that night on a mattress on the floor in a large hall adapted for the use of the forces. My next stop was at Cardiff where I was lucky enough to obtain a free ticket given to servicemen for the local theatre. Here, I shared a box with three ATS ladies (Auxiliary Territorial Service, the women's branch of the British Army) which made the evening so much more interesting. Finally arriving at Pembroke Dock, I was able to see the famous Short S25 Sunderland Flying Boats. On my return, I stopped at Tenby where I spent several days.

At other times I took a warrant to Blyth in Northumberland, to Manchester, or to Sheffield. In Wolverhampton I made friends with a young man my age who invited me to his home in Clacton-on-Sea for Christmas. He showed me around nearby 'Constable Country' in Suffolk and also took me to the ancient borough of Colchester with its famous castle, said to be the largest castle keep in the whole UK. Unbeknown to me at that time, one day I would live and work in Colchester.

I was very fortunate to be able to visit my brother fairly regularly. Sometimes he visited me, and other times I met him at whichever station he was currently based, for instance at Newton Ferrers near Plymouth where we went boating on the sea together, or at Hardway near Portsmouth where he was seconded to serve on the Air-Sea Rescue speedboats. On one visit, when Stach's girlfriend and another young lady were with us, we went swimming in the sea in heavy rain in Brighton. It was warmer in the sea, as is often the case in England. In the evening we went to a dance in the Regal Ballroom.

Early in the summer of 1946, now aged 20 years old, I was selected to attend an Entrance Examination for the Polish University School of Architecture in London. Despite being the youngest candidate, I did not find it too difficult to pass this exam. In October that same year

I was presented with a Certificate of Completion of the Wireless Mechanics Course by the Royal Air Force and was then provisionally transferred to RAF Dunholme Lodge in Lincolnshire, the home of the Polish Settlement Corps.

Dunholme Lodge had been a Bomber Command Station but after Hiroshima and the Japanese surrender, all flying from there ceased and in 1946 the Polish Air force in Britain was disbanded. Dunholme Lodge, No. 3 Polish Resettlement Unit, was then used to prepare Polish airmen for their next stage in life. Those servicemen who didn't want to return to a communist Poland trained for civilian life in Britain. They continued to be paid while learning the English language and various trades, or were supported into further education. This is where I learnt about the Polish School of Architecture.

After completing various resettlement forms at Dunholme Lodge, I was allowed to proceed to London for my new studies. During my first year at the Polish School of Architecture, until July 1947, I was still in uniform as a full member of the Polish Air Force and had to re-apply every four weeks for an extension of my leave. After that date I was transferred to Reserves and had to travel to York to collect my first civilian clothing. I was handed a suit, some shirts and underwear, shoes and a hat!

# IN THE SPOTLIGHT: SETTLING THE POLES IN BRITAIN

## 1946 –1948

*LINDA GALLAGHER*

A volatile situation was rapidly building up in Britain between the Poles and the British. So many Polish troops had refused to be repatriated after the war that the British government finally decided to bring all of them back to England; no one wanted to force them to go back to Poland, now under a Soviet puppet government, against their will after their experiences in Siberia and war-time Poland.

In May 1946, the Foreign Secretary, Ernest Bevin, announced that the British Government was to form the unarmed Polish Resettlement Corps (PRC) in order to prepare the Polish troops for demobilisation and British Citizenship. This was as much a face-saving solution for the British as it was a noble and generous act. Setting the PRC up required the support of the Governmental Departments of Education, Employment, Health and Pensions as well as Trade Unions and Professional Associations. Also involved were other Commonwealth Countries and even Vatican City in Italy because the Poles were predominantly of the Roman Catholic religion.

**Polish Resettlement Corps**

Intended to function for just two years from 1946-48, the Polish Resettlement Corps was run with a military structure. Altogether 40 Polish Resettlement Camps were set up in the UK and the Poles were provided with military uniforms that had Polish insignia on the shoulders. Comfort may have been lacking somewhat in the camps, but they offered a large degree of security and an empathetic environment. Vocational training and English language learning was provided, and help was given to those who wanted to emigrate to other countries.

Approximately 250,000 Polish servicemen and women, with their dependants, were eligible to enrol in the PRC and the majority of them did so; this number included war veterans from the Middle East and Monte Cassino campaigns, from the Polish Navy, the Polish Air Force, and the Polish Women's Auxiliary Air Force.

Dunholme Lodge, where my father was stationed for a very short while, was the main home of the Polish Resettlement Corps; the Polish Records Office was moved there from Blackpool too. Of Dunholme Lodge's 11,000 members, about 3,000 decided to return to Poland and almost 3,000 emigrated to other countries. About 5,000 wanted to stay in Britain, and of those, 500 flying personnel joined the British RAF.

For the Poles, the prospect of leaving the PRC at the end of the two years, was daunting. They had to make a difficult decision concerning where they wanted to be in the future.

Of the Polish troops who had come from the west of Poland and had escaped the Germans, approximately 37,000 volunteered for repatriation, but of the 85,000 former prisoners of the Soviets, only 300 volunteered to go back to Poland.

### Becoming British Citizens

The Polish Forces in Britain had thus sent a very clear message to the British Government that there couldn't, and wouldn't, be a wholesale repatriation of Poles. However, after the war, Britain was suffering from an acute shortage of labour and employable skills, and needed massive reconstruction itself. The government soon came to realise that far from being a problem, a well-organised Polish community could become a vital labour source. Over 150,000 Poles altogether were welcomed to settle in England and another 8,000 in Scotland.

Polish people are generally very hard, reliable workers and after the initial, favourable reception many had received, this trait brought some hostility as they started to be perceived as being in competition with the local population for employment. Many people in the UK didn't understand either why the Poles were in Britain in the first place, nor why they hadn't returned to their homeland after the war. Many Poles also felt that they were overlooked for work opportunities, or marginalised for promotion once in employment.

There was a tendency to treat the Polish people 'like the British' with a complete ignorance of the cultural differences, and this had a major impact of their mental welfare.

The war had torn these Poles away from their families and friends; they'd had no news of what had happened to their loved ones, many of whom had died or been killed during the conflict. They were witnesses and recipients of such atrocities that no one should ever have to experience. The vast majority of Polish people were Roman Catholic, unlike the English, while a small minority either declared they were unbelievers or would not state their religion. They all preferred to be called 'Political exiles' because they fervently believed that a return to Poland would place their own freedom in jeopardy.

The majority of Poles initially expected their stay in Britain to be temporary, and that they would return to Poland once the Soviet Government had been removed, but the decisions made at the Yalta Conference about Poland's future, and the legitimisation of the communist puppet government, brought a devastating blow to their dreams. They had fought for Poland's freedom in the war and yet here they were, still in exile.

They were now left feeling like aliens in a country with different customs, and the yearning to return one day to their homeland affected everything they did. They suffered cultural and linguistic isolation as they tried to adopt the British life-style, due to not having many friends to converse with in the Polish language, nor to share experiences with. And inevitably, the painful and laborious process of trying to trace relatives, needed to begin. Today, many of these Polish people could have been said to be suffering from Post-Traumatic Stress Disorder.

Most Poles made a lot of effort to adapt to their new country but few were prepared to let their children lose a knowledge of Polish culture and history, and so the Polish Saturday School movement came into being in 1948 and in many places, the schools are still in existence. My older siblings and I can remember attending one briefly.

## Making Sense of the War

Making sense of the past is very difficult for a person who has experienced such extreme traumas. They may try to block out the terrible memories, never speaking of them aloud while continuing to suffer much inner, emotional pain. In some situations, a non-Polish spouse or partner might be fairly unsympathetic and unsupportive and not want to hear about their memories, while others may show much more understanding.

Selective memory, perhaps, helped some Polish people begin to feel comfortable with who they are and why they were here in Britain. I think my father lived like this, blocking out much of the pain and horror until he was finally able to write everything down in his Memoirs, and thus bring a measure of healing to himself.

As they get older, many people from all walks of life generally want to explore their own life story to find meaning in it. They may want to rediscover their true identity in difficult life circumstances which were never chosen nor planned for, but imposed on them. Polish nationals will have wanted to find friends and relatives from their earlier life in Poland, to revisit the places they had known there, and to reconnect with those people they had shared the war with. Writing down their memories is important for them personally, but it is also important for others to read so that future generations can learn from history and hopefully never repeat it.

# IN THE SPOTLIGHT: SOVIETS AT THE NUREMBERG TRIALS

## 11/1945 – 10/1946

### LINDA GALLAGHER

Before the Nuremberg Trials, held between November 1945 and October 1946, there had never ever been an international trial of war criminals. The Palace of Justice in Nuremberg, Bavaria, was chosen for the trials because it was relatively undamaged by the war and it also had a large prison area. It had previously been a base for Nazi Propaganda Rallies so symbolically this was showing the death of Nazism. Once Hitler was dead, the Allies, initially, wanted to severely punish the Nazi leaders without a trial because they had caused such mayhem in Europe for the sake of their own 'Lebenstraum'; during the war, the Germans had destroyed much of the continent and had exterminated millions of Jews, Poles and other nationals.

Stalin, though, started with the premise that the Nazi leaders were guilty and deserved death and that the whole German nation should be destroyed for their betrayal of Russia. The Nazi invasion called Operation Barbarossa, had left millions of Russian troops and civilians dead or homeless, and had 'dragged' the Soviets into the conflict. Stalin wanted to execute upwards of 50,000 German officers with only a show trial, a 'Grand Political Spectacle' that had a pre-determined result, just like the Soviet purges of 1936-38, in order to expose the enormity of what the Nazis had done, and the evils of fascism. For him, this show trial would cement Soviet unity and show what immense sacrifices the 'courageous and peace-loving'

Russians had made in defeating the Germans. He also hoped it would establish the Soviet Union as one of the world's superpowers alongside America.

In opposition to this, America, Britain and France, all politically democratic, said that if there was to be a trial of any sort, then there had to be due process, including a legal defence. The mismatch between these ideologies showed up the widening cracks in the relationship between the Allies and the Soviets, sowing the seeds for the forthcoming 'Cold War' between USSR and USA.

## The Soviets were unprepared for the Nuremberg Trials

The Russians were totally unprepared for the democratic nature of the war crimes trials, led by the ITM (the International Military Tribunal set up for this purpose in 1945). While Britain, America and France could work freelance, the Soviets were under intense surveillance the whole time from their government in Moscow. Their delegation included the same chief judges and prosecutors as had sat at the Communist 'Purges' before the war and was handicapped by the same procedure of always having to report back to Stalin and receive orders from him. Like then, Stalin wanted to control the proceedings, and he also tried to control the other leaders.

The Soviet delegation, under Stalin's orders, provided their 'allies' with a list of taboo subjects that were not to be mentioned at the trials and requested that the word 'Totalitarian' was removed from any descriptions of Nazi Germany. The US and Britain agreed not to mention either the 1939 Soviet Ribbentrop-Molotov 'Non-aggression Pact' with Germany, nor the Katyn Forest Massacres which the Soviets continued to pin on the Germans, when they themselves had been responsible. Many members of the Soviet delegation itself did not even know the true facts of these matters.

The truth of these banned clauses did not come to light at the time of the trials because the other western prosecutors continued to keep quiet – as they had during the war – in order to appease Stalin – showing that they were actually complicit in the lies.

## 'Tu Quoque'

The Soviets, in reality, were just as guilty as the accused Nazis, who strongly used the defence of 'Tu Quoque' which means 'and you also'. This was an intent by the Germans to discredit the Soviets by attacking their behaviour as hypocritical, being inconsistent with the fact that they also had been part of the secret protocol to divide Poland up in the first place. This protocol, surprisingly, was only finally discovered by the Allies during the Nuremberg Trials.

Also, the Russians had deported millions of people from Poland and other countries to exile in Siberia, yet wanted to expose the German deportations to the concentration camps. As they liberated Europe alongside the Allies in the last years of the war, the Russians mistreated their POWs and raped thousands of German women, partly in retaliation for how the German soldiers had raped Soviet women.

## An Anti-Soviet Agenda

America and Britain were uncomfortable with the Soviet participation at the Nuremberg Trials and they gradually pursued an anti-Soviet agenda when they saw Russia making a post-war power-grab in other Eastern European countries and parts of Asia. The Russians were really no different to the Germans. At the end of the war, they already occupied Poland, Hungary, Bulgaria, Romania and Eastern Germany, and were seeking to establish their influence in other nations.

Some incriminating evidence against the Soviets was allowed to be introduced at the trials, but the 'war-crimes' of the American atomic bombing of Japan, the British firebombing of certain German cities like Dresden, and the Allies' invasion of Iran were not mentioned.

The Soviets finally lost any control of the proceedings at Nuremberg when the verdicts were announced. They were repeatedly out-manoeuvred and increasingly isolated as events unfolded, making Stalin furious. He then withdrew and focussed his energy on his attempts to restore post-war order on Europe in other, totalitarian, ways. One Soviet idea that came out of the trials that was not totally dismissed, however, was the suggestion that 'the planning and waging of an unprovoked war of conquest was a punishable criminal act'. This idea had much influence on future thinking about how to judge 'Crimes against Peace' and 'Crimes against Humanity' and as part of the tenets of the International Military Tribunal (ITM), it served to change international law forever.

## The Katyn Admission and a Soviet Apology

In an attempt to keep Stalin on board, the Katyn Forest Massacres were not mentioned during the Nuremberg Trials. However, 44 years later, in 1990, a year after the Berlin Wall fell and the day after the new East German parliament formally apologised for the Jewish Holocaust, Mikhail Gorbachev, the then Soviet Prime Minister, finally admitted that the Soviets had killed all the Polish Officers and Intelligentsia in the Katyn Massacres. This confession was to underline Gorbachev's new ideology of 'openness', and was intended to improve diplomatic relationships for the rest of the world with the Polish nation.

His successor, Boris Yeltsin, also formally apologised for the Soviet's atrocious lack of intervention during the Warsaw Uprising of 1944, when the Russians had waited on the opposite side of the River Vistula while the Germans decimated the

Polish capital, only coming to 'help' the Poles once the worst was over.

# CHAPTER 16: ARCHITECTURE, A WIFE AND A DEATH

## 24/10/1946 – 11/05/1950 (AGE 20-24)

### *JERZY DĄBROWSKI*

The day of my departure to start my studies in London finally arrived. It is incredibly difficult to describe my feelings at parting with so many friends with whom I had spent the last four and a half years, from age 16 to 20 years old. Those years had been very challenging but also very interesting, from leaving the Soviet Union across the Caspian Sea, through Cadets School and then service in the Polish Air Force in Britain. Our ties of friendship were strong and were bound to last until the 'end of time'. On the several occasions that I met up with them, either during my studies, or later in the *Polish Social and Cultural Club* in West London, we always had so much to say to each other.

For the first two weeks in London I was able to stay in the *Union Jack Club* for servicemen near Waterloo Station while looking for permanent accommodation. This club, founded in an Edwardian building in 1907 for non-commissioned members of the armed forces, provided over 1000 beds and had many public rooms. Commissioned Officers had their own clubs but ordinary servicemen had nowhere reputable to stay in the capital until King Edward VII officially opened this building. Lawrence of Arabia reputedly often stayed at the *Union Jack Club*. It was within walking distance of London with its sights and 'night life' and so I was often able to go dancing at the *Lyceum*, or see a show at *The Stage Door club*. Sometimes I was able to obtain free unsold tickets to theatres such as the *Windmill*.

Eventually I found a small, top-floor room in the World's End area in Chelsea. This room had a tiny window facing the backyard, and a small gas burner for making tea or cooking very simple meals on. My landlady treated me like a son and started giving me breakfast, then a regular evening meal so although my student grant was only £20 a month, I doubled my rent to her. I used to take my personal washing to a laundry near Waterloo Station. One hot summer day, I was cycling there wearing just shorts with my dirty clothes stuffed into my leather briefcase – which I had bought in Egypt – tied to my cycle rack. I was stopped by a policeman who wanted to know what was in the brief case. He didn't believe me when I told him, in my Polish accent, that it was my dirty clothes, and thinking I was just being funny, he made me open it. When he saw I was telling the truth, he looked so embarrassed and disappointed that he let me go on my way.

The Polish School of Architecture was part of the Polish University College in London and shared some lecturers with the University of London. At first it was in a facility near Sloane Square, about a mile and a half from my digs, but was later transferred to a building near the Royal Albert Hall facing Hyde Park. Close by were the famous Victoria and Albert, Natural History and Science Museums all of which I found very interesting and educational. Also nearby there were two Polish Clubs, *The White Eagle* and *The Polish Hearth* in South Kensington.

I was one of the very few still wearing my uniform at the college, and I was also the youngest student because all the others were ex-servicemen. Even all but one of the ladies there were also older than me. Most of the other students already had some knowledge of architecture from before the war so I found it quite difficult to keep up at first. The end-of-year exams could be taken in either Polish or English, but my lecturer for the History of Architecture course was not so young and was not very good at English, so I wrote my exam in that language, adding many free-hand drawings, and therefore always received a good mark for that subject. Other lecturers were younger and knew both languages well so I had to revise properly for them.

There was so much to learn in Britain. Guy Fawkes night, fireworks and burning a 'guy' were completely outside my understanding! Street fairs were also new to me – I wasn't interested in buying any unnecessary second-hand 'junk', but I did have a go at the shooting range. I noticed that, at first, all my bullets landed too far to the left and too low, so I adjusted where I aimed, ignoring all the bullseyes, and suddenly found, to the cheers of the onlookers and the disappointment of the stall holder, that I was winning a prize with every shot!

I used to spend much of my free time swimming in Hyde Park and getting a lovely tan. One day I met up with one of my old friends from the Cadets School to go boating with him. The boats had sliding seats similar to those I had learnt to row on before the war, so my friend, who was still in the Navy, and I decided to race each other in these boats. In no time at all, and with very little effort, I soon left my friend a long way behind because he had only learnt to row boats in the conventional manner. It gave me real satisfaction to beat a 'sailor' who should have known how to row.

At weekends, during the summer evenings, I went swimming at various indoor and outdoor pools. I loved diving from high boards, and tried many different tricks especially doing double somersaults. I was just about to perform a 'dead man's dive' from the top board of the indoor pool in Chelsea when someone shouted. I thought there might be a swimmer below me so I turned my head to see as I left the board but I had no chance of stopping. The moment my head hit the water, it was pushed against my shoulder bone. Stunned, I stayed under the water for a short while but when I finally emerged, everyone stared at me because blood was pouring from my face. My cheek had received a deep cut. The pool staff patched me up and sent me to the nearest hospital where nobody believed I had received the wound at a swimming pool; they all decided I had been in a fight.

In the evenings I often went ice-skating in Streatham, or dancing at Hammersmith Palace and various Town Halls which enabled me to meet a variety of girls. I had many different girlfriends, but only one at a time! I didn't want to be tied down yet so sometimes I said goodbye to them, or if they'd had enough of my company, they gave me up. One day, soon after my brother Stach, who had been visiting me, departed to return to his RAF Station, I went dancing alone at Hornsey Town Hall. It was now Friday 30th July 1948. As I went in, I noticed three English girls standing together at the edge of the dance floor. Like the three bears, one was too tall for me, and one was too short, but the one in the middle was about the right height so I invited her to dance with me.

During the dance, I asked her 'What is your name?' She said 'Gwen', which sounded very much like 'When?' to me. I had never come across that name before, and so, thinking she was joking, I asked her, 'What is your name now?' Again she replied, 'Gwen'. I still thought she had said 'When?'

'What do they call you at home?'

'Gwen!'

'What does your brother call you?'

'Gwen!'

Each time she gave the same answer, which to my Polish ears sounded like 'When?' Finally I asked her to spell it so I would know she wasn't teasing me. Ah, Gwen, short for Gwendoline! We went out together for eighteen months and visited many places of interest around London. As part of my University course, I had to join a camp at Godalming in Surrey with the other students from my class, to learn the practical application of land surveying. I enjoyed playing volleyball in my spare time, but one day this caused me to badly sprain my ankle. I had to spend a few days in the camp hospital and Gwen wrote very nice letters to me every day. We were looking forward to meeting up again very soon.

Finally, I was fully demobilised in January 1949 and was able to start to live as a civilian for the first time in ten years, since the beginning of the war. On Christmas Eve that year, Gwen and I, and my brother Stanisław went to a party at the house of one of my friends from the School of Architecture. Gwen and I sat quietly in a corner, chatting to each other, but everyone kept topping up our glasses with vodka, wine, whisky and beer until we were properly 'sloshed'! I had to take Gwen home then return to my digs on the crowded all-night tube train and I felt totally sick, so I left the train at Knightsbridge and walked the last two miles home. The following Christmas, I was invited to stay with Gwen's family and was able to sample her father's reboiled and twice brewed strong cups of tea – it was very hard to avoid being given a second cup.

Gwen and I were married on 18$^{th}$ February, 1950, in the Roman Catholic Church of St. Peter-in-Chains in Stroud Green, London. She was 22½ years old and I was almost 25. Gwen was a skilled seamstress, working for a company making quality clothing; her employers thought very highly of her and in appreciation of her work, made her a beautiful wedding dress. Her two cousins, Valerie and Pat, were her bridesmaids. Unfortunately my brother was in Egypt and unable to be present, so one of my friends from the School of Architecture was chosen to be my best man.

Our Wedding Reception was held in a local café after which Gwen moved into my current digs at Bayswater with me. We deferred our honeymoon until Easter when we had a lovely week in Eastbourne. Gwen continued to work for the same firm in London, making beautiful clothes for adults and children that were sold in West End shops such as *Harrods* and *Dickens and Jones* among others. I continued to cycle across Hyde Park for my lessons and as I was usually first home, I did most of the daily shopping.

As I mentioned, Stanisław was serving in the Royal Air Force in Egypt as a pilot, being stationed at that time at RAF Deversoir in the Suez Canal Zone, NE of Cairo. This base was originally built in 1930 as part of the defences for the Suez Canal which was being constructed on the NW shore of the Great Bitter Lake. During WW2, RAF Deversoir was used as a military airfield by the RAF and the USAF (United States Air Force) during the North Africa Campaign and continued to be used by the RAF until 1956, when it was turned over to the Egyptian Air Force. In 1950, when Stach was there, it operated as 324 Fighter Wing and was the home of three squadrons of De Haviland Vampire aircraft.

Stach often sent us photos from Egypt. The last one I received showed him bathing in the Suez Canal, waving his hand as if saying 'goodbye'. On the back of it he wrote: 'Don't worry about me. Nothing will ever happen to me'. A few days later, however, and less than three months after our wedding, I received a telegram from the War Office advising me that my brother had failed to return from his flight on 11th May 1950. He had been the pilot of a Vampire Mark 1 jet; the first time he had flown this very same plane was six months previously on 24th November 1949, the day our sister Halina had died in Poland under the Soviet occupation.

Stanisław had been involved in a head-on collision with a Lincoln Bomber, the largest war-plane Britain had at the time. Apparently, during 'friendly' exercises, he was 'attacking' the bomber with a camera (he had had really good results from all his previous exercises) but this time was unable to pull up after a dive and crashed. I learned later that the Vampire Mark 1 had this tendency after it had reached a certain speed. (This was corrected on the Mark 2 Vampire). Stanisław's remains were collected up from a large area and were buried in the cemetery at RAF Fayid. The War Office sent me his belongings and his Service Records but were unable to send me anything he had on him during that fatal flight.

Both my new wife, Gwen, who had met Stach on several occasions, and I, were considerably upset by this tragic news. While we were young, Stach and I had had our squabbles but once we left Poland in the deportation, we were always very close. Being older, he looked after me very well, through all our unsought-for travels from Poland to Siberia, Soviet Asia and the Middle East to Britain.

My father had died in Siberia, my mother had died in January 1943 aged 47, while under the terrifying German occupation in Poland, and my sister, who had barely survived that ordeal, had died after the war only few months previously. The loss of those three was somehow easier to bear than the death of my brother with whom I had gone through so much during the war. Even today, after all those years, I sometimes have the feeling that he may still come through the door to visit me.

# IN THE SPOTLIGHT: THE POLISH SCHOOL OF ARCHITECTURE

## LINDA GALLAGHER

The Polish School of Architecture, a higher education facility, was originally established in Liverpool University in 1941 as part of the Liverpool School of Architecture. It initially took in exiled Polish architectural students who had fled to Britain from their studies in Germany when it first invaded Poland. They needed to consolidate or complete their training so that they were ready to return to Poland and start reconstructing towns and cities there once the war had ended.

General Władisłav Sikorski, the Polish Prime Minister, who was in exile in Britain at that time, inaugurated the actual Polish School of Architecture itself in 1942. It was part of his broader plan for the Poles, which was to see many different academic disciplines placed in various universities in the UK, in preparation for rebuilding the Polish nation. The establishment stayed in touch with current architectural thought while emphasising the teaching styles and methods of traditional building design. Staff and students alike worked on many theoretical themes such as building hospitals, factories, flats, civic buildings and even Polish villages. It was specifically Polish in its cultural expression while engaging with contemporary designs and practices. Many qualified Polish Architects, however, decided to remain in Britain after their training.

The Polish School of Architecture moved to London in 1945 and operated there until 1953. My father trained in London during those years but on completing his studies, stayed in England working as an architect with various County Councils, initially to help with rebuilding and rehousing after the war in this country.

# CHAPTER 17: A CAREER AND A FAMILY

## 11/05/1950 – 31/12/1958 (AGE 24-32)

### *JERZY DĄBROWSKI*

Soon after receiving the sad news about my brother's death, we received some good news. Gwen was pregnant with our first child! We moved to slightly better accommodation in North Kensington owned by a Polish gentleman, and then after a few months moved again, to New Cross in South London, to a two-roomed flat on the first floor of a house owned by yet another Polish man who lived on the top floor. A Polish family with a little daughter and a grandmother, lived underneath us. We had to go downstairs to use the shared bathroom and for water but at least we had a small cooker. From New Cross, we were able to visit the seaside on several occasions. One particularly enjoyable trip was a week we spent at Littlehampton with its sandy beaches from where we also enjoyed a boat trip up the River Arun to visit Arundel Castle.

In February 1951, our son Christopher decided to make his appearance. Having very little money, I had to take Gwen the 12 miles on the bus to the nearest hospital at Hammersmith. She was quite petite and had a difficult time giving birth to a big baby, and she needed blood transfusions. The only way I could get her home after a ten-day stay in hospital, was on the bus again – poor, tired lady! But my late brother's camera came in handy for taking photos of our new-born.

When Gwen and I first got married, I was in my fourth year at the Polish School of Architecture. I had to leave early from New Cross every morning to cycle eight miles across London for my studies. My class of six people had a large project to design – the Redevelopment of South London. We were divided into three groups and my group came up with a detailed design for the Elephant and Castle area. The groups recombined to make a large model of our ideas. Another project I took part in was the design for a 200-bed general hospital in East London. In my fifth and final year, I worked on my Thesis Design, for which I selected a planning scheme called 'Dartford – Neighbourhood Unit and Sports Centre'. My project was to provide homes for over 17,000 people, with a main neighbourhood centre, three smaller shopping centres, a Sports Centre and a large school campus containing primary, secondary and technical schools. Another student, who was redeveloping Dartford Town Centre coordinated with me. None of these projects were actually built!

I sat my final exams in June 1951 and the external examiner was a Professor William Holford, a lecturer at the Liverpool School of Architecture, who had distinguished himself by winning a national competition for a Master Plan for Central London. Students from the Polish School of Architecture took second place in the same competition to design plans for rebuilding the capital after the war. Holford is particularly known for his redevelopment of Paternoster Square, the area around St Paul's Cathedral in London, which had been devastated by the Germans in the aerial Blitz. He was knighted in1953, the year of my graduation, and later made a life peer as Baron Holford.

Shortly after passing my exams, I was presented with my Diploma Certificate which I carried home in my bicycle saddlebag. Somehow, near Victoria Railway Station, the certificate fell out and I thought I'd lost it, but to my relief, someone picked had it up and sent it back to my school.

In 1951, for the first time, all the British Schools of Architecture, as well as the Polish School of Architecture, had many students who had finally completed their studies which they had begun before the war started, or had taken up since. All these graduates were discharged at the same time as myself, making it very difficult to find work. I wrote in excess of 150 applications before I was lucky enough to obtain an architectural appointment. While applying, I had to take temporary work in order to support my wife and son. It seems like a coincidence, but shortly after I received my diploma, I managed to get a job in the *'Diploma Laundry'* loading and unloading bagwash from around the city! My second temporary job was working in a furniture factory in Charlton, unloading sawn timber among other things. The wood was full of splinters so I took to wearing gloves in order to protect my hands for future drawing work. People thought I was just being funny but my foreman believed my story. I was glad to terminate this job when I obtained my first architectural post with Hornchurch Urban District Council in Essex.

It was really awkward to travel to Hornchurch by public transport – both on the underground and on buses – and I had to leave home really early and returned late. It was a twelve-hour day away from home, so I had very little time to spend with my wife and son. Being very shy, being left alone so much with a new baby in a house full of Polish people with whom she couldn't communicate, and possibly suffering from post-natal depression, this arrangement led to Gwen suffering a nervous breakdown. She had to spend time in hospital while Christopher was looked after by some kind people in Eltham. My free time was thus fully occupied with work, and with visiting both Gwen and my son as well as trying to look after our home.

I was beginning to find out what architectural work in practise was really like. I made several surveys of building sites and existing buildings in Hornchurch, designed a layout for over 500 houses and prepared many building specifications. Hornchurch Council were unable to help me find nearer and more appropriate accommodation for my family so after only a year I left for a job with Dartford Rural District Council which was able to provide us with a two-bedroom house in Wilmington, near Dartford which is 18 miles SE of London and is famous for its tunnel. Although there were 28 applicants for this post, apparently I was offered the post because one of the local councillors was interested in my unusual surname.

It was a condition of this employment that I should be able to drive a car, so I took lessons which were paid for by my employers, while my friends helped me to practise before I took and passed my Driving Test. This was essential for, from time to time, I had to inspect building contracts on various sites or carry out land surveys. For a week during the very hot summer, an assistant and I had stripped to the waist to do some surveying on a very large and difficult site, and we both acquired an amazing suntan. In the winter, we did another survey when the temperature was below freezing. My hands were so frozen from operating the theodolite, that we had to go to the nearest cafe every half hour to have a cup of tea and thaw out.

During the two years we lived at Dartford, I designed many new houses and flats, prepared layouts for housing estates for over 2000 houses and created the plans for various other buildings and projects which could continue after I left. One of my last jobs for Dartford Council was to design an indoor swimming pool which gave me the opportunity to visit several new swimming pools in other towns to learn how they were constructed. The pool was eventually built a few years after I had moved on.

Our second child, a daughter we named Linda, was born in January 1953, while we were in Dartford and she was followed only 17 months later by a third child, another son whom we called Andrew, born in June 1954. Gwen was still only 26 years old while I was 28! Across the street from our home was a rather lovely, elderly lady who took our family under her wing. We nicknamed her the 'Flower Lady' because she often gave us flowers from her garden which was full of them. She sometimes baby-sat for us and on one occasion, when Christopher was about 2½ years old, she enjoyed watching him splashing in a rather large puddle and only brought him home when he was thoroughly soaked!

In November of 1954, we moved from Dartford to Corby in Northamptonshire where I had secured a post with the Borough Council. Corby has been mined for iron ore since Roman times and this industry developed massively with the invention of the railways. Early in the 20th century, workers came from all over Britain to work in the steel-making factories. In 1950, Corby was designated a 'New Town' and William Holford, the external examiner for my finals exams in the Polish School of Architecture, was employed as its architect. He had designed a car-friendly plan for the town, with many open spaces and woodland. In 1954, the first 500 houses were being built and we were provided with a house on a new estate about a mile and a half from the centre, up a hill and close to a forest. There was mud everywhere, even around the four nearest shops on the estate. For major shopping we had to travel by infrequent buses to Kettering, changing in Corby centre. Life was a challenge, especially for Gwen with three tiny children and no friends.

For my official visits to building sites, I had the use of a small Ford van and I could occasionally visit home for lunch on my journeys. Most of my travelling for work was once again by bicycle. However, my work contract was not well developed and I often found I had little to do. This played on my mind as I still had to fill in forms daily saying what I'd done. My wife struggled too with the whole situation and once again became ill and very unhappy so after less than 9 months we moved once more! I managed to get work in Stratford-on-Avon where I was put in charge of the Architects Section under the Borough Engineer and Surveyor.

From the very beginning, we both really liked Stratford-on-Avon and Gwen's health improved a lot. Stratford is famous because Shakespeare was born and died there; every year, on Shakespeare's birthday in April, the town was decorated with flowers and the flags of approximately 90 nations. Ambassadors or representatives of those countries took part in a grand floral parade which started from the Guildhall and went to Shakespeare's grave at Holy Trinity Church. We were able to make many new friends in Stratford and there was always something to do. For instance, we were presented with two complimentary tickets for the The Royal Shakespeare Company Theatre and were able to watch previews of Shakespeare's plays for free! Our three children started school at St Gregory's RC School in Stratford, opposite Shakespeare's Birthplace.

My work in Stratford was far more interesting. As well as being responsible for several new housing projects, I was also involved in work on some historical buildings. I prepared a scheme to update the facilities in some almshouses for the elderly, and carried out improvements to the old buildings of the Public Library. I designed internal alterations to the Town Hall, including the provision of new kitchens and cloakrooms, and organised the rebuilding of a 400 year old roof. So many of the buildings I worked on had ancient problems like dry rot, or 'wonky' bricks, or thin walls held together by thick plaster. Some walls had to be rebuilt with old bricks because new bricks were too 'straight' and they had to match the wavy lines of old brickwork. I had the old bathing place on the river dismantled and designed a new swimming pool there. I also had the old Corn Exchange next to the Town Hall demolished, and designed a new small town square which included exposing the old timbers of many of the adjoining buildings. However, both these projects were only completed once I'd moved on, but the town square development actually won an award!

My boss, the Borough Engineer and Surveyor was very pleasant and often liked to come to my desk and talk to me just before the end of the day, to fill in the time before he had an evening committee meeting. I could hardly tell him to go away even though I knew my wife, with 3 small children at home, would be anxious for me to return. One of my sympathetic office colleagues sometimes stood unseen outside my office window, and in a childish voice called out 'Daddy! Daddy!' at which my boss used to look at his watch and apologise for keeping me. When I left the post, my boss said he would really miss me because I was his scape goat; sometimes he referred to me in his committee meetings if something had gone wrong, saying it must have been because I did not know English all that well!

In May 1956, I bought my first motor car, a 1934 Austin 10 Coupé. At 22 years old, it looked very old-fashioned so the neighbour's children started calling it 'Genevieve' after the 1953 comedy film of that name. The film is about two veteran cars, including the one called Genevieve, competing in the London to Brighton Veteran Car Run which is still held every year. Our 'Genevieve' had a soft top, leather seats, hardwood fascia, and a small boot with the spare wheel fixed on the outside. It also had trafficators that popped up to indicate which direction we were going to turn. The brakes worked on a flat road but were useless on hills. One time, trying to go up a steep, 1 in 5 hill, I could not get it into the unsynchronised first gear and the brakes refused to hold so the car rolled backwards down the hill. I managed to stop safely on a grass verge and then we all pushed it up the hill. I did manage to get Genevieve up that same hill on another occasion.

We used to go on camping holidays in this car, all five of us. Genevieve would be well and truly loaded, with a tent and luggage on the floor and the small boot filled to capacity. The three children sat on all the blankets and pillows, their heads nearly touching the roof. In 1957, we had a camping holiday near Barmouth in Wales. The weather was so good that we decided to stay just one more day and night. We went for a long walk across a railway viaduct and up a hill, but just as we reached the furthest and highest point of the hill, it started raining. It got heavier and heavier on our return to the car so, soaked to the skin, we drove to a teashop in Barmouth to get warmed up before going back to the campsite. Opposite the entrance to the site there was a petrol station. I stopped here to fill the tank up before the long journey home the next day, but then the engine flooded and the car would not start. We had to push it through the campsite and back to the tent.

There was no flysheet on the tent. The rainwater had penetrated the canvas and all our belongings were completely sodden. While I was hammering the tent pegs more firmly into the ground so that the tent would not fly away in the wind in the night, lightning struck the underground power lines about 30 yards from our tent, cutting out the electric supply for the whole area. We decided we all had to spend the night in the small car, but it was rocked from side to side by the strong gusts of wind and the roof started leaking. We were able to borrow a large groundsheet from another, kind camper so we covered the car and fixed it to the ground. But we felt like we were suffocating.

In the morning we packed up to leave for home but again, like many cars on the site, the car was damp and still refused to start. Someone helped me dry the spark plugs out and a local farmer towed us around the site until the engine finally fired. We were unable to get any more petrol on the way home because the power was still not reconnected and the petrol pumps were operated by electricity. The floor of the car was made of plywood which leaked and soaked my feet every time I drove through a puddle. In addition, we had to take a longer route home because the shortest way was blocked by large boulders that had rolled down the hills in the storm. This was *the* holiday to remember! I was finally able to update the car in 1958, and bought a black 1955, 6 cylinder Vauxhall Cresta with white wall tyres and two tone leather seats; it never leaked in the rain.

Just after Christmas, 1958, we packed up all our belongings again ready to move to Ilford in Essex where I had secured a new and better-paid position. We were really sorry to move from Stratford on Avon which was such a lovely place, and felt very sad to be leaving all the good friends we had made. On my very last day of working there, I took in a bottle of rather strong, Polish cherry vodka to share with my colleagues. It was very smooth and pleasant to drink but my boss did not realise how strong it was and after drinking it, couldn't 'find his legs'. As he moved towards the door, he had difficulty finding the handle, but when he finally went out, we all burst out laughing!

# CHAPTER 18: MOVING AND MORE MOVING

## 31/12/1958 – 28/02/1990 (AGE 32-64)

### *JERZY DĄBROWSKI*

Ilford, in Essex, seemed to have just one claim to fame; the only complete skull of a mammoth in the UK was found there in 1864! The town lies on the main route from London to Colchester and used to be a major coaching stop. In Ilford, as Deputy Head of the Architectural Division of Ilford Borough Council, more interesting work came my way and I was dealing with buildings other than housing. For instance, I designed a park pavilion, a new library, a covered swimming pool and several multi-level buildings of shops and offices some of which had underground car-parks.

The neighbours called us 'The Royal Family of Easternville Gardens' because of my smart, black Vauxhall Cresta. There was an old air-raid shelter in the garden, that the children loved climbing in and out of, but which was full of mouldering apples from the tree! Gwen had a severe bout of appendicitis here when she was four months pregnant, but recovered well from the operation, and gave birth, on Leap Year's day, 29th February 1960, to our fourth child, a second daughter we named Hazel.

I continued to advance in my career and was appointed to the post of Chief Architectural Assistant in Esher, Surrey, in the south of London. My office looked out on Sandown Racecourse, which was created in 1875 and was the first purpose-built enclosed racecourse in the UK for the nobility. On race days the traffic was so heavy it was difficult to drive home. We moved to Esher in 1962 and enjoyed living amongst the film stars, famous sportsmen and stockbrokers with their tennis courts and swimming pools, although we felt very out of place in our provided council accommodation! In front of our house was a green open space which the children enjoyed playing on, and behind it was a small wood in which there was a derelict house. Squirrels emerged from the trees and came right up to the back door of our home for food. We usually shopped at Kingston-on-Thames at the weekends, treating ourselves to lunch at Bentalls Department Store.

Family walks around the beautiful Claremont Lake to feed the ducks were also popular; this lake is now owned by the National Trust. Queen Victoria was a frequent visitor to Claremont Mansion, both as a child and as queen. She lent it to the exiled French King, Louis-Philippe, after the French 'February Revolution' of 1848 which had overturned the restored monarchy and brought in the French Second Republic. Hampton Court Palace was only two miles away from our home and we visited it frequently. It was built by Cardinal Wolsey in the early 16$^{th}$ century but somehow became the property of King Henry VIII who brought all his six wives there to live – but not at the same time! It had lovely gardens, an orangery, a maze and the first Tudor tennis court.

During my employment in Esher, I designed and supervised several housing estates and also a number of building schemes for residential homes for the elderly. Esher Council allowed me to spend a little more money on these projects than was usually granted, so I was able to use better quality materials and add trees to the streets and parks. Council Estates had never looked so classy.

Our next move, in 1964, was to Colchester in Essex where I was appointed Deputy Borough Architect. Colchester claims the title of 'oldest town in Britain', and as Camulodunum, it was the capital town of Roman Britain. Colchester has always had a military base since Roman Times and is still home to the Colchester Garrison. The castle is the biggest 11$^{th}$ century Norman keep in Britain and 'Jumbo' is the largest Victorian water tower. The house provided for us in Colchester was on the very busy by-pass near a roundabout. It was not at all suitable for our four growing children, and so I purchased a piece of land on a quiet estate in an area called 'Prettygate', and designed our next house myself. We moved in on my 40$^{th}$ birthday, March 1966, and I also took possession of my new car, another Vauxhall Cresta, which was big enough for all six of us. Colchester was fairly close to the sea so we often drove to the east coast, to Clacton-on-Sea, Walton-on-the-Naze or other seaside towns. For holidays we chose to go to other coastal resorts such as Cromer in Norfolk, Scarborough in Yorkshire, or Grange-over-Sands near the Lake District.

Gwen had always enjoyed sewing and was very skilled at it. She discovered that she could earn some 'pin' money by working from home, making clothes for well-known companies, and so an industrial sewing-machine provided for her found a home in the front room. She also made dresses for her daughters, knitted tiny jumpers for babies, and designed children's and doll's clothes. Unfortunately, also in 1966, Gwen had became very unwell again, suffering another major nervous breakdown which affected the whole family in different ways, for many years to come.

A fairly considerable part of my time in the office at my new job was spent advising planning officers on the architectural aspects of Planning Applications. I was asked to prepare a list of buildings with outstanding architectural or historical value in the area, and I made several designs for new houses and new housing estates, which included pubs and churches. I was part of a group working on the design of a new swimming pool and sports complex which was to include a new central library, and I also had to do some restorative work on really old timber-framed buildings, some of which had proved to be unsafe.

Some Polish people who lived locally were organising a new Polish Club in Colchester, and finding my name in the telephone directory, talked me into becoming a member. At the very first meeting, in 1966, I found myself elected onto the committee and was asked to speak a few words in my by-now very rusty Polish but fluency soon came back to me. Each year the club held a Christmas party and I had the privilege, on occasion, to act as St Nicolas, who was the Polish Santa Claus, and give presents to the children.

I attended the Roman Catholic Church of St Teresa in Lexden, Colchester which served a large diocese to the west of Colchester, and which included many villages. In 1969, I was asked if I would be willing to design a new church for them because the existing one, built before the war, was too small for the growing congregation. The Parish Priest wanted something traditional without any towers, and the Parish Committee wanted it to look modern. Somehow I managed to please everyone! My contemporary design had seven gables on each side, a glazed lantern above the altar, and could accommodate 400 people. The church was completed in 1971 and in January 1972, held the very first ecumenical service for all Christian denominations in the area. That same year, the Bishop of Brentwood celebrated Mass there himself rather than at his cathedral!

By 1971, the three older children had completed their schooling and the youngest had completed her Primary Education. Christopher had won a place in Glamorgan Polytechnic college in Pontypridd, South Wales, to do Computer Science – this was right at the start of the computer revolution; Linda started her training to be a PE and Music teacher, at Dartford College of Physical Education in Kent, and Andrew started work in Tollesbury, Essex, working on car radios, sparking a life-long interest in radio, TV and electronics.

Two years later, the local government was being reorganised and Colchester itself was to be enlarged. The Borough Architect decided to retire too and because they usually appointed people from outside the area for these top jobs, I knew I would not be in the running to take over from him. I decided therefore to look for another appointment.

I commenced working for a large, private Architectural Firm, John Brunton and Partners, in Bradford, West Yorkshire, in March 1973. Bradford lies in the foothills of the Pennines. The water is soft and was well suited for the first cottage industries of wool spinning and weaving during the Middle Ages. In the 19$^{th}$ Century, Bradford became prominent as an international centre of textile manufacture, rapidly becoming the 'wool capital of the world'. Through the industrial revolution, many industrial mills were built for the manufacture of textiles. The largest and most famous was Lister's Mill in Manningham which employed thousands of women and children. The mill was originally driven by huge steam boilers and the chimney is an enormous 250 feet tall and so wide that apparently a horse and cart could be driven around its very top! During the second world war, Lister's Mill produced miles of parachute silk. In 1853, Titus Salt, who owned five mills, built a model village for all his workers at Salt's Mill and named it Saltaire, a few miles from Bradford. It is now a UNESCO World Heritage site.

After a few weeks, I found a suitable five-bedroomed house with a large garden to buy and we moved in on the 25th of April. Only our youngest two children moved to Bradford with us because Christopher was working first in Stevenage then Coventry, and Linda was still studying in Dartford. In Bradford, Andrew was able to continue with his City and Guilds course in TV and audio equipment while Hazel continued with her schooling. As we were unpacking our possessions, to my surprise the telephone rang – I didn't even know it had been connected already! Our oldest son, Christopher was on the phone. 'Dad, you're a grandad!' he announced. So our very first grandchild, Cheryl, arrived on our moving day.

My new firm, Bruntons, was very generous: in addition to providing me with a car and giving me a petrol allowance, they also paid for all the legal expenses connected with buying the house and moving to Bradford. The countryside in Yorkshire was beautiful and we enjoyed driving to the moors and walking on the hills. We visited many historic towns including Harrogate and Ripon, and Howarth, home of the Bronte sisters and the book 'Wuthering Heights'.

A large number of Polish people lived in Bradford; they had their own Catholic church and two Polish Clubs. I soon found out that one of my friends from the Cadets' School in Palestine was celebrating his birthday at one of the clubs. I hadn't seen him since 1944 so we had plenty to talk about and we shared many pre-war Polish jokes. I was warmly welcomed with lots of drink top-ups and went home rather 'merry'.

My main project with Bruntons Architectural Partnership, was to help design a 9-storey high office block called Jacob's Well. When it was complete, it was taken over by the new Bradford Metropolitan District Council for their principal offices. I was also given the responsibility of adapting over thirty buildings for their new use, including Town Halls and old Council Offices at, for instance, Keighley, Bingley and Ilkley. I found this work very satisfying because, for the first time, I was able to select suitable contractors without obtaining competitive tenders.

Following the three-day working week in 1974, many firms got into financial difficulties. Bruntons lost the contracts for several multi-million pounds schemes, including the £6 million allocated for an extension to the Jacob's Well Project. The firm decided to make all of their employees who had been there for less than two years redundant. I had held my post for only 18 months so early in September 1974, within a few days of returning from my first, emotional trip back to Poland, I found myself out of a job, with only two months notice to help me find another and relocate.

I applied for many jobs further south where it was warmer. I actually accepted a post in Redditch at first, as Principal Planner with the Urban District Council, but within two weeks of starting there, I received invitations to attend interviews for another twelve posts. However, the newly formed Vale of White Horse District Council, based in Abingdon, Oxfordshire, was advertising for an Architect to the Council and this post seemed ready-made just for me. The designation was later changed to Chief Architect! Twenty eight people had applied, and six were shortlisted. I put my success in winning the job down the fact that I was already a Fellow of the Royal Institute of British Architects (FRIBA) and also because I had made everyone laugh during the interview. The sun had been shining fully into my face and I said jokingly, 'I know I am under the spotlight, but this is ridiculous!'

Gwen and I, with Andrew and Hazel again, finally moved to Abingdon early in 1975. Abingdon is a historic market town which used to trade extensively in wool and textiles. Roman remains lie beneath the town and the Abbey dates from the 7th century. The MG car factory found its home in Abingdon from 1929-1980, and Abingdon's brewery, Morland, named its most famous ale, 'Old Speckled Hen' after an early MG model.

The Vale of White Horse District Council was responsible for a large area which included 69 parishes from Swindon to Oxford. My work was to advise on all the architectural aspects of planning applications, of which there were over 400 a year. I took charge of all new building contracts, the restoration of old and historic buildings, and large scale improvements to the social housing stock. I also had to attend a very large number of committee meetings. In 1976, I became a member of the Society of Chief Architects of Local Authorities, and attended several conferences with them as well as visiting many important new developments. In addition, I went to many of the conferences of the Royal Institute of British Architects and just happened to be in York the day before York Minster was set on fire by a bolt of lightning. It wasn't caused by me looking for a new building to design!

From 1976 – 1989 I represented the Council on SEMLAC (South East Midland Local Authority Consortium) which was a group of twelve different councils working together. The last few years before my retirement I went back to the drawing board and personally designed several schemes of sheltered homes for the elderly. My final project included 60 flatlets, which adjoined 5 bungalows for more able elderly people, and a wing for the Alzheimer's Disease Society for specialist care. The complex was named 'Vale House' and was in Botley near Oxford. I retired in February 1990, but this building was finally opened in November of the same year by HRH Diana, Princess of Wales. I still have a photo with us both at the opening ceremony.

In 1989, the Vale of White Horse District Council decided to use private architectural firms for their future building works, and all members of my staff were made redundant. I was the last to leave at the end of February 1990, taking early retirement. I was given a great send off in the presence of most of the staff of every department of the Council, many friends I had worked with, and representatives of the local press! I was presented with an encyclopaedia, and with the *Times Atlas of the World* to tempt me to travel more and further afield. The presentation was made by the top man, the Chairman of the Council and the Director of Planning and Development. They made long speeches about the success of the Architects' Division since it was formed in 1974, with myself as the first, last and only Chief Architect.

So just before my 64$^{th}$ birthday, I suddenly found myself an OAP!

# IN THE SPOTLIGHT: JERZY DĄBROWSKI'S MAJOR ARCHITECTURAL PROJECTS

*LINDA GALLAGHER*

### St Teresa of Lisieux RC Church, Colchester, Essex, 1971

My father was invited to design a new building for the church he attended regularly while living in Colchester, Essex. The original St Teresa's RC Church in Lexden, Colchester, was built in 1937 and still survives as the Parish Hall. A larger, modern building but with traditional elements was required for the growing congregation, and so Jerzy designed a contemporary church which could accommodate a congregation of 400 people. It was opened in September 1971.

The unusual building has seven gables on each side so the interior is very well-lit , and it has a cross-over roof-beam design which adds an internal dramatic effect. There is a raised lantern made of glass above the altar and some quality artwork within the church, including a statue of the Risen Christ made of bronze by a local artist which is placed above the outside entrance canopy. The church building has more recently undergone some essential refurbishment.

### Jacob's Well, Bradford, Yorkshire, 1973

John Brunton and Partners architectural firm in Bradford, which employed my father for two years from 1973-5, was well-known for its design of 'Brutalist' structures built as part of the reconstruction of the nation after WW2. These buildings were not always well received in towns such as Bradford which had a strong Victorian heritage. The style emerged from the modernist movement of the early 20th century, and consisted of very large, blocky, geometric constructions built of poured concrete. The buildings had few or small windows and were commonly designed for government use or as public buildings.

My father designed one large and important structure in Bradford, named 'Jacob's Well', after the public house that was originally built on that site in 1830. Jerzy's design had a prefabricated, reinforced concrete frame and apparently was rather banal in appearance. It was built in 1973 and opened a year later, housing offices predominantly for Bradford Council. It later became vacant and was demolished in 2016.

## Vale House, Botley, Oxford, 1990

This specialist facility for people with Alzheimer's Disease and dementia, designed by my father, was opened in 1990 by Diana, Princess of Wales, who actually met my father at the event. At the time of writing, it is the only care home in Oxford to be rated 'outstanding'!

The building was founded with one clear purpose in mind, to care for people with dementia, however severe and complicated, and to support their families. It was so popular that the facility moved to an enlarged and more central location in Littlemore, Oxford, in 2012.

It is ironic that my father, who suffered with Alzheimer's Disease himself for the last few years of his life, and lived only a few miles away, wasn't able to reside in the place he had designed.

# CHAPTER 19: BACK TO POLAND AT LAST

## 1974, 1979, 1990, 1993
## (AGES 48, 53, 64, 67)

### JERZY DĄBROWSKI

As I mentioned earlier, it was only in the summer of 1974 that I finally felt able to return to Poland for a visit, 35 years after I had been deported. Gwen and the younger two children came as well. We drove to Harwich, caught the all night ferry to Bremerhaven in Germany, and then continued driving through West Germany, to East Germany which left a very gloomy impression on us. Nobody smiled and everyone seemed to be alert, looking over their shoulder rather than face-to-face. The motorways that had been built by Hitler's government were full of pot-holes and there was very little traffic – the majority of cars seemed to be police cars. When we got to the Polish border at Świecko near Frankfurt on the River Oder, it was a relief to see that the Polish guardsman was cheerful and jokey.

It would be impossible for me to describe my feelings upon stepping on Polish soil for the first time since the beginning of the war, when I was only thirteen. I was quite apprehensive and a bit afraid that the Communist Authorities may arrest me again and send me back to Siberia; even though I had a British Passport and had been a British Citizen for many years, according to them it seemed I was still a citizen of Poland. Many who did return had been branded as traitors, imprisoned or deported again, or executed, even years after the war ended. Luckily, they let us continue to Poznań, one of the oldest cities in Poland, where my first cousin lived. One of the city's most renowned landmarks is the famous ancient Poznań Town Hall with its head-butting Frolic Goats clock.

We were given a marvellous reception at Poznań and so decided to stay a day longer with my relatives than we'd planned to give ourselves time to catch up on the missing years properly. My cousin gave us a tour of the area and we visited Gniezno with its cathedral, swam in a lake in a beautiful forest, and went to a museum packed with many historic beehives built in various shapes such as buildings, trees and people, each with a swarm living inside. While in Poznań, we visited my mother's youngest sister who greeted us with open arms. Typical of Polish hospitality, she had made a magnificent four-course meal for us, after which she presented us with some wonderful cakes. We were so full that when we refused them, she asked 'Don't you like my cooking?' When we first arrived in Poland we only had three addresses to visit, but after Poznań we had another twelve, and at every place the ladies made us special Polish cakes and gateaux which pleased us all.

From Poznań we drove to Racibórz, Silesia, where another of my cousins lived. He was a well-known surgeon and his wife was also a doctor in the same hospital there. We visited Krystyna, who was my mother's sister's daughter, as well as towns, castles, mountains and lakes. One very hot day, when the temperature was about 42° C, I parked the car in the sun and when we returned it refused to start. I opened the bonnet but then a police officer came and helped us push the car into shade. Once the engine had cooled and could start, he provided a police convey for us to the nearest garage, at which point he saluted and left us!

My cousin in Racibórz booked us into one of the best hotels in Zakopane, the luxurious Kasprowy Hotel that overlooked the mountain of the same name which was part of the Tatra range. The Tatra Mountains are home to much wildlife including the chamois, marmot, lynx and bears. Zakopane is a charming town that has many examples of the typical regional, traditional, wooden architecture with its pointed roofs. One of my Polish friends from Bradford in England had arranged for me to meet the Town Architect of Zakopane; this kind gentleman enabled us to park in a private car park then took us onto the cable car up Krasprowy Wierch mountain without queueing. The mountain is at the crossroads of four crests with many footpaths and steps, which are the boundaries of both Poland and Slovakia. At the top is a large restaurant and information building with ski lifts outside.

This new friend also took us to the two famous deep lakes, Morskie Oko (the eye of the sea) and Czarny Staw (the black pond) that I had visited with my school just before the war started. You are not allowed to swim in either lake, nor feed the trout! Morskie Oko is reached either by a two-hour walk on foot, or by horse-drawn carriage. Legends suggest there was an underground passage joining it to the sea but this is unlikely for the distance is over 700 km. Czarny Staw is very clear, deep blue and has no fish and from a nearby rocky edge there is an amazing view of it in the deep valley.

Our British car was, of course, a right-hand drive car. One day, my son Andrew sat in the front passenger seat and fell asleep. Two Police Officers standing near the red traffic lights saw the car starting to move as the lights changed green but they thought that the driver had fallen asleep. They rushed over, drawing their guns and then realised they had made fools of themselves. We could not stop laughing!

From Zakopane, we drove to Kraków, the beautiful old capital of Poland. Here we visited Wawel Castle with its cathedral which was the first UNESCO World Heritage Site in the world. It was built by King Casimir the Great and is one of the largest fortified complexes in Poland, representing nearly all European architectural styles of mediaeval, renaissance and baroque periods. Many Polish kings were crowned, and later buried beneath the cathedral in the grounds. The Polish Pope, Jean Paul II, was previously the Archbishop of Kraków, based at Wawel Cathedral.

Just outside the castle, on the banks of the River Vistula, there is a statue of the mythical Kraków dragon which breathed out 'fire' every few minutes. This statue was built to commemorate the tale of how Kraków was founded. There are many variations of the story. Apparently the legendary King Krak (or Krakus) had to supply either some cattle (or maybe young maidens) every week to feed and appease the evil dragon who lived in a cave overlooking the river, or else the dragon would beat a path of destruction across the countryside, killing the civilians, pillaging their homes, and devouring their livestock. The King promised his daughter's hand in marriage to any brave knight who could kill the dragon, but many knights lost their lives trying. Finally, a cobbler named Skuba filled a sheep skin or a calf skin with sulphur and placed it outside the cave. The dragon swallowed what looked like an animal but the sulphur in his stomach burnt him so much that he kept drinking the water in the river until his stomach burst. Not a tale for the squeamish! Of course the shoemaker married the princess and everyone lived happily ever after!

Kraków market square is the largest in Europe; we drove right around it in an open landau and then visited the famous Cloth Hall which has a marvellous art gallery on the first floor, while the ground floor is full of tiny souvenir shops, many of which sold beautiful leather and wooden goods, and chess sets galore!

Later, on the way to Kielce to visit my nephew Andrzej, my sister's son, we drove through the magnificent Jurassic highlands of the Kraków-

Częstokowa chain of hills, seeing many unusual rock formations, such as the famous Club of Hercules, on the way. We were well received by Andrzej and his wife, Mira, and their 7 year old son Michał. We drove altogether one day to Skarżysko-Kamienna, my old home town where I used to live before the war. Andrzej's father, my sister's husband, also called Michał, lived there on the ground floor of a new block of flats built on a new housing estate.

The devastation the war had brought was still very much in evidence in Kielce. The town centre itself left such a sad impression. All the old buildings which had contained shops mainly owned by Jewish people, were still shut, and bullet holes could be seen in the walls. The streets were empty and the roads full of potholes. I visited my old grammar school which now looked so small. We found the three-storey flats where I had lived as a child and actually met the sister of one of my pre-war friends!

We all went to the cemetery in Kielce, and for the first time I visited the tomb of my mother, Albina, who had died during the war, in 1943 at age 47, while Poland was still under German occupation. She had suffered a great deal, being separated from her husband and two sons, not knowing what had happened to us, not knowing if she would ever see us again. In the last photo I had of her, which my sister had sent me, she looked as if she had doubled in age.

Seeing my mother's grave was a very traumatic experience for me. When I touched her gravestone I could not let go for over ten minutes. I sensed her telling me to send everyone else away so we could have some time alone. For those ten minutes we seemed to have some sort of spiritual communion. Afterwards, I placed some flowers on the gravestone, lit some candles and said prayers for her soul, then with great sadness in my heart, I left the cemetery with the others.

In Skarżysko-Kamienna, we visited the R C Church where I had been baptised, confirmed, and later served at the altar. We saw my old primary school, and the artificial lake in Rejów, with its dam rebuilt. Later we drove to the ancient oak tree called Bartek, which is in the Mountains of the Holy Cross. The woodlands here are full of the graves of the many members of the Polish Underground Army, including a few of my friends, who lost their lives fighting for freedom against the German invaders.

Our next significant stop was in Warsaw. Our hotel this time was the newly-built 32 storey Forum; from the top you could feel it sway in the wind. It faced the 'Palace of Culture', an ugly and typical building 'donated' by the Soviet Union. The people of Warsaw had made a joke about it.

*'Where is the best view point of Warsaw?'*
*'The top of the Palace of Culture because that is the only place where you cannot see it!'*

The old town of Warsaw, the capital of Poland, had been razed to the ground by the Nazis. But now, it was such a lovely surprise to see it all rebuilt apparently exactly as it was before the war. We were able to visit the Royal Palace where some internal restoration work was still taking place. Also the famous market square where all the buildings were rebuilt from drawings and paintings hidden from the Germans in the sewers. The following day we went to visit one of the most beautiful palaces, the Lazienki Palace, which is surrounded by water and a small lake.

The Forum Hotel was very expensive so after one night, we went to stay with Myszka, the youngest daughter of my mother's sister, who lived in Wołomin, near Warsaw. After a few more days sightseeing and shopping, we returned to Poznań, passing the tallest structure in Poland on the way, the Radio Raszyn

Tower near Płock, standing 2028 feet high. We also stopped at Toruń, the town where Nicolas Copernicus, famous for working out that the earth went round the sun rather than vice versa, was born. Early the next day we left Poznań for Bremmerhaven to catch the ferry back to England, having travelled over 300 miles by road that day, and arriving with two hours to spare.

My second trip back to Poland was undertaken 5 years later, in 1979, soon after the Polish Pope, John Paul II had visited it. Gwen, Andrew and Hazel accompanied me once more. This time we took the ferry from Felixstowe for a two-day journey across the North Sea to Świnoujście on the Baltic coast of northern Poland, sailing first all the way around Denmark where we hit a storm and took to our beds to prevent seasickness. Arriving late that afternoon, we discovered all the nearest hotels were full but finally found overnight accommodation at Szczecin (Stetin).

We repeated some of my first journey, staying with my cousin in Poznań for several days; this time our visits included the cathedral in which were the tombs of Poland's first two kings, and the mediaeval town hall where an urn containing the heart of my namesake, the famous 18th Century General Dąbrowski, was kept at this time. General Dąbrowski fought in the Napoleonic wars and is celebrated in the chorus of the Polish National Anthem – which is also known as 'Poland is Not Yet Lost' and 'Dąbrowski's Mazurka'.

From Poznań we went to Częstokowa, to the well-known Jasna Góra monastery of Roman Catholic pilgrimage, which looks after the famous and miraculous picture of the Black Madonna. This four-foot high painting, is also known as Our Lady of Częstochowa, and is a venerated icon of the Blessed Virgin Mary, whose painted face probably darkened over time and with the smoke of many candles lit before her. In the icon, the Virgin directs attention away from herself, gesturing with her right hand toward Jesus as the source of salvation. In turn, the child extends his right hand toward the viewer in blessing while holding a book of gospels in his left hand. The icon has been intimately associated with Poland for the past 600 years. Its history, prior to its arrival in Poland, is shrouded in numerous legends which trace the icon's origin to St Luke who apparently painted it on a cedar table top from the house of the Holy Family. It was rediscovered in Jerusalem in 326 by St. Helena who presented it to her son, Constantine the Great. It eventually made its way to Częstochowa.

We attended Mass at Częstokowa, in front of the icon, and for a split second I felt the eyes of Our Lady fixed on me and she seemed to be saying to me, 'Most of the people here need my help but you are alright and don't need anything from me!' This experience made a lifelong impression on me.

We continued travelling through Kraków to Zakopane and stayed a few days in a villa belonging to the friend of yet another of my many cousins. On the river Dunajec near the Tatra Mountains, we joined a rafted contraption of five boats to 'Shoot the Rapids'. Unfortunately, halfway through the two-hour journey, a thick mist descended and we were unable to see Trzy Czorsztyn (The Three Crowns), the highest peak of the Pieniny mountain range, with its steep, forested drop towards the river in the valley.

On leaving Zakopane, we travelled to Kielce to stay with my nephew, Andrzej, my sister's son, with whom we had stayed previously. Once again we drove to Skarżysko-Kamienna to see my mother's grave in the cemetery, but this time I did not have any traumatic experiences. From Kielce we returned to Warsaw via the small historic town of Kazimierz named after the 14th Century King of Poland, Casimir the Great. I managed to discover the address of the only cousin on my Father's side who lived in Łodz and we really enjoyed visiting them for the first time since the war. We drove back to Poznań then had a relaxing woodland walk while waiting for our ferry back to England.

I went to Poland alone on my next two trips. In May 1990, just after I retired, I wanted to visit the members of my family again, since my last trip had been 11 years ago and we were all getting older! Things had changed and it was a joy to drive part of the way on the smooth German Autobahn. At this time, since the Berlin Wall had fallen, East and West Germany were being united so I had no trouble at the borders. I stayed once more with my Mother's youngest sister, now 87 years old, in Poznań; this was the last time I saw her alive. I also visited my relatives in Łodz, Warsaw and Kielce. We travelled once again to Skarżysko-Kamienna where, this time, I was pleased to meet one of my pre-war school friends who was able to tell me what had happened to so many of the people we had known.

My final journey to Poland took place in 1993, when I was 67 years old. At the time, I didn't know that it would be my last trip there. I caught the night ferry to Hamburg which allowed me to get to Poland without any over-night stops. This time I stayed in a woodland house near Poznań with Marek, the grandson of my mother's sister who had now died. Near here was a chapel erected by grateful parishioners to the memory of my Father's brother who was a Parish Priest and a Canon in that village. Alone, I found I had the freedom to visit many relatives, close or distant both family-wise and geographically, some of whom I had seen on my previous trips to Poland. It was amazing to catch-up and feel that once again I really belonged in Poland. Sadly, many of my relatives had died already, or would die over the following few years, because of old age or illness. While travelling around, I also visited several towns and places of historic interest.

Of course, I had to see my nephew, Andrzej in Kielce. Unfortunately, his wife Mira had had a stroke which had left her partially paralysed. We went to the historic city of Sandomierz with its famous cathedral, and then on to Skarżysko-Kamienna, where I had spent my early childhood up till the war. We visited my mother's grave again, and also the grave of my brother-in-law, my sister Halina's husband.

With Andrzej, I also spent some time with the old school friend I'd met last time, who was able to supply me with the addresses of other schoolfriends I had known. One of them, whom I hadn't seen for 54 years, still lived in Kielce, and we had an amazing reunion. He had been a leader of one of the Polish Underground Units fighting the Germans. However, when the Soviets invaded, to 'liberate' Poland from the Germans, he was put in prison for 5 years because he wasn't a grateful communist sympathiser.

Once again, I went to Warsaw, this time with my cousin's daughter, and heard Mass, celebrated by Cardinal Glemp, the Catholic Primate of Poland in the presence of Lech Wałęsa, the President of Poland, in the Cathedral of St John. We stopped at Frederick Chopin's mansion on the way back to Łodz, where I was able to relax for a few days with my cousin on my Father's side, before my long drive back to England.

Although I did have many other holidays abroad both before and during my retirement, this proved to be my last trip to Poland but I still felt it was my real home.

# IN THE SPOTLIGHT: REBUILDING WARSAW

## LINDA GALLAGHER

The razing of Warsaw right to the ground had long been planned by Hitler, as part of his Germanisation of Western Europe. The capital city of Poland had been selected for destruction and then major reconstruction, but once they realised that the war was lost, the Germans abandoned the idea of rebuilding the city, and their final act of flattening it was done solely in reprisal.

Hitler and his troops virtually destroyed Warsaw on two occasions; the first time was during their initial invasion of Poland in 1939, which initiated Poland's surrender. The second time, when the Germans were retreating from the 'victorious' Soviet Army, was in retaliation for the Warsaw Uprising of 1944, during which 20,000 Nazi troops died. During this battle, over 16,000 members of the Polish Resistance and over 150,000 civilians were killed or executed in the 63 days of the land battle and the air strikes. Warsaw and its cultural heritage was systematically plundered and destroyed to ground level, and thousands of corpses were later found buried in the rubble.

British Pathé film archive footage from 1950, and photos of the wreckage taken at the time, show the extent of the shocking devastation. Across much of Warsaw, 80-90% of the buildings were destroyed and all that remained appeared to be the ruined walls of ground floors and basements. Many of the Varsovians, the citizens of Warsaw, who had not fled, inhabited these basements. Only about 175,000 Polish citizens were left alive in Warsaw, less than 6% of the pre-war population. Clouds of dust continually threatened to asphyxiate all who ventured outside, and someone calculated that each person had inhaled the equivalent of four bricks per year! The authorities initially suggested that the remains of Warsaw should be left as they were to memorialise the war, and the entire capital of Poland relocated, but the inhabitants loved their city so much they were willing to suffer with their every polluted breath to help rebuild it and bring it back to life.

The Old Town of Warsaw was particularly affected by the destruction. Once the war was over, local Varsovians rallied together to clear the vast amounts of debris. Any fragments of the original Old Town buildings were recovered to be used in the reconstruction, and various architectural features were kept to be copied onto the rebuilt facades. The former Jewish Ghetto area, which had already been completely flattened by the Nazis after the 1943 Warsaw Ghetto Uprising, provided much of the material for new bricks, and more building supplies were brought in as needed from neighbouring ruined towns. Much of the detailed work was done off-site by construction workers and specialist builders from all round Poland.

**Reconstruction of Old Warsaw**

Even the Soviet puppet government – as well as the Polish people – was interested in restoring Warsaw to the beauty of its 'Golden Age' of 200 years before rather than creating a modern concrete, communist town. Many local people still possessed photos of pre-war Warsaw in their family albums which helped in the restructuring. These, along with the expertise of Polish architects, the knowledge of art historians and the encouragement of conservators, as well as the committed builders, meant that the reconstruction of Old Warsaw was completed in an impressively short time.

The architects were able to copy the beautiful paintings of Bernardo Bellotto, a nephew of the Italian artist Canaletto. In the 'Golden Age' of the 18th century,

Bellotto was Court Painter to the King of Poland and his pictures show, with great accuracy, the historic buildings, city-scapes, squares and gardens of Warsaw at that time. For unaccountable reasons, all of Bellotto's 22 street scenes of Warsaw survived the war, despite the Nazis stealing them from Warsaw's Royal Castle in 1939 in order to destroy them. The pictures, which were found by the American Art Protection Service in Callenberg Castle, the summer residence of the Dukes of Coberg, were reclaimed by Poland in 1946 and returned to Warsaw where they were finally reinstated in the newly rebuilt Royal Castle in 1983. The modern city is not an entirely accurate re-creation of his paintings; Bellotto had traced pencil drawings of the architecture using a Camera Obscura, which led to some minor inaccuracies, and then transferred them on to canvas, before finishing them off with watercolour paint. However, he had paid almost excessive attention to architectural detail and so these paintings could be used, almost 200 years later, as a reference for reconstructing each building as accurately as possible in approximately its original place. Most of the rebuilding of the city was completed by 1955, though some work is still on-going even today. One church, The Visitants' Church, still retains some of the original pipes of the organ played by Chopin! Today, reproductions of Belloto's paintings line the streets of Warsaw's Old Town, on boards which explain their crucial role in the rebuilding process. Everywhere in the city there are pertinent reminders of Poland's history of devastation and reconstruction. The wreckage of the war has now been transformed into what is now a UNESCO World Heritage Site.

# CHAPTER 20: TRAVELS AND RETIREMENT (EPILOGUE)

## VARIOUS DATES UP TO 2018 (AGE 92)

### LINDA GALLAGHER

The final chapter of this impressive story had to be written by me, and not my father. In his original memoir, which ended in 1994, my father wrote at length about his many holidays abroad, and about his children; although that may be of great interest to his family, it is not so captivating for the general reader. Instead, I have taken the liberty of condensing the final few years of life into this short narrative which shows how his zest for life continued until it became impossible to sustain.

Jerzy always loved maps and spent much time studying them, whether World Atlases, maps of different countries, or local OS maps. He also loved geography and travelling; this passion stayed with him despite his war experiences. So it is no surprise to know that apart from visiting Poland four times, he also travelled quite extensively while still working and in early retirement. He visited his eldest son, Chris, twice in South Africa, and took holidays in places such as the Canaries, the Algarve and Yugoslavia.

While living in Abingdon, Jerzy and Gwen enjoyed driving locally to visit delightful formal gardens or beautiful countryside, and eating meals out in picturesque country pubs, as well as seeing their children and grandchildren.

The year 2007 was very eventful for the Dąbrowski family. First of all, in May, Jerzy fell off a step ladder and fractured his skull on the edge of a paving slab, causing much bleeding in the brain. The doctors said that, at age 81, he only had a 1% chance of surviving this, and if he did survive, he would probably be a 'vegetable'. Of course we all said that he was an incredible survivor from his war experiences and that he would recover. After 4 months he was back at home with Gwen and beginning to take charge of his life once more. Amazing!

In the June of 2007, Oxford and Abingdon were severely affected by flooding. It was a year of tremendous rainfall in the UK and just one month after Jerzy had had his fall, and while he was still in hospital, our parents' house in Abingdon was flooded which caused much additional distress to Gwen. A small flat was found for her and when Jerzy was discharged, he joined her there until their home could be dried out, redecorated and furnished and made more suitable for them to live in.

By the year 2012, at the age of 86, Jerzy was showing signs of memory loss and a couple of years later was subsequently diagnosed with Alzheimer's Dementia. Gwen had never really recovered from the flooding and began to get very depressed. Also, they both had underlying physical health issues of various kinds and began to need more help at home. In May 2015, for her own health and safety after several falls, Gwen was accommodated in a Residential Home in Oxford. She died there in December, 2015 at the exemplary age of 87. A gentle and sensitive funeral service was held on January 12th 2016.

Jerzy's dementia progressed quite rapidly after Gwen's death and in July 2016, he was offered a place at a Care Home near Abingdon. He settled down well but the disease progressed and Jerzy, being such an independent man, became rather difficult to deal with. A year later he was moved to a specialist dementia unit at a Residential Home near Abingdon. Here he used his charm to great effect and everyone liked him: he was very well cared for during his whole stay. By the following summer, we could all see a marked deterioration in his condition; he became unable to walk or do anything for himself, and his speech was very confused.

Jerzy died peacefully in this home, aged 92, in August, 2018. He left behind four children, eight grandchildren (two of whom were adopted) and seven great-grandchildren (all of whom are my grandchildren). He certainly deserved his rest!

His Funeral Service was held three weeks later by a very kind and thoughtful priest, Father Rob, at St Edmund's Roman Catholic Church in Abingdon which Jerzy had attended for over 40 years. All four of his children were able to attend. The priest gave up trying to pronounce the Polish names of towns and people in Dad's homily when he saw how much we were all laughing at his efforts, and he was relieved when we told him that for almost of all of his life in England, Jerzy had been known as 'Terry'! Jerzy's committal took place at a Crematorium in South Oxford.

In February the following year, 2019, I arranged for there to be an interment of both parents' ashes together in a wooden casket. Unusually, because the graveyard of St Edmund's church was already very crowded, we were granted permission to do this in recognition of Jerzy's long membership there of over 40 years. Apparently there was just enough space for the casket and a smart memorial stone! The same priest, Father Rob, officiated at this simple ceremony.

Jerzy wrote his original memoirs between 1992 and 1994, aged 66 - 68 years. We, his wider family, would like our father's story to be available for future generations, to add to the growing number of stories that are now being written about the terrible fate of the thousands of Polish people deported to Siberia during the war. For many, these harrowing stories are either unknown or unacknowledged but the world needs to know how the Polish nation was treated and let down.

Jerzy Henryk Dąbrowski was an amazing man who picked himself up when he had lost everything he'd had in Poland, and made a very successful life for himself in England.

Linda, Chris, Gwen, and Andrew in the pram

Camping with Genevieve at Barmouth

Jerzy's new Cresta

Dąbrowski Family at Lavenham

Jerzy's nephew (Halina's son) Andrzej and wife Mira

A childhood friend – 54 years later

The grave of Jerzy's mother, Albina, in Kielce

Andrzej (pictured earlier) is buried with Albina

Jerzy at work

The Dąbrowski Family 2005. From the right – Front row - Gwen and Jerzy. Back row (and in order of age) - Chris, Linda, (the author), Andrew and Hazel.

Jerzy's 80th birthday, 2006

Jerzy's 90th birthday, 2016

Photos from funeral programmes – both pictures are from when they were about 80 years old. Gwen died in 2015 aged 87, and Jerzy died in 2018 aged 92 years.

# Jerzy's Unplanned Wartime Journey

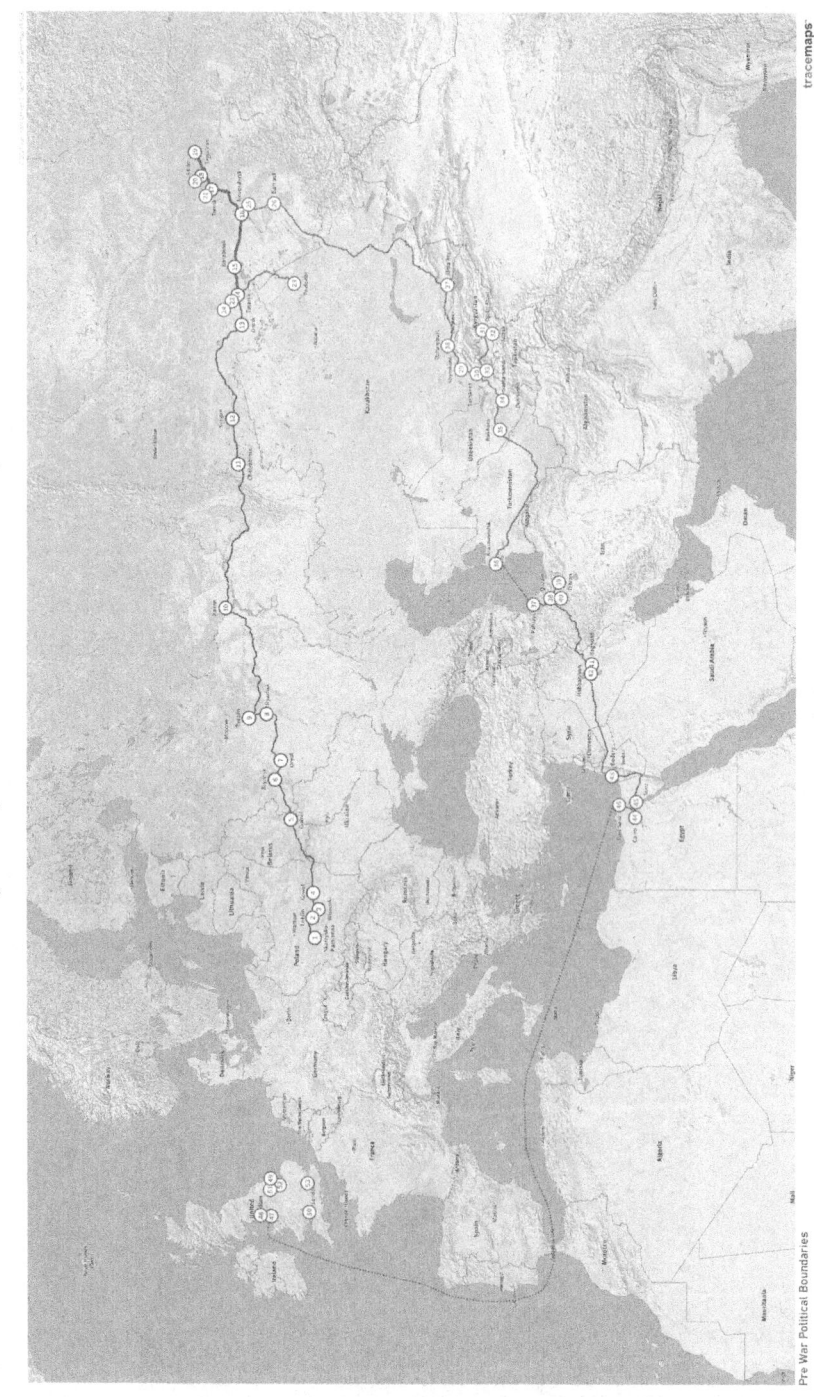

# Map Legend

## Invasion of Poland - September 1st 1939

1. Skarzysko-Kamienna to Lublin
2. Lublin to Wiszenki
3. Wiszenki to Kowel
4. Kowel to Gomel
5. Gomel to Bryansk
6. Bryansk to Oryol
7. Oryol to Ryazhsk
8. Ryazhsk to Ryazan
9. Ryazan to Kazan
10. Kazan to Chelyabinsk
11. Chelyabinsk to Kurgan
12. Kurgan to Omsk
13. Omsk to Tatarsk
14. Tatarsk to Barabinsk
15. Barabinsk to Novosibirsk
16. Novosibirsk to Tomsk
17. Tomsk to Asino
18. Asino to Teguldet

## Amnesty - August 12th 1941

19. Teguldet to Asino
20. Asino to Tomsk
21. Tomsk to Tatarsk
22. Tatarsk to Pavlodar
23. Pavlodar to Tatarsk
24. Tatarsk to Novosibirsk
25. Novosibirsk to Barnaul
26. Barnaul to Alma Aty
27. Alma Aty to Dzhamburl
28. Dzhamburl to Shymkent
29. Shymkent to Tashkent
30. Tashkent to Djalal Abad
31. Djalal Abad to Suzak
32. Suzak to Taskent
33. Tashkent to Samarkand
34. Samarkand to Bukhara
35. Bukhara to Krasnovodsk

## Freedom - March 28th 1942

36. Krasnovodsk to Pahlavi
37. Pahlavi to Qazvin
38. Qazvin to Tehran
39. Tehran to Qazvin
40. Qazvin to Baghdad
41. Baghdad to Habbaniyah
42. Habbaniyah to Gedera
43. Gedera to Cairo
44. Cairo to Suez
45. Suez to Port Said
46. Port Said to Liverpool

## Life in England - October 22nd 1944

47. Liverpool
48. Blackpool
49. RAF Faldingworth
50. RAF Locking
51. RAF Cammeringham
52. RAF Dunholme
53. Polish School of Architecture

tracemaps™

# TIMELINE OF THE KEY EVENTS OF WW2 AND JERZY DĄBROWSKI'S JOURNEY

| Key Events of WW2 | Before the war | Jerzy's Story |
|---|---|---|
| | 1922 | Stanislaw (Stach) Dabrowski born |
| | 1926 Mar 14 | Jerzy Henryk Dabrowski born in Skarżysko-Kamienna, Poland |
| Germany annexes Austria | 1938 Mar 11–13 | |
| Munich Agreement allows Nazi Germany to re-arm and invade the Sudetenland of Czechoslovakia | 1938 Sept 29 | |

| Key Events of WW2 | 1939 | Jerzy's Story (aged 13) |
|---|---|---|
| Molitov-Ribbentrop Pact – signed by Nazi Germany and the Soviet Union which includes a secret protocol dividing Poland between them | Aug 23 | |
| Gleiwitz incident - fabricated excuse by Nazis for invasion of Poland | Aug 31 | |
| Germany invades Poland, starting World War II in Europe | Sept 1 | Bombers attack the Polish Munitions factory in Skarżysko-Kamienna |
| Great Britain and France declare war on Germany | Sept 3 | |
| | Sept 6 | Jerzy, his father and brother + 40 others flee - they cycle to Polish border with Ukraine |

| Key Events of WW2 | | Jerzy's Story (aged 13-14) |
|---|---|---|
| The Soviet Union invades Poland from the east without warning | Sept 17 | |
| | Sept 13 | Jerzy, Stach and their father arrive at Wiszenki village |
| | Sept 22 | Red Army soldiers plunder Wiszenki |
| Warsaw surrenders to Nazis and the Polish government flees into exile | Sept 27–29 | |
| Soviet elections in East Poland falsified | Oct 22 | |

| Key Events of WW2 | 1940 | Jerzy's Story (aged 13-14) |
|---|---|---|
| Katyn Forest Massacre begins – Soviets murder 22,000 Polish army officers | March 5 | |
| Operation Dynamo – Dunkirk evacuated | June 4 | |
| Third Wave of Deportations to Siberia | June 29 | Jerzy with brother Stach and their father deported to Siberia in cattle trucks by Soviets |
| The Battle of Britain – defeat for Nazi Germany | Jul 10 – Oct 31 | |
| | July 15 | They arrive at labour settlement at Sibyriak, Siberia |

| Key Events of WW2 | 1941 | Jerzy's Story (aged 14-15) |
|---|---|---|
| Operation Barbarossa - Nazi Germany breaks Molotov-Ribbentrop agreement and invades the Soviet Union | June 22 | |
| | May 27 | Jerzy's Father Michal dies in Siberia |
| Sikorski-Mayski Agreement between Soviets and Poland – Amnesty for Poles | July 30 | |

269

| | | |
|---|---|---|
| General Anders starts to form a Polish Army in Exile | Aug 4 | |
| | Jul 31 | Jerzy and Stach hear news of Amnesty - Raft building starts at settlement |
| Official Proclamation of the Amnesty – Poles in Siberia to be released | Aug 12 | |
| | Sept 18 | Jerzy and Stach and hundreds of others set off on rafts on the River Chulym – 2 weeks |
| | Oct 3 | They arrive at Asino and catch train to Pavlodar – |
| | Oct 15 | They arrive at Pavlodar – spend a month there |
| | Nov 16 | Jerzy and Stach register to join Polish army, catch train to Uzbekhistan |
| Japan bombs Pearl Harbour | Dec 7 | |
| | Dec 15 | Jerzy and Stach arrive in Dzhalal Abad to join army but instead sent to Susak to pick cotton |
| **Key Events of WW2** | **1942** | **Jerzy's Story (aged 15-16)** |
| German Wannsee Conference and the "Final Solution" to annihilate all Jews | Jan 20 | |
| | Feb 13 | Stach joins army, Jerzy becomes a batman. They have to split up. |
| | March | Jerzy travels to Krasnovodsk |
| Anders orders formal evacuation of Polish POWs from Soviet Union to Persia (Iran) | Mar 24 - Apr 4 | |

| Key Events of WW2 | | Jerzy's Story (aged 16-17) |
|---|---|---|
| | Mar 28 | Evacuation – Jerzy catches coal ship for a 2 day journey across Caspian Sea |
| | Mar 30 | Jerzy arrives in Pahlavi, Persia, and stays for 2 days - a free man |
| | Apr 1 | He travels through Iran and Iraq |
| | May 5 | He arrives at Habbaniyah, Iraq for 2½ weeks |
| | Late May | Jerzy arrives at Gedera in Palestine. He meets up with Stach again |
| Battle of Stalingrad between Nazis and Soviets starts | Aug 23 | |
| British troops defeat the Germans and Italians at El Alamein in Egypt | Oct 23 – Nov 11 | Jerzy's Cadet School moves to Qasina in Palestine |

| 1943 | | Jerzy's Story (aged 16-17) |
|---|---|---|
| | 20 Jan | Jerzy's mother, Albina dies under German occupation – aged 47 |
| German discovery of the Katyn Massacre | Apr 13 | |
| | Apr 23-25 | Jerzy is in Guard of Honour at Tomb of Christ in Jerusalem at Easter |
| General Sikorski, inspects Jerzy's camp at Qasina in Palestine | Late May | Jerzy is in the Guard of Honour when Sikorski inspects the Polish troops in Qasina, Palestine |
| Grand Military March in Cairo to celebrate El Alamein victory | Jun 14 | Grand Military March in Cairo – Jerzy's platoon of cadets represent Poland |

| Key Events of WW2 | | 1944 | Jerzy's Story (aged 17-18) |
|---|---|---|---|
| *General Sikorski killed in an air accident near Gibraltar* | *Jul 4* | Summer | Jerzy moves to Barbara Camp near Gaza in Palestine |
| | | Autumn | Jerzy starts final schooling for the Full Matriculation |
| *Tehran Conference – Roosevelt, Churchill and Stalin – appeasing Stalin with ideas for new Soviet/Polish border* | *Nov 28 – Dec 1* | | |
| | | Apr 1 | Jerzy leads April Fool trick – his cadet platoon march 4-5 miles to the Mediterranean Sea |
| | | Jul | Jerzy takes his Full Matriculation Exams and passes |
| D-Day Landings – British, US, and Canadian troops land on the Normandy beaches | Jun 6 | | |
| The first Nazi concentration camp, Majdanek, discovered by Soviet army | Jul 23 | | |
| Warsaw Uprising | Aug 1 – Oct 2 | | |
| | | Late Aug | Jerzy travels to Al Qassasin Camp, Egypt |
| | | Oct 3 | He travels to Suez and is made Platoon Leader |
| | | Oct 10 | Jerzy travels from Port Said, Egypt on the SS Strathmore Ship to UK |
| | | Oct 22 | Jerzy arrives at the Port of Liverpool, UK |
| | | Oct 24 | He travels to Blackpool – stays for 4-5 weeks |

| Key Events of WW2 | 1945 | Jerzy's Story (aged 18-19) |
|---|---|---|
| The Battle of the Bulge – Germany's last major offensive | December | |
| | Dec 16 | Jerzy is posted to RAF Bomber Command Station at Faldingworth, Linc, and joins Polish Bomber Squadron 300 |
| Yalta Conference to decide how to stop the war | Feb 4 - 11 | |
| Dresden bombed by UK and USA | Feb 13-15 | |
| | Early April | Jerzy transferred to RAF Locking, Weston Super mare, to train in Wireless Mechanics and Radar |
| Hitler commits suicide | Apr 30 | |
| Germany surrenders to the Allies | May 7 | |
| VE Day | May 8 | |
| Germany surrenders to the Soviets and all of Poland is under the Soviet puppet government | May 9 | |
| | May | Jerzy is transferred to RAF Cammeringham in Lincolnshire to continue Wireless Mechanics training |
| Potsdam Conference – to decide Poland's border with Germany | Jul 17 – Aug 2 | |
| US drops an atomic bomb on **Hiroshima** | Aug 6 | |
| US drops an atomic bomb on **Nagasaki** | Aug 9 | |
| Japan formally surrenders, **ending World War II** | Sept 2 | |

273

| Key Events | After the War | Jerzy's Story (aged 19-24) |
|---|---|---|
| *Victory Parade in London – Poland not invited in order to appease Soviets* | **1946** Jun 8 | |
| | **1946** Summer | Jerzy passes his Entrance exam to Polish School of Architecture in London |
| | **1946** | Jerzy is transferred to RAF Dunholme Lodge in Lincs – Polish Resettlement Corps. |
| | **1947** Oct 24 | Jerzy starts Architecture Studies in London |
| | **1948** Jul 30 | Jerzy meets his future wife, Gwen |
| | **1949** Jan 29 | Jerzy is finally demobbed from air force |
| | **1949** 24 Nov | Jerzy's sister Halina dies |
| | **1950** 18 Feb | Jerzy and Gwen get married |
| | **1950** 11 May | Stanislaw Dabrowski, Jerzy's brother, dies in his Vampire Jet mark 1 in a head-on air-crash in Egypt |

# Jerzy Dabrowski's Family Tree
(Mother's side)

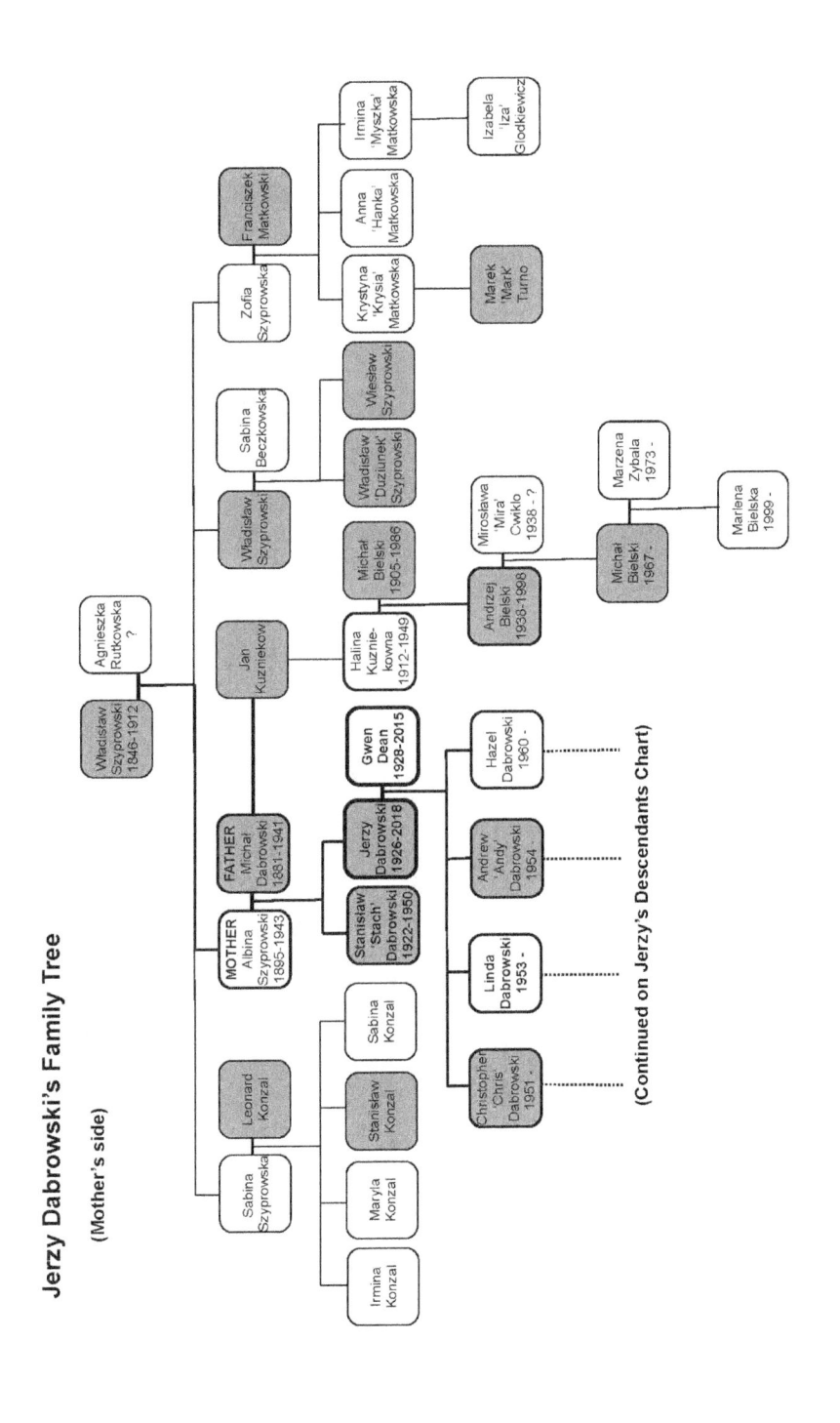

- Wladyslaw Szyprowski 1846-1912
- Agnieszka Rutkowska ?

Children:
- Sabina Szyprowska
  - Leonard Konzal
    - Irmina Konzal
    - Maryla Konzal
    - Stanislaw Konzal
    - Sabina Konzal
- MOTHER: Albina Szyprowski 1895-1943
  - FATHER: Michal Dabrowski 1881-1941
    - Stanislaw 'Stach' Dabrowski 1922-1950
    - Jerzy Dabrowski 1926-2018 — Gwen Dean 1928-2015
      - Christopher 'Chris' Dabrowski 1951 -
      - Linda Dabrowski 1953 -
      - Andrew 'Andy' Dabrowski 1954
      - Hazel Dabrowski 1960 -

(Continued on Jerzy's Descendants Chart)

- Jan Kuzniekow
  - Halina Kuzniekowna 1912-1949
    - Andrzej Bielski 1938-1998 — Mirosława 'Mira' Ćwikło 1938-?
      - Michal Bielski 1967 - — Marzena Zybala 1973 -
        - Marlena Bielska 1999 -
  - Michal Bielski 1905-1986

- Wladyslaw Szyprowski — Sabina Beczkowska
  - Wladyslaw 'Duziunek' Szyprowski
  - Wieslaw Szyprowski

- Zofia Szyprowska — Franciszek Matkowski
  - Krystyna 'Krysia' Matkowska — Marek 'Mark' Turno
  - Anna 'Hanka' Matkowska
  - Irmina 'Myszka' Matkowska
    - Izabela 'Iza' Glodkiewicz

275

# Jerzy Dabrowski – Descendants

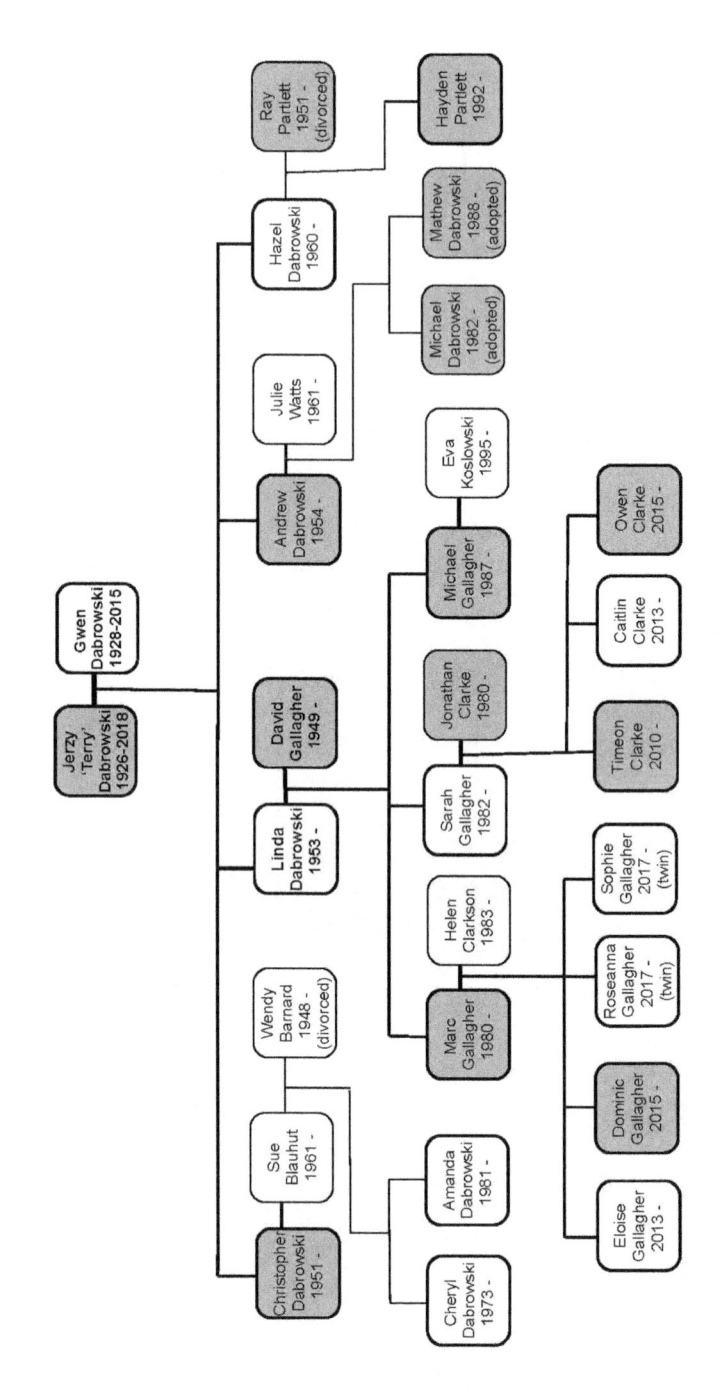

# FURTHER READING

## BIOGRAPHIES/AUTOBIOGRAPHIES

Adamczyk, Wesley *When God Looked the Other Way*, University of Chicago Press, 2004

Greenwood, Marylyn Gwizdak *The Whistler*, C. M. Greenwood 2017

Hunter, Georgia *We Were the Lucky Ones*, Viking 2017

Kelly, Matthew *Finding Poland*, Vintage Books 2011

Kossakowski, Irena *A Homeland Denied*, Whittles Publishing Ltd 2017

Maczka, Stephan B *Goodbye Poland*, Stefan B. Maczka 2012

Mowrer, Lilian T *Arrest and Exile*, Pickle Partners Publishing 2016

Rewitz, Slavomir *The Long Walk*, Robinson 2007

Taylor, Elizabeth *Next Stop Siberia*, Grosvenor House Publishing Ltd 2012

Waydenfeld, Stefan *The Ice Road*, Aquila Polonica 2010

## HISTORY AND REFERENCE

Applebaum, Anne *Gulag: A History* Penguin Books 2003

Binns, Stewart *Barbarossa: And the Bloodiest War in History*, Wildfire (an imprint of Headline Publishing group) 2021

Czapski, Josef *The Inhuman Land*, New York Review Book 2001 Eng Translation by Antonia Lloyd-Jones 2018

Davies, Norman *Trial of Hope*, Rosikon Press 2015

Hastings, Max *All Hell Let Loose*, Harper Press 2012

Hirsch, Francine *Soviet Judgment at Nuremberg*, OUP USA 2020

Kerrigan, Michael *Russia – Crime and Corruption*, Amber Books Ltd 2018

Kochanski, Halik *The Eagle Unbowed*, Penguin Books 2013

Rees, Laurence *World War II - Behind Closed Doors*, BBC Books 2009

Smith, Tim and Winslow, Michelle *Keeping the Faith*, Bradford Heritage Recording Unit 2000

Zamoyski, Adam *Poland, A History*, William Collins 2015

Zawodny, J K *Death in the Forest*, Pickle Partners Publishing 2014

## TOURIST GUIDES TO POLAND

*Poland – The Rough Guide*, Rough Guides 2009
*Poland – Insight Guide* APA Publications 2000

## WEBSITES

Global News – This Day in History - 01/09/1939
Kresy-Siberia Foundation
Polish at Heart
WWII Casualties of Poland
General Anders – Difficult Choices

## TELEVISION

World War II Behind Closed Doors – Stalin, the Nazis

and the West, 2008

## MAGAZINES

*Blitzkrieg – Invasion of Poland* History of War Issue 71 – 80th Anniversary Special - 2019

*History of Communism* The History Collection Issue 41 2020

## PHD THESIS

Winslow, Michelle *War, resettlement, rooting and ageing: An oral history study of Polish emigrés in Britain*, White Rose eTheses online 2001

# ACKNOWLEDGEMENTS

I am very grateful to my many friends and close family who have encouraged me in the writing of this book. I would like to thank my special friends Carol Gallagher and Mary Bangs for being willing readers of the initial draft of my manuscript – their first impressions really helped me to keep going, to improve the book and make it more accessible to all readers. Special thanks also to my daughter Sarah Clarke for finding time to sensitively use Jerzy's own original pictures to design the front cover. I would also like to thank my brothers, Christopher and Andrew Dąbrowski, who have given me much encouragement along the way and have provided anecdotes, information, artefacts, and photos, many of which have brought our father's story to life.

I am especially appreciative of the input by one of my oldest friends (in both senses of the word!) David Matthew, who painstakingly read through two versions of the work-in-progress; his many pertinent and creative suggestions have vastly improved the book in every way. Thanks too, to Ben Childs of 'Tracemaps', who has been brilliant in producing the accurate map of my father's journey during the war – his interest in my project has really motivated me to keep going and get it published. And also, thanks to Jonathan Puddle, my publisher, who has done all the hard work of bringing my manuscript to print.

And finally, I thank my amazing husband, David Gallagher, who always shows me much love and patience, and has been my enthusiastic and interested listener throughout the whole process.

Printed in Great Britain
by Amazon